MISSION TO CHINA

Mary Laven lectures in History at the University of Cambridge, and is a Fellow of Jesus College. She grew up in Canterbury, and – apart from interludes in Venice and York – has spent most of her subsequent life in Cambridge.

She loves Italy, archives, beer, and walking around the suburbs of unfamiliar cities. Her first book, *Virgins of Venice: Enclosed Lives and Broken Vows in the Renaissance Court*, won the John Llewellyn Rhys Prize.

Praise for *Mission to China*:

'Laven carefully unpicks some of the compromises with Chinese civilisation made by Matteo Ricci who led the Jesuit campaign in China . . . Absorbing and moving.' Julia Lovell, *Guardian*

'Compelling reading . . . Laven artfully and playfully chooses topics that arouse the reader's curiosity, and makes interesting use of some of her sources.' Ana Carolina Hosne, *Times Higher Education Supplement*

'This is by no means the first study of (Ricci). There is, however, much to commend it, especially the deft way in which its narrative of Ricci's early years In China are interspersed with reflections on the issues raised by his remarkable career.' T. H. Barrett, *Independent*

'An important account of the first Jesuit mission to China.' *Traveller Magazine*

Mission to China

Matteo Ricci and the Jesuit Encounter with the East

MARY LAVEN

faber and faber

First published in 2011
by Faber and Faber Limited
Bloomsbury House
74–77 Great Russell Street
London WC1B 3DA
This paperback edition published in 2012

Typeset by Faber and Faber Limited
Printed and bound by CPI Group (UK) Ltd, Croydon, CRO4YY

A CIP record for this book
is available from the British Library

ISBN 978-0-571-22518-7

2 4 6 8 10 9 7 5 3 1

For Jason, Daniel, and Benjamin.

Contents

List of Illustrations

Clearing'. National Palace Museum, Taiwan, Republic of China.

11 Ex-voto (1582). Museo degli Ex-voto, Convento degli Agostiniani, Piazza San Nicola, Tolentino.

12 The Basilica of the Holy House, Loreto. Photo: author.

13 'The Apostle in the Waves'. From *Master Cheng's Garden of Ink-Cakes* or the *Chengshi moyuan* (1606). Needham Research Institute, Cambridge.

14 Engraving of Christ and disciples from Jerome Nadal, *Evangelicae historiae imagines* (Antwerp, 1593), plate 144. Cambridge University Library, Syn.3.59.3. Reproduced by kind permission of the Syndics of Cambridge University Library.

15 *Biblia sacra, Hebraice, Chaldaice, Graece, & Latine*, 8 vols (Antwerp, 1569–72), I, 2–3. Cambridge University Library, BSS.100.B69.4. Reproduced by kind permission of the Syndics of Cambridge University Library.

16 Ricci's grave, Jesuit cemetery, Beijing. Photo: author.

Maps

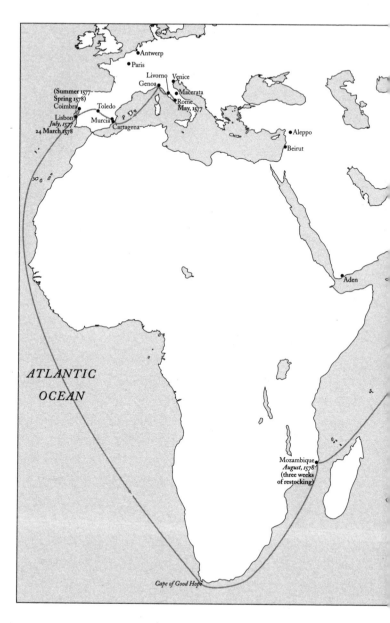

Antwerp

Paris

Livorno Venice
Genoa Macerata
Rome
May, 1577

(Summer 1577-
Spring 1578)
Coimbra Toledo
Lisbon Murcia
July, 1577 Cartagena
24 March 1578

Aleppo

Beirut

Aden

*ATLANTIC
OCEAN*

Mozambique
August, 1578
(three weeks
of restocking)

Cape of Good Hope

From Rome to Macao: Ricci's Voyage Out

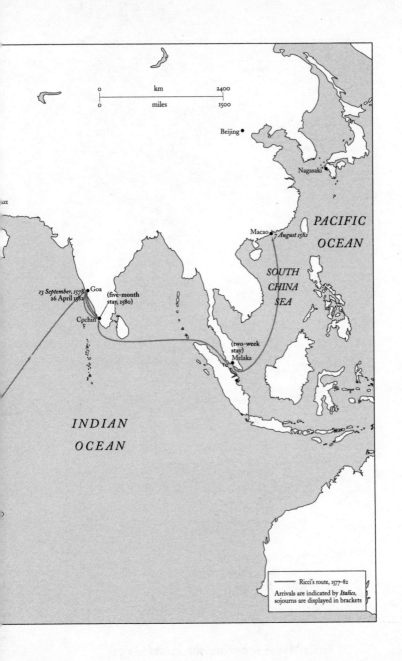

km
0 ——————————— 2400
miles
0 ——————————— 1500

Beijing •

Nagasaki •

PACIFIC
OCEAN

Macao • *7 August 1582*

SOUTH
CHINA
SEA

13 September, 1578 • Goa
26 April 1582 (five-month
stay, 1580)

Cochin

**(two-week
stay)**
Melaka

INDIAN
OCEAN

—— Ricci's route, 1577–82
Arrivals are indicated by *Italics*,
sojourns are displayed in brackets

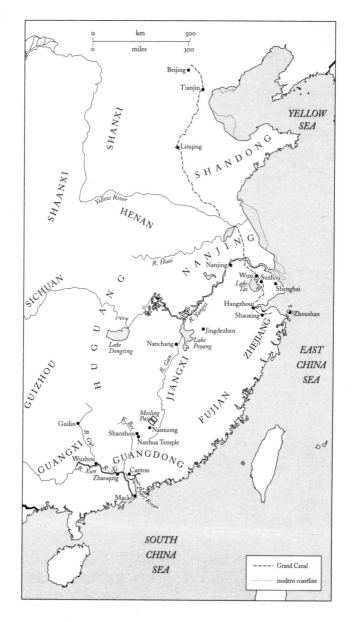

From Macao to Beijing: the Jesuits' China

A Note on Spellings

I have adopted the modern pinyin system of romanisation for the transcription of Chinese names and terms. There are a few exceptions. For example, I write of 'Canton' rather than Guangzhou, because the former term was so resonant with Europeans who travelled to southern China during the period of the Jesuit mission. On the other hand, I have opted for Beijing rather than Peking (Ricci's *Pacchino*), because the latter now sounds jarringly old-fashioned. Inevitably, alternative romanisations appear in some passages of quotation; I have silently emended these so as to avoid confusion.

Introduction: Mapping the World

Cambridge is a city in the south-east of Great Britain, the administrative centre of the county of Cambridgeshire and one of the country's oldest university centres. It is situated on the River Cam (actually a tributary of the River Ouse), 75 km north of London. There are 90,000 inhabitants (1981); the area of the city is 25 km².

The city is surrounded by cultivated hills or flat plain (absolute height up to 70 m) traversed by rather shallow river valleys. The altitude of the hills and ridges is 10–50 m, the summits of the hills are rounded or flat with gentle slopes. The predominant soil in Cambridge is boulder clay, with large areas of sand to the north of the city. When wet, the clay becomes waterlogged and severely impedes off-road movement of mechanised transport. The most important water obstacle in the city and its surroundings is the River Cam (or Granta), which is navigable north of Cambridge . . . The rivers do not freeze and are in full flow all year round . . . Practically all land surrounding the city is under cultivation, with crops of wheat, barley, potatoes and sugar beet . . . Fields are bordered and roads lined with high hedges, which significantly impede observation of the countryside. A dense network of motor highways in the region of the city ensures the movement of transport in all directions throughout the year. The London–Cambridge motorway is dual carriageway with asphalt and ferro-concrete surfacing, each carriageway being 11m wide, with a dividing strip 2.5–5 m wide . . . From the air Cambridge is easily recognised by its shape, its situation on the River Cam and the pattern of the road network . . . Cambridge is an important scientific centre of Great Britain . . . The Cambridge railway junction includes two stations, with comprehensive facilities and many warehouses, including storage for inflammable materials and lubricants.[1]

These extracts come from an account of Cambridge published in 1989 to accompany a 1:10,000 city plan. It is one among many thousands of descriptions of cities and regions that were produced by the Soviet military authorities as part of their extraordinary and top-secret project to map the world. This global mapping project was underway before World War II, but intensified during the Cold War. In every embassy, a diplomat was given the responsibility of gathering as much information as possible regarding the topography of the land to which he or she was posted. All available published maps, guides, and directories were collected and sent to Moscow. In addition, any mode of espionage that might uncover the location of significant buildings, resources, and defence structures was encouraged. The plan that survives for Cambridge is fuller, more detailed, and more up to date than any Ordnance Survey map that was available at the time.[2] It was also one of the last such maps to be published, since in the very same year the Berlin Wall came down, reorienting the world anew.

The sinister implications of the Soviet enterprise have faded fast. Since the first batch of secret maps was discovered in the early 1990s in Latvia, they have become collectors' items, curios that provoke laughter more than fear. In the United Kingdom, their quaint transliterations ('Perli' for Purley, 'Sarri Doks' for Surrey Docks) and occasional errors ('Timlico' for Pimlico) have attracted much discussion among amateurs of cartography.[3] Nevertheless, to view what is familiar through foreign eyes is an unsettling process. It is astonishing how the superimposition of place names in Cyrillic script can render alien the well-known shape of one's home town, the coastline of a favourite seaside resort, or the curve of a major river. Meanwhile, the descriptions offered in the accompanying texts, though

2

unarguably accurate, are eerily detached. 'The predominant soil in Cambridge is boulder clay.' 'The rivers do not freeze and are in full flow all year round.' 'Fields are bordered and roads lined with high hedges, which significantly impede observation of the countryside.' These statements do not come readily to the mouth of a Cambridge-dweller.

Although belonging to a very particular moment in twentieth-century international relations, the Russian maps provide a striking comparison with a more remote episode in the history of global mapping. Five hundred years earlier, the world was riven by another iron curtain, which separated Europeans from the vast and secretive empire of China. The so-called Middle Kingdom, ruled by the Ming and rumoured to be extremely rich and highly civilised, was a land prohibited to foreigners. But in 1583 two men from Italy took a boat from Macao up the Pearl river and settled in the ancient city of Zhaoqing. The men who dared to penetrate the forbidden country were Jesuits, members of the recently formed Society of Jesus, and their intent was to convert the Chinese to Christianity. It was a plan perhaps no less brazenly imperialistic than that nurtured by the Soviet authorities in the twentieth century. In order to achieve their goals, the Jesuits (like Russian spies and diplomats) would need information. Thus they set about mapping the lands, customs and beliefs of the Chinese. Their accounts are inevitably those of outsiders. For all that the Jesuit missionaries were astute and conscientious observers, their attempts to make sense of (for example) Chinese religion or government would have seemed strangely alien to those whose practices they described. But that is not to say that their insights hold no validity, nor that relations between the missionaries and their would-be converts were as consistently chilly as the cold-war analogy might suggest.

This then is a book about encounter and mutual perception: about the understandings and misunderstandings, conversations and confusions, descriptions and distortions that arose from the meeting of two worlds.

The two Jesuits who entered mainland China in 1583 belonged to an order that had originated among a group of students at the University of Paris fifty years earlier. There were ten companions to begin with: Ignatius (a former soldier from Loyola in the Basque country, who – following a battle injury in 1521 – had determined to devote himself to religion and learning), Francis Xavier (another Basque and Ignatius's room-mate) and eight others, a majority of Iberians and a minority of Frenchmen. They spoke, they prayed, they planned, and one day, on 15 August 1534 (the Feast of the Assumption), they met in the Church of Saint Denis in Montmartre, bound themselves by vows of poverty and chastity and pledged to go to Jerusalem, or – failing that – wherever else the pope might direct them. Unable to obtain passage to the Holy Land, they went instead to Rome, where in 1539 they presented a proposal for a new religious order, the Society of Jesus, to Pope Paul III. Despite the objections of some cardinals, Paul was persuaded of the benefits of supporting this new order, distinguished as it was by its direct accountability to the papacy. There was even to be a fourth vow (in addition to the conventional obligations of poverty, chastity and obedience) that bound members of the order to journey anywhere in the world, when ordered to do so by the pope. According to the papal bull that gave formal approval to the Society in 1540, the purpose of the 'Jesuits' was 'the propagation of the faith and the progress of souls in Christian life and doctrine'. In 1550, a further bull spelled out that 'the defence and propagation of the faith' would include 'public preaching, lectures . . . the education of children and unlettered persons in Christianity, and the spiritual consolation of Christ's faithful'. Besides the faithful, however, the Jesuits were now explicitly urged to direct their ministries to 'the Turks or any other infidels, even those who live in the region called the Indies, or . . . any heretics whatever'. [4]

It is often presumed that the Society of Jesus was founded in direct reaction to the Protestant Reformation that was coursing through Europe at the very time that Ignatius and his friends were gathering in Paris. 'Shock troops of the Counter-Reformation' is how the Jesuits are sometimes described. True enough, by the 1550s, campaigning against heresy had become a crucial aspect of their vocation. The 'Collegio Germanico' was founded in Rome in 1552, specifically to train up German Jesuits to combat Protestantism back in their homelands. And in 1555 Peter Canisius, the Dutch Jesuit famous for his conversion work in the heartlands of Protestantism, would publish a Catechism in German, in order to propagate the doctrines of the true Church among those most susceptible to heresy. However, the first Jesuits were more focused on pilgrimage and crusade to distant lands than they were on fighting heretics at home. The order grew and spread with rapidity and, by 1555, there were 55 Jesuits based in Goa on the west coast of India, 25 in Brazil and 15 in Ethiopia. [5] Their vocation was a uniquely mobile one. Eschewing the monastic conventions of eating and praying in common, it was said that the Jesuits' 'best house' was their pilgrimages and missions. [6] According to the Society's *Constitutions*, the Jesuit's calling was 'to travel through the world and to live in any part of it whatsoever where there is hope of greater service to God and of help of souls'. [7] It was to 'the region called the Indies' that founding father Francis Xavier would journey. Arriving in India in 1542, he proceeded to Japan in 1549, where he described the people as 'the best that have as yet been discovered', although complex politics and an unfathomable language were to prove major obstacles to the Jesuit's success.[8] Next he set his sights on the even less welcoming territory of China. He made it to the island of Shangchuan, 14 km from the south coast of China. But there, in 1552, he died of a fever while he was waiting for a boat to take him over the water to his promised land. It was to Xavier's elusive quest, the conversion of the Chinese, that the two Italian Jesuits Matteo Ricci and Michele Ruggieri were to return thirty years later.

In a frenzy of correspondence conducted in the weeks prior to his death, Xavier wrote of the 'preparations and anxieties' relating to his passage to China: 'The voyage will be most painful under my present straitened circumstances; it is full of a thousand dangers, of very doubtful issue, and full of terrors. How it will turn out I know not, but I have a firm confidence, and a strong inward assurance, that however things may go, the result will be good.'[9] What was the allure of China, and what did the Jesuits know of that xenophobic land? Throughout the late Middle Ages and into the Renaissance, European information about this distant territory had derived from accounts such as those left by the Venetian traveller Marco Polo, who spent seventeen years at the court of the Great Khan of Tartary in the later thirteenth century. Polo depicted a prosperous and sophisticated civilisation. His description of Dadu (the court capital, built on the site where Beijing stands today) emphasised its rectilinear plan and orderly streets and praised a city that was 'arranged in squares just like a chessboard'. Here, on the occasion of the new year or 'White Feast' (so named on account of the dress code), the emperor received magnificent gifts from his subject peoples: gold and silver, pearls and gems, and more than 100,000 white horses. Meanwhile, there paraded before the Khan 5,000 elephants, bedecked in 'rich and gay housings of inlaid cloth representing beasts and birds', each carrying on its back splendid coffers filled with silver plate and other luxury items.[10] If such exorbitant reports at first attracted scepticism, those of a later, rival description made them look like the acme of reliability. *The Travels of Sir John Mandeville*, written in 1356–7, was a fictitious account that drew on the works of learned Latin authors, especially Pliny, and on the fabulous imagination of its unknown author. According to the record of 'Sir John', the outer edges of the world were populated by cannibals, Amazons, and one-legged men whose enormous feet served them for parasols.[11] China had its own monstrous race, indigenous to the Yangzi valley: pygmies 'only three spans tall', with a life expectancy of eight years, much of which might be spent fighting a 'perpetual war' against cranes.[12] The age of print would see Mandeville's *Travels* reissued time and again, often studded with fantastic illustrations.

Despite the persistent appeal of such images, European understandings of China were about to undergo a revolution, thanks to transformations in the structure of global trade. For centuries, the Middle Kingdom had stood at the starting line of the spice route that linked western Europe to eastern Asia in a mammoth relay race that was both complicated and costly. Junks from Canton had crossed the South China Sea to Melaka, the great eastern entrepôt on the west coast of the Malay Peninsula, and the distribution centre for spices from the Moluccas. There the pepper, cloves, cinnamon, nutmeg, mace and ginger that titillated European taste buds were loaded onto the ships of the Muslim merchants who controlled the Indian Ocean. Their next stop was Calicut, on the Malabar Coast of India. Then the spices were shipped to the Mediterranean by one of two ancient routes: either via Ormuz and the Persian Gulf, up the Euphrates to Aleppo and Beirut; or via Aden and the Red Sea, and then overland to Suez and Alexandria. Imported into Europe via Venice, the goods – and the final slice of the profits – were received by Christian merchants.[13]

In the fifteenth century, circumstances on each side of the globe challenged the supremacy of the old routes. In China, the flow of spices was stemmed by the Ming Dynasty's new policy of economic isolationism. Fear of Japanese pirates on the eastern seaboard and the perpetual threat of Manchus and Mongols in the north prompted China's rulers to close their borders. A series of 'sea bans' placed tight restrictions on international trading, and China's coastal provinces were vigorously policed to prevent smuggling. The state-sponsored voyages of discovery led between 1407 and 1433 by the famous eunuch admiral Zheng He, whose splendid fleet had journeyed as far as Calicut, Ormuz, and Aden, were never to be repeated.[14] At the same time, in the west, the comparatively tiny state of Portugal was embarking on an unprecedentedly grand policy of expansion. At the very time that Zheng He was voyaging towards the east coast of Africa, Portuguese adventurers were exploring that continent's west coast. Initially their sights were set on the gold of Guinea; they hoped to bypass the Muslim middlemen who brought the precious metal across the desert to the north African ports. And, by the sixteenth century, Portugal's success in this respect had plunged the 'infidels' of the Maghrib and the Sahara into recession. But by 1480 Portugal's ambitions had shifted eastwards, their new goal to seize the lucrative trade in exotic spices from those merchants who controlled the Levant and the Mediterranean. In 1488, Bartolomeu Dias was the first European to sail around the southern tip of Africa. He called it the Cape of Storms, but this new opening to the East was soon rechristened the Cape of Good Hope. And in 1498, Vasco da Gama successfully brought his fleet into the port at Calicut on the west coast of India. Thereafter, as well as setting up numerous trading posts along the new route to the East, the Portuguese used force to capture the ports of Goa (in 1510), Melaka (1511) and Ormuz (1515).[15] They now dominated the major spice routes in the Indian Ocean, and had strategic bases across the southern rim of Asia.

The result of the push-pull of isolationism and expansionism in the early sixteenth century was to move China nearer to the centre of European attention. The Portuguese urgently craved a base in China, a craving that would be satisfied in 1557 by the acquisition of the port of Macao, a peninsula on the southern tip of the empire; in order to achieve this objective, they needed a better understanding of this closed-off country and its peoples. As in the work of the Soviet mapmakers in the twentieth century, the threat of violence was but thinly veiled. Diogo Lopes de Sequeira, sent from Portugal to reconnoitre Melaka in 1508, was instructed to

ask after the Chijns, and from what part they come, and from how far, and at what times they come to Malacca . . . and the merchandise that they bring, and how many of their ships come each year . . . and if they are wealthy merchants, and if they are weak men or warriors, and if they have arms or artillery, and what clothes they wear, and if they are men of large build . . . if they are Christians or heathens, if their country is a great one, and if they have more than one king amongst them . . . and if they are not Christians, in what do they believe and what they adore, and what customs they observe . . .[16]

In these instructions, the desire for knowledge and the quest for power went hand in hand; it is hard to determine where curiosity stopped and self-interest began. A comparable blend was compounded by Tomé Pires, the Melaka-based apothecary who in 1512 began writing his *Suma Oriental*, which included a substantial account of China based on information provided by his Asian trading contacts.[17] For Pires, China was an immense country, 'as stately, impressive and wealthy' as any in the East.[18] Although China enjoyed a thriving economy, Pires explained, the authorities there presided over a peculiar trading system, which forbade native merchants to leave the country and banned foreigners from entering it. All foreign trade had therefore to take place at the twice-yearly fair in Canton, the southern port at the mouth of the Pearl river, 'where the entire empire of China unloads all its wares'.[19] Pires went on to itemise in detail the commodities that underpinned the Chinese economy. Pepper surpassed all other exports by some long way. But cloves, nutmeg, sandalwood, aloes wood (for use by apothecaries), incense, elephants' tusks, and tin might also be sold to the Chinese. Meanwhile, China exported massive quantities of silk and other textiles, seed pearls, musk, 'apothecary's camphor' and rhubarb, this last also prized for its curative properties. ('Though', Pires added with the cynical eye of a professional, 'this is wholly valueless: what I have seen so far arrives rotten.') The list ran on: alum, saltpetre, sulphur, copper, iron, bowls and pans, fans, needles, countless copper bracelets, and 'an inexhaustible supply of porcelain'.[20] Pires did not restrict his interest to commerce. Following de Sequeira's model, he also attended to the physical appearance and dress of the Chinese, dwelling particularly on the men's winter wardrobe (knee-length boots, felt leggings and fur cloaks) and on the fashionable accessories sported by women (golden headdresses, jewellery, fans, and silk shoes). Reassuringly, Chinese men were found to 'look somewhat like Germans' while the women resembled Castilians. For, as Pires confidently remarked, 'Like us, the Chinese people are white.'[21]

Then, the note of threat. With the exception of the war-like Tartars in the north, Pires reported, the Chinese were weak and fearful. It would not be difficult for the governor of Melaka to bring the empire under European control, he wrote, 'because the people are very weak and easily routed'. Several years after writing this, Pires was chosen to take part in a Portuguese embassy to China, led by Fernão Peres de Andrade. The limitations of their diplomatic skills were suggested when, approaching Canton in 1517, the emissaries announced their arrival with blasts of cannonfire. There was worse to come when Fernão's brother Simão de Andrade was soon afterwards caught building an unauthorised military base in the Pearl river delta. Imprisoned in Canton, Pires and his associates smuggled out letters that offered further intelligence about China's governance, administration, commerce and communications, and about the diet, dress, customs and courtesies of the people.[22] Across the sixteenth century, the Iberian fantasy of conquest in the East was fanned by communications such as these.

The final, inevitable ingredient in this amalgam of curiosity and power was religion. Since the launch of the European 'voyages of discovery' in the fifteenth century, the quest for gold had always gone hand in hand with the quest for converts to Christianity. As one of Cortés's soldiers would later remark, when he set foot on American soil, 'We came here to serve God and the King and also to get rich.'[23] The relationship between religion and information was bilateral. On the one hand, the religious

imperative demanded information; on the other, missionary priests became crucial agents in the European intelligence operation and ushered in new methods and new criteria for establishing geographical truth. In a description of
China, penned following a visit to Fujian province in 1575,
the Spanish Augustinian friar Martín de Rada solemnly
reassured his readers, 'The things which we will treat herein concerning this kingdom will be part of them seen with
our own eyes, part taken from their own printed books and
descriptions of their country.' 'Hearsay' was to be scrupu-
lously avoided. De Rada – who, in the manner of a Soviet
diplomat, had clearly done his homework – was in possession of seven books of Chinese geography, 'wherein are
described in detail all the provinces, cities, towns, and fron-
tier posts and garrisons, and all the particularities thereof,
and the families and tributaries and tributes, and the gains
which the King derives from each one of them'. Unfortunately, these works were not uniformly accurate: their illustrations were 'very crudely' drawn, and their information
regarding distances was often unreliable. He therefore used
his sources critically, trying to isolate verifiable data, and
discarding less secure evidence:

Thus as regards the size of the country and the distances, what
is stated hereafter will be much less than what is found in their
books, but I feel it will be more exact, and I leave the truth to
subsequent experience when all the country will have been travelled.[24]

Less careful authors, meanwhile, began to attract severe
criticism. The pioneering Jesuit historian and Latin scholar
Gian Pietro Maffei was lambasted for his scholarship when
in 1571 he produced a Latin translation of a Portuguese
manuscript about the history of the Asian missions up to

1568. Unsurprisingly perhaps, the author of the original text, Manuel da Costa, was especially offended by the errors imported into the translation, and exclaimed in frustration that 'so many lies would distress even a man who prided himself on them'.[25] Maffei, who was the recipient of much advice and information from his colleagues in the East, persisted in his scholarly efforts and the resulting *History of the Indies in XVI Books*, published in 1588, received a far more positive critical response.[26]

The Jesuits had a particular set of motivations in attempting to gather and report as much trustworthy information as possible regarding the unknown corners of the world. As we have seen, these roaming priests experienced little of conventional monastic life, in which community was nurtured through the shared rituals and spaces of chapel, cloister, refectory and dormitory. Nor were they obliged to wear a particular habit that displayed to the world their membership of a common body. Instead, members were urged to conform to the style of reputable priests in the regions where they found themselves.[27] As the Society of Jesus grew within its first three decades from the group of ten men who had met at the University of Paris in 1534 to 3,500 members scattered throughout Italy, Germany, France, Portugal, Spain and India, the order's sense of community and identity was energetically reinforced through the practice of letter-writing.[28] Missionary activity, whether to the wildest parts of southern Italy or to the new worlds of America and Asia, cast Jesuit priests still further from the physical reach of their 'family' of religious brothers, and rendered the need for letters closely detailing their circumstances yet more acute. To handle this volume of correspondence, a special office was established in Rome with responsibility for communicating with missionaries, sifting incoming letters, selecting, editing and translating those to be circulated throughout the order. Juan de Polanco, who became permanent Secretary of the Society in 1547, and who co-ordinated the Jesuits' corresponding activities across the world, wrote of the critical importance of passing news and information between Jesuits and their superiors in order to promote a 'thorough knowledge of each other'. He urged the General and Provincials to take a 'special care' of this letter-writing, so as 'to obtain that in every place they should know about the things that are being done in other places, which knowledge is a source of mutual consolation and edification in our Lord'.[29]

So Jesuits wrote for themselves. Reporting on the circumstances in which they found themselves, they participated in a bonding exercise, a kind of group therapy, whereby members of their tight-knit but far-flung community could empathise with one another and engage in 'mutual consolation'. And yet the Jesuits did not write only for themselves. They also wrote in order to interest the European laity in their work. Their intended readers here were members of the social and political elite, potential patrons whose support in part depended on the fulfilment of their curiosity. In 1554, Ignatius Loyola, the founder of the Society of Jesus, specifically addressed the demand for knowledge about Asia:

Some leading figures who in this city [Rome] read with much edification to themselves the letters from India are wont to desire, and they request me repeatedly, that something should be written regarding the cosmography of these regions where members of our society live. They want to know, for instance, how long are the days of summer and of winter; when summer begins; whether the shadows move towards the left or towards the right. Finally, if there are other things that may seem extraordinary, let them be noted, for instance, details about animals and plants that either are not known at all, or not of such a size, etc. And this news – sauce for the taste of a certain curiosity that is not evil and is wont to be found among men – may come in the same letters or in other letters separately.[30]

It was for this reason that the Jesuits used print to circulate their letters and reports far beyond the limits of their order.

Finally, the Jesuits wrote – in a roundabout way – for the people whose lands they described. For mapping the world was a fundamental plank of their missionary strategy. If they did not know and understand a people, how could they hope to convert them? This was partly the reasoning of the imperialist, akin to that of the Soviet officials operating in the UK in the 1980s: missionaries, like potential invaders, needed to know the lie of the land, and to gather information about roads and rivers, climate, demography and food supplies in order that they could plan their assault. It was as important to identify cities served by excellent communications and natural resources as it was necessary to locate areas suffering from insalubrious air or poor climate. Only by research of this kind could the Jesuits target their mission effectively.[31] But whereas the Russian surveys of the late twentieth century were characterised by a lifeless detachment, the Jesuit observers of the late sixteenth century aspired to a far more interactive engagement with the people they sought to know. The ethnographic approach was pioneered by the Italian Jesuit Alessandro Valignano, who in 1573, at the age of thirty-four, was appointed 'Visitor' to the province of 'India' (a term used to cover the whole of East Asia, not just the subcontinent). Charged with directing that handful of priests who were attempting to bring Christianity to Asia, he would spend the remaining thirty-three years of his life hopping between Goa, Melaka, Macao and Nagasaki.[32]

When he died in Macao in 1606, Valignano left behind a large repository of writings on the peoples and parts of the world that he had visited during the course of his long and exacting career. His first pieces of reportage related to the Africans whom he had encountered in Mozambique, and his impressions were grimly negative. The people of the Monomotapa tribes, he wrote, 'are of very limited ability . . . I am told, in fact, that they are completely incapable of grasping our Holy Law and customs . . . which can be accounted for not only by the naturally inferior capacity of their intellect . . . but also by their savage conduct and the vices which plague them, for they do live like brute beasts.'[33] The land was 'sterile and reprobate' giving no hope of fruits to be yielded. Valignano was at first equally pessimistic about the people of India, who were not, alas, 'motivated in their behaviour by reason' and who were consequently 'very difficult to convert'. (This was a view that he would subsequently alter, judging in 1583 that the inhabitants of the subcontinent were, after all, 'rational beings', 'capable of learning and of grasping [Christian] doctrine'.)[34] But even before he had got there, he was confident that 'the white people' of China and Japan were going to be of an altogether different order. Following his first visit to Japan in 1580, Valignano was delighted by the morality and sophistication of the people whom he found there: 'It can truly be said that no pagan people (including the Romans when they were pagans) were ever so modest and decent as the Japanese.'[35] Valignano immediately set out to itemise the conventions and courtesies that defined Japanese civility, in a work entitled *Observations on the Habits and Particular Customs of Japan.* This detailed account provided Jesuits in the field with a

vade mecum on local etiquette that covered such crucial
subjects as food, dress, table manners, cleanliness, and the
use of honorific forms when addressing people of a different
rank from one's own.[36] This was not just a book to be read; it
was a set of rules to be practised.

Across the water, Valignano's approach rubbed off on his
colleagues and compatriots, Michele Ruggieri and Matteo
Ricci, both of whom composed lengthy accounts of Chinese
society. Their shared belief in the importance of observation
is well illustrated with reference to the topos of urban transport. In the course of their writings on China, both Ruggieri and Ricci remarked on the fact that anyone who was
anyone disdained to walk on the streets, and instead insisted on being carried around by sedan chair.[37] At one level,
their comments slotted neatly into the 'communications'
box, thereby conforming to one of the enduring expectations of city description. Whereas the inhabitants of late
twentieth-century Cambridge might avail themselves of
either the train or the asphalt-and-ferro-concrete-clad MII
in journeying to London, city-dwellers in late Ming China
hired either horses (or other pack animals) or sedan chairs
and porters to carry them around from A to B. But, unlike
the Soviet descriptions, the Jesuits' remarks also functioned
at an anthropological level, and were expressly concerned
with understanding the practices and motivations of the
people they were observing. Take Ricci's description of the
streets of Beijing. According to the Jesuit, these were rare-
ly paved, and were consequently thick with dust or mud,
depending on the season. This was why only the very poor-
est people walked the streets, with mules available for hire
for just a few pence, and sedan chairs reserved for literati
and other members of the social elite. Furthermore, everybody, regardless of their gender, social station and means of

transport, covered their heads and faces with a black hood and veil. Ricci went on to explain that what had begun as a practical measure to keep the dust out of one's face had taken on a social function: 'This practice also serves to prevent one from being recognised on the streets, and so excuses one from having to engage in so many salutations and courtesies with friends along the way, causing one to dismount at every step.' The convention was advantageous to the Jesuits, both because 'it was dangerous in these times for foreigners to go about the streets uncovered' and because the European priests were plagued by people following them out of mere curiosity. Thanks to the black veils, Ricci and his colleagues were able to traverse the entire city without being seen by anyone.[38]

The Jesuits' observations about Chinese mores had a direct impact on their own behaviour. As Ricci informed the General of the Society of Jesus Claudio Acquaviva in a letter sent from Shaozhou (known today as Shaoguan) in 1592: 'In order to gain greater authority, we no longer go about the streets by foot, but we are carried in chairs on the shoulders of men, in the manner to which important persons of consequence are here accustomed.' Without the authority that this custom lent the Jesuits, Ricci claimed that they would be bound to fail in their attempts to gather 'fruit among the gentiles'.[39] Mapping the world, and reporting on the social customs therein was therefore an essential precondition of the Jesuit policy of 'accommodation', the label that is often used to describe the mission to China, and which earned the Society praise and blame in equal measure.[40] When in Rome do as the Romans do. According to this principle, Jesuit priests were asked to assimilate as much as possible of their hosts' culture and to adopt the *modo soave*, the gentle method, in their dealings with non-believers. Would-be

Jesuits had to be screened for their 'flexibility', their ability to adapt to unfamiliar ways of life.[41] Rather than seeking to eliminate local culture, missionaries were encouraged first to study and then to participate in it.

*

Matteo Ricci stands as the icon of the Jesuits' approach to mission. The most famous portrait of Ricci, painted immediately after his death in 1610 and based on sketches of his corpse, spells out as clearly as any written document the terms on which this man was to be remembered.[42] Fittingly, the image is itself a cultural melange – the work of a Chinese artist, You Wenhui, trained in the school of the Italian Jesuit, Giovanni Nicolao, and known professionally by his European name, Emanuel Pereira. His work melds the conventions of European portraiture with the calligraphy and flattened perspective of Chinese art, and the result is of dubious aesthetic appeal. But, whether or not one likes the portrait, its hybrid style admirably befits its subject. The Western priest is depicted as a Confucian scholar, a pose that Ricci in fact adopted for the last sixteen years of his life. He sports a distinctive pointed cap (reminiscent – said Ricci – of a bishop's mitre), an abundant beard, flowing robes, and capacious sleeves that conceal his hands in a gesture of respect, all of which signal his integration into Chinese elite society. This was the second sartorial transformation effected by Ricci and his colleagues. When they arrived in mainland China, they had been persuaded by Chen Rui, the principal administrator of Guangdong and Guangxi provinces, to assume the garb of Buddhist monks. Writing in 1585 to his college friend Giulio Fuligatti, Ricci proclaimed, 'I have become a Chinaman.'[43] A decade later, however, Ricci was no longer convinced that it paid for the

European priests to dress as Buddhist monks, since it turned out that these indigenous clean-shaven clergy were held in low esteem by the ruling elite. It was time for the Jesuits to re-identify as literati, the scholar-officials trained in Confucian philosophy, who were elected to office on the basis of success in the civil service exams. Valignano concurred, and instructed members of the China mission to grow their hair and beards, and to procure appropriate robes. The effect, claimed Ricci, was immediate. Those who had spurned the Jesuits now invited them into their houses. Thanks to his newly acquired beard and flared sleeves, Ricci found a foothold in Chinese society.

It is Ricci's adaptability, his receptiveness to foreign mores, his embrace of difference, his determination to enter into conversation with another world, that have won the sixteenth-century missionary a sort of cult status among promoters of global harmony and cultural exchange. Institutes set up in the name of Matteo Ricci flourish today in San Francisco, Macao and Macerata (the Jesuit's home town), each one dedicated to the causes of intercultural understanding and dialogue. They testify to our enduring admiration for the man who entered 'so fully into another culture without losing himself'.[44] But of course there are many ways of spinning Ricci's slippery image. The sinologist Jacques Gernet, who has painstakingly pieced together Chinese reactions to the Jesuit mission, stresses the deceitfulness of the European priests, who used every means to make friends with the local literati while concealing their true motives. The words of seventeenth-century pamphleteers writing against Christianity provide a necessary counterbalance to hagiographic descriptions of the Jesuits and suggest the superficiality of European respect for Chinese culture. As one particularly virulent critic pronounced,

'They conceal their scheming beneath an appearance of honesty . . . They appear to be quite unpretentious but their hearts are devious.'[45] In particular, Chinese critics of the Jesuits warned their readers to be wary of the priests' intelligence and learning, and of their bamboozling displays of technological and scientific expertise. On the basis of this compelling evidence, Gernet concludes that Ricci's mission was none other than 'an exercise in seduction'.

In proffering his verdict Gernet risks simplifying Ricci's mission strategy, which was constantly evolving and riven with ambiguities. There are certainly moments at which it seems plausible to understand the Jesuit's appearance as a Confucian scholar as a kind of disguise, the Christian wolf adopting native sheep's clothing. At other times it looks like a far deeper transformation, which leads Ricci to comment as if helplessly on the changes that his travels have wrought on him ('I have become a Chinaman'). Such speculation invites fundamental questions about the nature of identity. Can we separate personhood from performance? What is the relationship between the inner and the outer self? These are questions that preoccupy historians as much as experts in philosophy and psychology, and they invite historically grounded responses. Rather than falling back on the extremes of cynicism and idealism, we need to register the importance of a peculiarly Renaissance style of self-fashioning to the mission. Ricci grew up in the Italy of Castiglione and della Casa, authors of best-selling works of 'conduct' literature – repositories of advice on every aspect of social deportment, from dancing and jousting to speaking and laughing. It was a culture in which everyone was an actor, shaping their behaviour so as to enhance their status in the theatre of the world. The Jesuits brought that developed consciousness of self-fashioning to their encounter with Chinese society. As Ricci put it in a letter to Duarte de Sande in 1595:

We are growing a good deal in credit and respect with the Chinese, which is extremely necessary in order to enter into contact with the rulers and to gain their esteem for our holy law and our doctrine. All this, not because we seek honours, but because in this land where the law of Our Lord is unknown, the reputation of that law depends to a certain extent on the credit and reputation of its preachers, for which it is necessary that we adapt ourselves externally to the local customs and uses.[46]

From this point of view, the Pereira portrait shows neither a saint nor a con man, but someone who was working to adapt himself to the values of an alien world. To legitimate his religion in the eyes of the Chinese, he first had to legitimate himself.

A similar story might be told from the piece of visual evidence that has perhaps done most to cement Ricci's posthumous reputation as a global citizen – an image this time not of himself but of the world. For among all the Jesuit's prolific publications, including works of philosophy, theology, mnemonics and mathematics, none was more celebrated in China than his *mappamondo* or world map, first sketched in Zhaoqing in 1584, and redrafted, refined and republished many times during the remainder of Ricci's life. It was soon after the Jesuits' arrival in Zhaoqing in 1583 that a map pinned to the walls of the mission house sparked Chinese curiosity about European cartography. The precise identity of that map remains unclear; in principle it could have come from one of the prestigious copperplate atlases circulating in the latter half of the sixteenth century, such as those of the Flemish map-maker Gerard Mercator or of his compatriot Abraham Ortelius. However, given Ricci's lament in 1585 about the shortage of books in his possession, and his subsequent gratitude at receiving a copy of Ortelius's *Theatrum Orbis Terrarum* in 1608, it is unlikely that he had access to such lavish volumes in China in the early 1580s.[47] The map on the wall in Zhaoqing was probably a cheaper and more functional navigational aid, produced in Goa or Macao by a Portuguese cartographer, and published on a single sheet.[48] In any case, it caught the fancy of a group of mandarins who had travelled upstream to visit the Jesuit residence, and Ricci was prevailed on by the governor of the city, Wang Pan, to make a copy with Chinese names and legends. This was the kind of opportunity that Ricci never turned down. By October 1584 he had prepared a new map, of modest dimensions, with notes adapted for the Chinese viewer. It showed the equator, the tropics and the five climatic 'zones'; it named all the countries, and described the customs of their peoples; and it was marked with degrees and parallels, unlike any Chinese maps before it. To European eyes, the most startling innovation was that, unlike the map that Ricci had posted on the wall of the Jesuit house, the new depiction of the world placed Asia in the centre. At the same time, Ricci deviated from conventional Asian representations and risked offending his hosts by radically diminishing the size of the 'Middle Kingdom'. As Ricci later commented, to persuade the Chinese that their country 'occupied anything less than three-quarters of the world' was a tough call.[49]

Ricci's risk paid off, at least with his immediate patrons. Wang Pan, now promoted to the position of *lingxi dao* (superintendent) of the provinces of Guangdong and Guangxi, was delighted with the map, and in November 1584 had it published at his own expense (jealously keeping the blocks that had been used in its production).[50] In the years that followed, Ricci would return again and again to his cartographic vocation. He could scarcely conceal his pride when he was greeted in Shaozhou in 1589 as 'a great astrologer and cosmographer who knew how to draw the entire world'.[51] There were reissues of the map, produced to a larger scale, in 1592, 1594, and 1598. By 1596, Ricci had gone back to the drawing board in an effort to produce a more accurate version. This second edition came out in 1600, and was followed by a third in 1602 and a fourth in 1603. The third edition, which Ricci described as 'made up of six plates, each one about a yard in width and two or more in length', was twice the size of the 1600 edition, itself twice the size of the 1584 edition.[52] It was printed secretly by Ricci's friend, collaborator and convert Li Zhizao, who added a fulsome endorsement and asked various friends and literati to contribute prefaces in support of the venture. The fourth edition was grander yet, an eight-plate version, published by another convert, Paolo Li Yingshi. New editions and reprints continued to fly off the presses throughout the final decade of Ricci's life and, in 1607, the map alighted on the walls of the imperial palace when a hand-coloured example was presented by one of the eunuchs to his master the Wanli emperor.[53]

Although the story of the *mappamondo* reads in its bare outlines as a triumphant success, it was in reality – like Ricci's portrait – more vexed and complicated. Ricci himself was on occasion ambivalent about his achievement, and feared the loss of control occasioned by the proliferation of pirated versions of the map. Writing to the head of the Society of Jesus, Claudio Acquaviva, soon after it was first published, he included a copy and expressed his embarrassment at the many errors in it – partly his own fault (for he had dashed off this rough version, he claimed, never intending it to be published) and partly the fault of the publishers who had imported fresh inaccuracies into the image while cutting the woodblocks.[54] At other moments he was more sanguine. Thanks to the *mappamondo* and other, similar projects, the Jesuits were gaining in 'credit', while they waited for the Lord to open the way to more important things. Furthermore, technological achievements such as the map were concoctions in which one could 'mix up many matters relating to God and our holy law'.[55] So those legends on the map which related to Europe took good care to draw attention to Rome (seat of the Holy Father, 'who is revered by all') and to proclaim, somewhat disingenuously, that the entire continent was united in its devotion to the religion of the Lord of Heaven. Palestine was singled out as the place where 'the Lord of Heaven was born', while Constantinople and Mecca were named but – significantly – not glossed.[56]

The *mappamondo* was simultaneously a source of anxiety, a reserve of cultural capital and a Trojan horse bringing the truths of Christianity to a salvation-starved people. Chinese opinions were once more polarised; while Li Zhizao celebrated Ricci's 'perfection' as a man and a scholar, and congratulated him on having dispelled the errors of traditional Chinese cartography, one anti-Christian writer presented a rather different view: 'So great is men's taste for strange things that they become ecstatic when they see Ricci's map of the world . . . But all he did was delude men over what they could not see with their own eyes and over places which were beyond their reach.'[57] Again we are confronted with a barrage of irreconcilable perspectives, none of which is easy to reject out of hand. Ricci doubtless was keen to inform his Chinese hosts, to raise his own status and to encourage conversions. And he might well have had darker purposes as well. In one fascinating glimpse into the Jesuits' embroilments with secular authorities, we catch Ricci dispatching his first full account of China (dated 1584) *not* to a colleague or a superior within the order, but to Giambattista Román, the Treasurer of the Philippines – arguably the most powerful European official in the Far East.[58] Ricci's description of China had been actively solicited by the Spaniard, no doubt to back up his nascent plans to organise an Iberian conquest of the Middle Kingdom. And Ricci, who clearly appreciated the diplomatic sensitivity of his intelligence, warned Román that 'if letters of this kind fell into the hands of mandarins, they could do us no small harm'.[59] In the same letter, he lamented the fact that it was not yet possible to send a copy of the *mappamondo*, since it would provide an excellent representation of 'all the provinces and cities' in China. But in the absence of a map, the Jesuit's description went on, in technical vein, to attempt to locate China in terms of longitude and latitude and to discuss the characteristics of the empire under the headings of 'fertility, beauty, wealth, knowledge, power and government'.[60] Some of his categories of analysis – natural resources, communications, urban infrastructure, population – bring us back to the twentieth-century Soviet accounts with which we began, although Ricci's emphasis on the administrative system, customs and beliefs perhaps suggests an intention to work with existing social structures rather than to obliterate them.

In grasping the riddle that Ricci presents us with today, two points need to be borne in mind. The first is that his aim, the saving of souls for Christ, was an end that could (and, in Reformation Europe, did) justify all manner of means. His enemies, in accusing him of hypocrisy, perhaps underestimated the imperative under which he laboured in his mission to the East. The second point is that the conflict we have been tracing here – between a Christianity that was open, accommodating, tolerant, pacific, and a Christianity that was closed, imperialistic, intolerant, hostile – is a conflict that was being played out in many other arenas in this period. Perhaps it was clearest of all on the spiritual battleground of late medieval Spain. In the wake of the conquest of Granada of 1492, Ferdinand and Isabella, the Spanish monarchs, first sought to convert the Muslims of the south through assimilation and persuasion. Under the liberal regime of Talavera, the first Archbishop of Granada, Catholic priests were instructed to learn Arabic, and to set pieces of Christian liturgy to Moorish harmonies. Muslim practices of bathing, fasting and circumcision were permitted to continue, since they could be accommodated alongside Christian doctrine. But within ten years, the policy was reversed. Frustrated by the slow pace of change, Ferdinand and Isabella summoned Cardinal Xisneros, the zealous Archbishop of Toledo, to assist with the conversion of the Muslim population. Under such pressures, Talavera quickly changed his tack, and demanded the dismantling of every aspect of Moorish culture – the creation of a clean slate on which the new doctrines of Christianity could be written bright and clear.[61] The same split could be pursued into New Spain, where the colleagues of Xisneros and Talavera confronted strange languages and customs among the native Americans. Back in Europe, the argument continued, both in relation to old infidels (notably, the Jews, whose ghettos often afforded them a surprising degree of religious freedom and cultural autonomy), and in response to new heresies. By the second half of the sixteenth century the conflict between Catholics and Protestants had created parallel dilemmas within the Christian world. Out of the chaos of the religious wars sprang a new 'politique' approach that put the stability of the state before the insistence on religious conformity; but, as in France, edicts of toleration could lead to the worst outbreaks of sectarian violence and to state-sponsored backlashes against minority groups.

The quandary in which Christian rulers found themselves is not altogether unfamiliar. Today, Western governments vacillate in their attitudes towards ethnic minorities and flit between policies that encourage cultural diversity (for example in the realms of language, dress and social customs) and an insistence on Western norms (hence 'citizenship' examinations and the enforcement of 'gender equality'). Nowhere has this been clearer than in relation to the vitriolic debate on the veil. This is why the story of Ricci's mission to China remains so compelling. We live in a world in which leaders once more invoke the language of mission and crusade, and in which our attitude to unfamiliar cultures is being tested on a daily basis. Four hundred years after Ricci's death, as we stand at the beginning of what many believe will be remembered as China's century, it is timely to consider how our European ancestors confronted and negotiated cultural difference. We may be surprised to discover that, in many respects, their approach was more honest and more open than our own. But we should not be shocked if it was shot through with anxieties and inconsistencies; the battle between domination and acceptance raged in the heart of every missionary.

*

Matteo Ricci was born in 1552 in Macerata, a walled city in the Italian Marches under papal rule, with a cathedral, law school and recently founded university.[62] He was the son of an apothecary, and in a rare letter to his father, written from Shaozhou in 1592, he commented on the copious supplies of rhubarb, that hotly prized ingredient of Western pharmaceuticals, that were to be found in China:

Among the other riches of this realm is rhubarb, of which there is such an abundance that they use it to dye cloth. Some want all European supplies to come from China, travelling via Persia, Armenia, Turkey and Venice; here, it is of little value, but the Portuguese merchants don't know how to transport it by sea, and nearly all of it rots on the voyage.[63]

It is an interesting moment when the usually deracinated missionary connects with his home background. In fact, Ricci's origins in the apothecary's shop were by no means unrelated to his fate. Indeed, it is significant that two of our most influential sixteenth-century writers on China, Ricci and Pires, should have shared a background in pharmacy (and an interest in rhubarb). For apothecaries throughout Europe were renowned not only for their trade in exotic eastern substances, deemed crucial to contemporary medical remedies, but also for their display of foreign curiosities and their importance as nodes in international news networks. Here, among the majolica pots, the recipe books, the pestles and the mortars, pharmacists provided a space in which news sheets could be pored over and intelligence of the wider world exchanged.[64]

The story of Matteo Ricci and the Jesuit mission to China has been told many times before, from a wide range of perspectives. There are insider accounts and outsider accounts, critiques and apologies, studies by European historians and by sinologists.[65] From out of this rich field of scholarship a single theme has come to dominate: the exchange of ideas between East and West and the hybrid intellectual world that grew up around the missionaries.[66] It is unsurprising that the mission of Matteo Ricci to China has proved such a rich seam for intellectual historians. Ricci was, after all, a thoroughly intellectual man. Thanks to his education at the Jesuit school in Macerata, and later at the Roman

College, he was steeped in the classics, and had an astute grasp of contemporary philosophy, mathematics, astronomy and theology. While none of that in itself would have earned him much notice, his pioneering role in bringing Western learning to China and vice versa has secured him a prominent place in the history of ideas. This study adopts a different approach. The focus here is on mental worlds more broadly conceived. Its premise is that what we have in our heads and what motivates our actions may include bits of Aristotle, Confucius, Cicero and Aquinas, but it also includes a lot of other stuff, picked up along the way (rhubarb, fathers and apothecaries' shops, for example). We therefore cannot limit the history of encounter to the history of encounter between learned ideas. We have to admit emotions and human relationships, amply documented in the extensive letters and reports that the Jesuits left behind them, and crucial to the everyday unfolding of the mission. We need to acknowledge a world of rituals, images and objects, which often speak more eloquently about the interplay between East and West than the learned texts for which the missionaries became famous. We need a more tangible history of the mission, grounded in the land and the people of China rather than floating in a realm of abstractions. But such a history will also be *less* tangible, shaped by psychic pressures and irrational energies rather than consciously and decorously controlled.

1 The Tower of High Fortune

On the banks of the River Xi, a mile to the east of the ancient walled city of Zhaoqing, two buildings stood, in mid-construction, side by side. One arose from an octagonal base; the other was rectangular. The first, initiated in 1582, was already a lofty structure, its delicate tiers providing views – when the mists lifted – across the busy river and to nearby limestone crags. The second, begun in the following year, was only two storeys high, but soon became an architectural curiosity. The layout of the building was peculiar: in contrast with the single-storey dwellings that characterised Chinese domestic architecture, this one had living quarters on the first floor, while its ground floor was given over to religious uses. Equally strange were the details of its design. In 1585, as construction work drew to a close, the style of the house, with its balconies, its windows, and its elaborately locking doors, was attracting a deal of comment. Only in the materials from which they were made did the two buildings have something in common. Early on, the builders on their neighbouring sites had seen the logic of co-operation, and had negotiated to use the same supplies of bricks and timber.[1]

Thus it was that in a corner of Guangdong province, 110 kilometres west of Canton, the first European-style house in mainland China took root amid a patch of market gardens, just a stone's throw away from the region's tallest pagoda. The Tower of High Fortune, as it was known, was the result of municipal fervour and faith in *fengshui*. The literati of

Zhaoqing had petitioned the city's *zhifu* or Prefect, Wang Pan, to erect a building that could prevent the good fortune of the land being carried away by the waters of the Xi. Wang Pan was at first hesitant, but eventually succumbed to their request, and the Sub-Prefect, referred to by Ricci as Tansiaohu, was put in charge of raising funds to pay for the monument. Three thousand taels were stumped up by the worthies of the city, many of whose names were recorded on a commemorative stele.[2] The result was a splendid tapering edifice, nearly sixty metres high, its nine tiers concealing (by means of a clever network of internal staircases) seventeen floors within, its roof topped with a gilded bronze globe.[3]

The European house and church also owed their existence to Wang Pan, who in 1583 had orchestrated the Jesuits' admission to his city and had offered to provide them with land on which to establish a residence. Michele Ruggieri set off for the city in the company of Matteo Ricci, who had only recently arrived in the Far East from Goa. Reaching Zhaoqing on 10 September 1583, the two priests were taken immediately to the palace of the Prefect. On their knees, speaking through an interpreter, the Jesuits announced that they were religious men, servants of God, from the furthest reaches of the west, come to witness the famed good government of China. Their desire was merely for a place to settle, away from the bustle of merchants in Macao; a place where they might build a little house and church, and serve God until the end of their days. If the *zhifu* could help them to achieve this, they would be obliged to him for the rest of their lives.[4] One site above all others seemed to suggest itself to the Jesuits' contacts in Zhaoqing, and they were led at once to the place where the Tower of High Fortune stood just one tier high. The location was pleasing to everyone for, as the Jesuits had requested, it was set apart from the noisy streets of the walled city, but by no means isolated. Proximity to the river would enable easy communications with Macao, Canton and the surrounding towns.[5] Wang Pan was delighted; in his view, the presence of the foreign priests would constitute the ultimate adornment of his pagoda.[6]

We may imagine that the Jesuits bit their lips at the news that they were being cast as 'adornments' to the pagan Fortune Tower. The committee in charge of the Tower was more vocal. Its President, the Sub-Prefect, made clear that it viewed the coming of the Jesuits as the thin end of the wedge. Before long they would bring other foreigners from Macao, and those foreigners were bound to spell trouble for Zhaoqing.

Strange neighbours: the Tower of High Fortune and the Jesuit house stood side by side, prefiguring the co-existence of a small group of Catholic priests and their Chinese hosts during the coming century and a half of attempted evangelisation. The Jesuits' period of residence in Zhaoqing, from 1583 until their expulsion in 1589, was characterised by the interplay of curiosity and hostility that would come to mark the mission as a whole. One minute, city notables, anxious to see the precious objects that the strange men had brought from Europe, queued up outside the Jesuit residence; the next, angry locals pelted the building with stones.[7] In a single letter, Ricci could praise China for its good government, rich resources, well-ordered cities and advanced transport systems, and condemn the debauchery of the mandarins, let alone the polygamy of that 'wretched Sardanapalus', the Emperor.[8] And so the small European house and the towering Chinese pagoda, though wrought of the same earth, were icons of two civilisations in contest.

*

The Jesuits' first foothold in China was not easily won. The building of the little house by the river was the culmination of a series of advances and setbacks that stretched back over many years. One could date the start of the Jesuit mission to China to 1551, when Francis Xavier, after a lifetime of proselytising in the East, set sail from Japan and reached the island of Shangchuan. Or one could go back even earlier to 1534, when the first Jesuits, or 'Companions of Jesus' as they called themselves, gathered in Montmartre and pledged to minister to the people of distant lands. But the story of the men who set up home in Zhaoqing in 1583 begins more precisely on 24 March 1578, when fourteen Jesuits departed from the port of Lisbon, headed for Goa, the city that lay at the heart of the Portuguese empire, on the west coast of India.

There were three ships in total, each carrying around five hundred people – a mixed bag of soldiers, merchants and adventurers. So as not to risk all the Jesuit eggs in one basket, the fourteen missionaries were divided between the ships, piously named *Saõ Gregorio*, *Saõ Luiz* and *Bom Jesus*. A Latin document recording the names, origins and ages of the missionaries on board each vessel notes the number of years each man had belonged to the order, and gives brief details of their education and training. Among the five holy men aboard the *Saõ Luiz* was Ricci: 'Italian – from Macerata – aged twenty-six – seven years in the Society – educated at the Roman College – degree in philosophy'. Ruggieri, his senior by eight years, was listed as a native of Capua, north of Naples, who had also studied in Rome. Their three remaining colleagues were all Portuguese, and all in the prime of life, aged between twenty-seven and thirty-one.[9] The journey ahead was, in physical terms alone, an immensely gruelling one; there was no place for the old and frail.

After being tossed on the high seas for nearly half a year – with a six-week break in the Portuguese colony of Mozambique, where the ships were restocked with provisions and a cargo of African slaves – Ricci and friends landed in Goa on 13 September. Praising God for their safety, several of the priests wrote letters to Rome, and provided graphic descriptions of the trials they had endured: seasickness, confrontations with pirates, periods of frustrating calm (eventually lifted in response to the prayers of passengers and crew, who at the Jesuits' instigation had processed with holy relics from stern to prow), and of course sail-lacerating storms, all of which difficulties had been overcome only by the grace of God.[10]

In Goa, the missionaries confronted different problems. They were deeply uncomfortable with the bullish conversionary tactics of the Portuguese authorities, who destroyed Hindu temples, prohibited Christians from keeping 'infidel' servants and forced 'converts' to attend sermons. More prosaically, the work of the Jesuits was hampered by disease. Ricci fell victim to a series of unspecified afflictions and was dispatched to the more southerly city of Cochin, where it was hoped that the clean air would help him to recover.[11] Here, in the well-established college, Ricci studied theology, taught grammar and took Holy Orders. Recalled to Goa at the end of 1580, he continued to study theology and to teach. Since the 1540s, the Goan Jesuits had undertaken the education of around six hundred local boys, all of whom were put through the paces of a thoroughly Western education, grounded in Latin, rhetoric and the Christian faith.

Life in Goa – that far-flung outpost of Christendom, where the Portuguese colonisers were developing a taste for a hot and vinegary dish that would become known as vindaloo – was a strange blend of the exotic and the familiar, by turns whetting and dulling the missionaries' appetite for their work. Ricci occasionally experienced the thrill of the fight, as when he reported how local infidels had attempted to burn down Christian churches along the south-eastern coast of India, only to be scared off by the sight of a cross that would not burn; or when he contemplated the pos- sibility that the Great Moghul – 'the most powerful ruler in all of India, Lord of seventy territories, commander of 300,000 cavalry and of 20,000 elephants' – might be on the brink of conversion.[12] But Ricci's letters from India also betray ennui, a sense of loss at being parted from his friends in Rome, impatience at some of his less high-minded col- leagues and dissatisfaction deriving from the routine nature of his teaching. Then, in April 1582, a letter arrived from Japan from Alessandro Valignano, summoning Matteo Ricci along with his friend Francesco Pasio to the Far- Eastern Portuguese settlement of Macao in preparation for a mission to China.

After a turbulent sea-voyage of three and a half months, during the course of which Ricci was so sick that he was convinced that his hour had come, the Jesuits arrived at the glittering sea port of Macao. Dubbed 'City of the Name of God' by its Portuguese rulers, the graceful peninsula on the southern coast of China, with its curving bays and green hills, might well have seemed to European travellers a divinely chosen place.[13] In reality, it was a settlement as much char- acterised by worldliness as religiosity. Its Christian name never really stuck, and Portuguese merchants continued to call the port Amacao, or 'Macao' for short, meaning Bay of Ama, the Buddhist goddess renowned for protecting sailors whose temple stood (and still stands) at the entrance to the inner harbour.[14] Perhaps it was to her that the Portuguese who sailed to east Asia owed their fortunes. For the wealth of Macao was derived from maritime enterprise. Ralph Fitch, an Englishman travelling in the East Indies in the 1580s, gave a succinct account of the lucrative commercial equation on which the city was founded:

When the Portugales goe from Macao in China to Japan, they carrie much white silke, Gold, Muske and Porcelanes: and they bring from thence nothing but Silver. They have a great Carake which goeth thither every yeare, and shee bringeth from thence every yeare above 600,000 crusadoes; and all this silver of Japan, and 200,000 crusadoes more in Silver which they bring yearly out of India, they imploy to their great advantage in China: and they bring from thence Gold, Muske, Silke, Copper, Porcelanes, and many other things very costly and gilded.[15]

By ferrying Chinese silk to Japan and Japanese silver to China, Portuguese merchants creamed off extraordinary profits from two nations that refused to do business directly.

Our image of 'historic Macao' today is dominated by the elegant colonial architecture of the eighteenth and nineteenth centuries. But in the late sixteenth century it might have felt more like a ghetto than a colony. The Portuguese who had settled in Macao, and who gained the right to establish a formal community there in 1557, were kept under close surveillance by the Cantonese authorities. For all their riches, the few hundred Europeans based in Macao lived a makeshift existence. Their lives were dangerous, their fortunes always at risk from piracy. Leaving their womenfolk in Lisbon, the Portuguese sailors set up home with Cantonese women, and sired children of indeterminate race and religion. The European settlement would remain, throughout Ricci's lifetime, a crucial anchor of the Chinese mission: the principal clearing house for communications between Jesuits, a vital source of financial support and a place of refuge. But Ricci, who did not see his future in service to the ex-pat community, was itching to get out of the city from the moment that he arrived.

It was, however, Ruggieri, the older Jesuit who had accompanied Ricci from Lisbon to Goa and who had continued eastwards to Macao in 1579 (three years ahead of Ricci), who led the way. As early as 1580, Ruggieri gained passage to Canton, in the company of the Portuguese merchants who were permitted to enter the city twice a year in order to trade with the Chinese. By 1581, he had befriended the *haidao*, the official in charge of policing the coasts of Guangdong province, with particular authority over foreigners, and had been granted temporary residence in the palace traditionally occupied by the Siamese ambassadors.[16] Ruggieri claimed to be making friends, even converts, among the Cantonese, but there were limits to what one missionary could achieve, and it was clearly frustrating to be tied to the rhythms of the trading year, forced to leave the city with the Portuguese merchants once the fair was over. Paradoxically, a worsening of diplomatic relations between China and the Iberian adventurers who stalked its coasts would give Ruggieri his next opportunity to step further into the prohibited lands of the Middle Kingdom.

In 1582, Chen Rui, the *dutang* or Governor of Guangdong and Guangxi provinces (referred to in European sources as the 'Viceroy') summoned the two principal figureheads of the Portuguese community to his seat in Zhaoqing. These were Leonardo de Sá, the Bishop of Macao, and the 'Captain-Major', the Portuguese merchant who, thanks to an annual privilege from the king, captained the yearly voyage to Japan and was de facto governor of the European community.[17] The *dutang* was responding to an imperial order to expel the Westerners from the peninsula. Yet Chen Rui, described in Ricci's account as 'a wise man, and a friend of

money', seems to have seen an opportunity for securing new
financial benefits from the Portuguese in return for special
privileges.[18] The Bishop and the Captain baulked at the idea
of leaving Macao. Lesser mortals were therefore selected
for this sortie: Mattia Penella, the principal magistrate of
Macao, was sent in place of the Captain, while the Jesuit
Michele Ruggieri was to represent the Church.[19] The del-
egates compensated for their deficiencies of status with lavish gifts: 'velvet, woollen cloths, crystal mirrors and other
things that are esteemed in China, worth more than one
thousand ducats'.[20] These expensive presents had the desired
impact on the *dutang*, who was 'placated and happy'. Seiz-
ing the moment, Ruggieri addressed Chen Rui by means
of an interpreter, and expressed his hope that one day the
Jesuits might be permitted to set up a church on Cantonese
soil. His bold proposal was not rebuffed, and when Penella returned on a second embassy to Zhaoqing, the *dutang*
was keen for news of the Jesuit. Ruggieri was lying sick in
Macao (a botched blood-letting had nearly killed him) but
sent word that the Jesuits had received a clock 'that chimed
by itself' which they wished to present to their new Chinese friend. This was a tactical triumph which prompted
the *dutang* to summon the 'Fathers of the Company', and
to invite them to build a church and house in Zhaoqing.[21]

Rather than joy, the long-awaited invitation caused con-
sternation in Macao, since it brought home to the Jesuits
their failure to master the Chinese language. Even Ruggieri knew too little, it was thought, to undertake such a
grave mission. And yet they could not pass up a heaven-
sent opportunity. It was decided by Valignano that Ruggieri
should travel in company with Francesco Pasio, 'a man of
great prudence, intelligence and authority', whose qualities might make up for the Fathers' linguistic inadequa-

cies.[22] Arriving in Zhaoqing two days after Christmas 1582, the two men at first made good progress.[23] Once again, the *dutang* was pleased with their gifts, including the clock and a 'triangular glass' or prism that split sunlight into many-coloured rays. In return, he gave them a room in a city-centre temple (a 'temple of idols', in the words of the Jesuits), and provided them with food. For four or five months, the two Westerners lived surrounded by 'the principal people' and mandarins of Zhaoqing, and nurtured 'grand hopes of staying in China for ever'. Their hopes were boosted when Chen Rui's secretary issued them with a licence permitting a third colleague, Matteo Ricci, to enter the city. But just as things were going so well, unexpected news reached Zhaoqing from the capital: Chen Rui, the Jesuits' patron, had lost his job. The Westerners were told to get out.[24]

Ruggieri and Pasio returned disconsolate to Macao. Pasio set sail for Japan, to apply his missionary energies to what – some fourteen years before the crucifixion of twenty-six Christians at Nagasaki – appeared to be far more fertile ground.[25] Ricci assumed the role of Ruggieri's new companion, and the two men, closely watched by Chinese officials, endured a nerve-racking period in bureaucratic limbo. In Zhaoqing, the new *dutang*, working his way through the archives of his predecessor, became aware of the arrangements that had been made to accommodate the foreigners. He tracked them down to Macao and called them to yet another meeting, this time with Canton's *haidao*, an old contact of Ruggieri's.[26] The European priests made their case: they were religious men, who had come from their land attracted by China's famous good government in order to live and die there. All they wanted was a piece of land where, supported by alms, they might build a small church and house in which they could serve the King of Heaven whom they adored; they would harm nobody, and would live off the alms that they had already collected.[27] The *haidao* listened to their speech sympathetically, but explained that he did not have the authority to grant their requests. Their fates lay in the hands of the new *dutang*, Guo Yingpin. As it turned out, Guo was in the process of issuing the first edict of his period of office, in which he made great play of his contempt for foreigners, and specifically condemned those who had facilitated the entry of two priests into mainland China. It looked like a hopeless case: Ricci and Ruggieri returned to Macao believing that the Jesuits would now never enter China, at least not if this *dutang* had anything to do with it.

Only a providential twist could save the mission. Less than a week after the Jesuits' return to Macao, a servant from the palace of the *dutang* came knocking on their door bearing the letter from Wang Pan that promised to provide them with a place on which they could build a house and church. The Jesuits, who had never before met the Prefect, expressed amazement at his intervention, and were even more mystified as to why the xenophobic new *dutang* was apparently backing their re-entry to China. (The large tips that the priests had promised to some of the servants at the *dutang*'s palace in return for their support might have had something to do with it). But, for now, theirs was not to reason why. The priests 'thought only of how God in his mercy had turned his eyes towards this miserable kingdom, and with a powerful hand had opened the door that had been locked to the preachers of the Holy Gospel, in order that they might here sow the seeds of Christian faith.'[28] On 10 September 1583 Ruggieri and Ricci re-entered Zhaoqing.

*

Although it is some way off the beaten track today, Zhao-qing was no backwater in the late sixteenth century. Francisco Cabral, Rector of Macao and Superior of the Chinese mission during the years 1582–5, visited the Jesuit house in November 1584, and described Zhaoqing as 'a city of 50,000 households'. Although Cabral spoke of hearths not heads, one can deduce that this was an impressive figure when one considers that the total population of Rome at this time was only 80,000.[29] A year later he was still holding forth about the delights of a city 'so fresh and so healthy, so fertile, and glutted with everything'.[30] Above all, Zhaoqing was a centre of officialdom:

That city where we have been given licence to live is a place more suited to spread the Gospel, in my view, than there is in all of China from the Royal City down. Since the *dutang* always resides in Zhaoqing, all the Mandarins of this province necessarily return there because of the custom and obligation they have to visit him at the beginning of each month, although those who live far away usually come every two months. And all, when finishing the three-year term of their office, before returning to the court of the king, must come to be licensed by him. And similarly, those who come from the court, provided with new assignments and duties, render him obedience before taking possession of them.[31]

Cabral was delighted to report on how easily the flow of literati was diverted to the Jesuit house, and shared the view of the missionaries on the ground that such contacts would lead in time to conversions:

This gives us the opportunity to deal familiarly with [the Chinese] and to share our affections in such a manner that our fame has already spread through the greater part of China, and they take more notice of us than of the ministers of idols. And in so far as I have understood the ease with which these Gentiles hear the things of our holy faith, it is to be hoped that the Lord has reserved for us a great harvest in this spacious land, if we on our part, with all humility and desiring the honour of the blessed Christ, dispose ourselves to cultivate it as it should be.[32]

With little money at their disposal, but copious supplies of 'courtesy', the Jesuits in Zhaoqing embarked on a punishing regime of hospitality.[33]

The elite male officials who crowded into the Jesuit house were exactly the constituency that the Jesuits hoped to attract: 'educated', 'noble', 'the principal persons' of the land.[34] The assumption from the outset was that the ruling classes were the people to target. Conversions in these ranks might cause Christianity to be imposed, as a state religion, on entire communities. But the scholar-officials who queued outside the Jesuit house were innocent of spiritual motives. They were drawn instead by curiosity and a fascination with the exotic. First there was the strangeness of the European building, esteemed for its 'delicacy', and considered to be one of 'the wonders of China'.[35] Then there were the 'unusual and strange' things to be found within: 'triangular crystals, the map with Chinese letters, and other things in which they take delight'.[36] Finally, there was the weird spectacle of the Western men themselves: the Jesuits were 'in appearance so different' from the Chinese that they were themselves worthy of a place on the tourist trail.[37]

Among the most pleasing signs of the Jesuits' apparent success in courting the literati was a gift of verses and two 'gilded tablets' from the Prefect who had facilitated their entry into Zhaoqing. Wang Pan, who the year after the Jesuits' arrival was promoted to *lingxi dao* (a prestigious administrative position within the provinces of Guangdong and Guangxi), was exactly the kind of friend that the Jesuits needed to cultivate. And in a letter of May 1584, subsequently distributed throughout Europe in a published version, Ruggieri made clear the significance of his gift:

The Mandarins love us and are very content with our staying here. One of the most learned of them composed some verses and sent them to me, together with two titles written on gilded tablets. The one is to be placed above the door of our house, and the other in the chapel. For the consolation of our brethren, I put them here as they sound in our language.

TITLES

Church and New Flower of the Saints
From the West there came to us, Fathers, Men Most Pure

VERSES

Let us give a song to the heavenly man.
From the western Kingdom, carried in a small ship for ten thousand miles, he crossed the vast ocean.
Only because he was human did he enter the celebrated solitude of the Chinese, that as holy man he might rest there.
In the dead of night a dragon descends into the lake: all around the violent wave grows dark.
When spring comes a guo bird is sent out into the wooded, green field.
Here he is forgetful of himself and his own; does he remember his dear place of birth?
As his heart knows the right, so alone he pours forth prayers to God, and reads books.
He came to see in the region situated in the middle, men preparing for themselves a road to Heaven.
How rare the man with strong and resolute mind who would spread forth an odour far and wide.[38]

With its lavish symbolism and its sympathetic portrayal of the sacrifices that the Jesuits had made in the cause of religion, the poem turns their presence into an elegantly ornamental affair.

Such friendly overtures were a huge fillip for Ricci and Ruggieri. But they also presented a challenge to the Jesuits' sense of identity. Wang Pan's poem touches on the problem: 'he is forgetful of himself and his own; does he remember his dear place of birth?' Even here, at the very beginning of their mission, Ricci seems to have imagined that he and Ruggieri were fitting in so well that their foreignness was scarcely perceptible. In a letter of October 1585 to Claudio Acquaviva, head of the Jesuit Order in Rome, he wrote that the local notables 'get on very well with us and are losing their fear of foreigners; many say that we are nearly the same as them, which is quite some compliment in a nation which is so closed and arrogant'.[39] The claim clearly contradicts Ricci's assertions elsewhere that the Jesuits' appeal lay in their strangeness, and reveals just how dizzying the European priests found the demands made of them to assume new identities in this alien land. If the pressure to 'go native' derived in part from Jesuit policy – the famous strategy of 'accommodation' that was being championed in the Far East by Valignano – it also stemmed from local influences. It was on the advice of Chen Rui, the *dutang* who had first invited the Jesuits to Zhaoqing, that they had decided to adopt the robes of Buddhist priests. In sixteenth-century Europe, a change of clothes could mean a change of identity. This was the context of Ricci's half-joking declaration, in a letter to his old Jesuit friend Giulio Fuligatti in Siena, that 'I have become a Chinaman. Already you will be aware that in clothing . . . in ceremonies, and in all exterior matters, we are now Chinese.'[40]

More testing than the Jesuits' assumption of Chinese dress was the obligation to acquire the Chinese language. This was, once again, key to Valignano's strategy in the East, as well as being a matter of pressing practical concern. Jesuits were renowned for their study of languages; when at school and college, they were expected to converse in Latin, and were encouraged to join 'academies' for the promotion of Greek and Hebrew.[41] But, as Ricci told his friend Martino de Fornari in 1583, shortly after his arrival in Macao, learning Chinese was not like learning 'Greek or German'; it was *altra cosa* – something else. First there was the ambiguity of spoken Chinese: 'Many words signify more than a thousand different things, and sometimes there is no way of distinguishing between these meanings other than by pronouncing them in a higher or lower voice, in four different tones.' As for the written language, 'There are as many letters as there are words or things – more than 70,000 in all – each one very different and complex in form.'[42] Round about the same time, Michele Ruggieri also wrote home of the trials of having to learn this seemingly impossible tongue, which was possessed 'of innumerable characters', and which was so difficult that the Chinese themselves spent 'fifteen or twenty years' at it. The particular problem experienced by Europeans seeking to acquire the language, explained Ruggieri, was the absence of bilingual instructors: 'thus it was necessary to teach me both the Chinese language and characters by means of pictures'; if, for example, his teacher wished him to learn how to say and write 'horse' in Chinese, he would 'paint a horse, and above it paint the character that signifies horse, and which is pronounced "ma"' – a process that Ruggieri considered utterly 'ridiculous'.[43]

But, despite the immense difficulties encountered by the Jesuits, early reports suggested the value of at least being seen to make an effort. As Ruggieri reflected after his first meeting with the new *dutang*, Guo Yingpin, in Zhaoqing:

Having understood how we have come from the Company of Rome sent by the Great Father, that is, by the Highest Pontiff, and seeing that we have desired to learn their language and their letters in order to be able reciprocally to share ours with them, he received me very lovingly.[44]

Ricci's grasp of Chinese, meanwhile, was evidently going from strength to strength. Within a little over two years of his arrival in China, he claimed to have made great progress in the language, and considered himself ready to confess and preach in Chinese.[45] Determined to gain fluency not just in speech but in reading and writing, he told Acquaviva that 'already I am speaking to everybody without an interpreter, and I am writing and reading Chinese books moderately well'.[46] But it was not all gain. The strides that Ricci was making in speaking and writing Chinese were apparently paralleled by a decline in his command of his mother tongue. This is something that Ricci commented on repeatedly in letters to his compatriots: 'Forgive me for writing so badly, since it is certain that I no longer remember the Italian language.'[47] Such claims have perplexed experts in Italian linguistics who insist that Ricci's abilities to write Italian were undiminished, and it has been suggested that his assertions of inadequacy were merely rhetorical.[48] Another interpretation would be that Ricci was suffering from acute disorientation. As he confided to Fuligatti, 'We go about here in such a mix of language that I do not know if I am writing in Italian, or in German, or in some other language . . . I think I have become a barbarian for the love of God.'[49]

*

Zhaoqing provided the Jesuits of the China mission with their first testing ground for the '*modo soave*', the 'gentle method' of conversion. Writing up the events of 1583 in the *History*, Ricci explained:

At first, in order not to excite any suspicion among those people regarding this novelty, the Fathers did not engage explicitly in preaching our holy law, but rather employed themselves, in the time available to them for receiving visits, in learning their language, their letters, and their courtesies, and winning the hearts of the Chinese, and moving them by their good and exemplary way of life to that which neither their linguistic ability nor the time at their disposal permitted them to express.

Or, as he put it more succinctly, a few paragraphs later:

With this means of speaking, more with deeds than with words, the good scent of our law began to spread throughout China.[50]

Unsurprisingly, however, the Chinese people were not impervious to the novelties of Catholicism, as was indicated by their reactions to the painting of the Virgin and Child that hung above the altar of the Jesuit church:

Everyone who came to visit the Fathers – the mandarins and other literati, as well as ordinary people, and, above all, the idolatrous priests – adored that image of the Madonna and her Son . . . pausing at the threshold to genuflect and bow down before it. And they admired the artifice of our painting.

The Jesuits were forced to take swift action, 'replacing the Madonna with another image, this time of the Saviour':

and this was because the Chinese, on hearing the Fathers say that they had to adore only one God, and on seeing the image of the Madonna on the altar, came to be rather confused, and many spread the word around that the God that we adored was a woman. For it was too soon to declare the mystery of the Incarnation.[51]

In Ricci's view, recorded many years later in his *History*, it was better to render the Virgin Mary invisible than to allow her image to promote misunderstanding.

Yet the evidence from the 1580s suggests that the Jesuits were, in fact, far more forthcoming about the mysteries of Christianity than Ricci's retrospective appraisal allows. The first work that Ruggieri and Ricci produced in Chinese was a translation of the Ten Commandments, the Paternoster and the Ave Maria. But it was in constructing a purpose-designed Catechism for the Chinese that the Jesuits were forced, for the first time, to confront the question of which doctrines they would choose to promote and which they would shroud in silence. The first draft of this important work – loosely framed as a dialogue between a Chinese and a Western scholar – was produced by Ruggieri in 1581. After Ricci's arrival, the two men would repeatedly edit and correct the text, before publishing it under the title *The New Compilation* in November 1584. This publication turned out to be remarkably explicit: it not only introduced the topics of the Lord of Heaven, the Creation, the Christian laws, the Last Judgment, and baptism, but also disclosed the 'truth' about the Incarnation and Virgin Birth. Thus the Chinese were taught how the Lord of Heaven became a real man, who lived for thirty-three years in the kingdom of 'India', before ascending into Heaven. His name was Jesus, and he talked, smiled, slept and ate just as common people do. His mother was 'a perfect woman, Mary, who conceived by the work of the Holy Spirit, and after nine months gave birth to Jesus. She remained pure, just as a woman who did not know the things of the man.'[52]

That these bold statements of Christian doctrine did not emerge in isolation is indicated by a short text, discovered in 1935 by the great Jesuit scholar Pasquale D'Elia, and

believed to be by Ricci himself. Appended to the manuscript of a Chinese–Portuguese vocabulary, probably dating
from 1585, are a series of paragraphs in Chinese detailing
conversations that Ricci had, or at least hoped to have, with
the literati visiting the Jesuit residence in Zhaoqing. The
text was presumably an aide-memoire for Ricci, a kind of
highly specialised phrasebook, which would help him to
come up with the right words for the right occasion. D'Elia
christened the text the 'catechetic conversations', although
inevitably they preserve only the missionary's side of the
conversations. Ricci first speaks of his love of China, and
the great distance that he has travelled. Then, having given
a brief account of Adam and Eve and the Fall of Man, he
launches into the topic of the Incarnation:

Fortunately, the Lord of Heaven, in His mercy, had compassion of
the pains of those in the earthly prison. He chose a fifteen-year-old
girl, named Mary, who conceived without a husband. After nine
months she gave birth to a son, Jesus, a European name that means:
Saviour of the world. Jesus made many good actions, cured many
people: the deaf, the blind, the mute and hundreds of sick people
. . . It would be difficult to report here all the single miracles. He
proclaimed and propagated the Gospel and trained many disciples.
Jesus, the Saviour of the world, was without sin. Unfortunately evil
people, of a certain place, did not want to listen to or believe in
Him. They took two sticks of wood and made a cross (the sign of
the Chinese character ten); they nailed His hands and His feet and
made Him die on the cross. His disciples took His corpse and buried Him in a grave of stone. In the three following days, the soul
of Jesus entered the earthly prison to judge the people. He allowed
the perfect saints, who in ancient times did good and venerated the
Lord of Heaven, to leave the place. Those who have not found the
Lord of Heaven entered the earthly prison, where they cannot see
the light. After three days, the soul of Jesus reunited with the body,
returned to life, left the burial place and appeared to everybody.
Once the 40th day arrived, in front of all the disciples, he ascended

in plain daylight, taking with him all the good souls, who ascended to enjoy happiness. He commanded all the disciples to spread out in four directions to preach the Gospel, to exhort all to do good, and give the holy water to those who believe, in remission of the old sins. The disciples spread out as clouds, not afraid of travelling a thousand *li* . . . The Lord of Heaven gave them the special gift of understanding the language of all nations, of saving souls, of cancelling sins and performing miracles.

And thus, concluded Ricci, 'I have humbly imitated my predecessors.'[53]

Whereas Ricci, writing his *History* towards the end of his life, proclaimed that 'it was too soon to declare the mystery of the Incarnation', contemporary evidence makes it clear that both he and Ruggieri had been notably upfront about the fundamental tenets of Christian teaching. So how did the Chinese respond to the Jesuits' revelations? The Cat-echism was apparently a literary success. On 25 January 1584, Ruggieri wrote to Acquaviva, 'I have now finished revising a *Doctrine* that I have produced in the Chinese language, which I started writing four years ago, and it pleases these Chinese governing lords so much that they have forced me to print it.'[54] Distributed in more than 3,000 copies, the Catechism demonstrated to the Jesuits the extraordinary power of print in China. In October of the following year, Ricci sent Acquaviva copies of the Catechism, together with the other Christian writings that had been published in Chinese – the very copies that still sit in the Jesuit archives in Rome. Like Ruggieri, Ricci was delighted by the recep-tion of the Catechism, and explained how the publishing project had been supported by the *lingxi dao*, Wang Pan. But although the tone of Ricci's letter is very positive, and the news is intended to be of 'consolation' to Acquaviva, it also betrays the complexity of Chinese reactions:

When a new book is published, it is the custom in China, as we do, to make some epigram in commendation of the book or the author; thus they get some man who has an important office in the kingdom to write a composition in prose. For this reason, when we saw the *lingxi dao*, who is our protector on this earth, and who last year was promoted from governor to the much higher office of *lingxi dao*, we asked him to write a composition for the Catechism, that was already published, without the first folio. He was very happy to see the work, saying that it was very good and full of good arguments, and yet he did not want to write such a composition, nor did it seem to him necessary for anybody else to write it, and that we should present it to the people as it was. For this we gave thanks to him and to the Lord, because this was a licence to spread the holy law throughout this land. Although this work includes refutations of the principal sects of China, and opposes many of the customs and sins of China, on account of which we were very frightened, from the moment that we started to distribute it among the people, especially to literati and officials, we have heard nothing but good about it. The same *lingxi dao*, when he comes to our house and brings others to see us and our possessions, reminds us – if we forget – that we should give them a copy of the Catechism; and thus he, as with all the others from there, more than ever before honours the image of our Saviour that is in our chapel.[55]

Wang Pan was surely attracted to the Catechism, as he and his colleagues were to the clocks and prisms in the Jesuit house, as a piece of exotica. He was happy to read and commend it, but had no wish to give it his imprimatur. While Ricci gives the impression that mandarins were queuing up at the Jesuit residence to get hold of the Catechism, he admitted in a letter of 1586 to his friend in Rome Ludovico Maselli that 'up until now we have not converted to Christianity any person of real consequence'.[56]

It was not that the Jesuits were failing to make converts; rather that they were making the wrong sort of converts.

The first baptisms were presided over by Francisco Cabral, during his visit to Zhaoqing, on 'the Feast of the Presentation of Our Lady' (21 November) 1584.[57] On this occasion, there were three candidates for baptism, one of whom was turned away on the grounds that he was not yet properly instructed. Of the remaining two, one was a *xiucai* or graduate from Fujian province who had spent four or five months studying with the Jesuits, while also teaching them Chinese. He took the name of Paolo. The other, henceforth to be known as Giovanni, who was evidently not a literatus, was nevertheless described in Ricci's *History* as a 'young man of fine intellect', who had been learning all about Christianity since Ruggieri and Francesco Pasio had first established themselves in the city. When they were forced to leave Zhaoqing in 1583, the Jesuits had entrusted him with their altar, and on their re-entry to the city they were delighted to learn that their friend had not only looked after it but had installed it, complete with seven or eight incense-burners, in his house, beneath a tablet on which were written the Chinese words meaning 'To the Lord of Heaven'.[58]

By October 1585, Ricci was able to tell Acquaviva that there were now twelve converts, 'the majority of whom are men of penitence, who fast in the Chinese manner, that is they do not eat either meat or fish'. Among these, the most prominent were another 'Paolo', baptised appropriately enough on the Feast of St Paul (29 June), and 'an old man' in his late sixties, known as 'Nicolao', baptised on the Feast of the Assumption (15 August).[59] Paolo was renowned for his penitential life, and was a committed vegan: 'He eats neither meat nor fish nor eggs nor milk.' He had adopted Christianity with great enthusiasm:

Upon seeing and reading the Catechism, he brought us his idol and his books to be burned; and getting down on his knees, and putting his head on the ground, he begged us to make him a Christian. And after having learnt the Credo, Paternoster, Ten Commandments, etc., that we had published in his language, on the day of St Paul, we baptised him; for this reason, he is called Paolo, and he continues with great edification to come to mass and to engage in other Christian exercises.[60]

Nicolao demonstrated 'extraordinary fervour' and was determined to have his entire family brought to the font. In November 1585, by which time the tally of Zhaoqing Christians stood at nineteen or twenty, Ricci reported that Nicolao had already 'made one of his sons, two of his nephews, and a son-in-law Christian, and soon he will convert his whole household that is full of men and women'. Ricci added approvingly, 'These Christians . . . gave us books and idols to burn, since for so long they had been deceived by them.'[61]

On 29 October 1586, Ricci told Maselli that 'our flock is growing, and now stands at nearly forty'. He went on to inform his friend that 'many come to enquire about our faith', including 'three mandarins or senior magistrates who are based in this land': the *buzheng shi* of Canton, whom Ricci described as 'the principal administrator of the province'; the *lingxi dao*, whose hospitality the Jesuits often enjoyed, and with whom they engaged in lengthy conversations about God (he was apparently especially curious about the Jesuits' meditative practices, and their ability to perform miracles); and the *zongbing*, or military commander of the Cantonese troops. But having enumerated these officials, and their perceived interests in matters divine, Ricci was forced to concede that the most significant conversion to date was the father of the second-most important magistrate in the city, 'an old man of over seventy years'.[62]

By the end of the Zhaoqing mission, the Jesuits had

apparently made nearly eighty conversions.[63] These included, in 1589, the first Chinese women to be baptised, who were described by Ricci as 'a great credit', who helped to 'sustain Christianity in their households'. Equally beneficial as ambassadors of Christianity were a number of children, brought to the font from their deathbeds, for these were subsequently 'sent to heaven as new intercessors for the people of China'. Among the other named converts from this final phase of the Zhaoqing mission were a man whose demonic delusions were cured when he was encouraged by the missionaries to burn all his idolatrous images, and a minor official who had sought the help of Ricci and his colleagues on account of his wife's infertility. It seems that the Jesuits' first converts in China were not the high-ranking mandarins that they had courted, but rather women, children, the sick and the old. And where able-bodied men came to the font, they were attracted either by the Jesuits' reputation for conducting miracles or by the missionaries' regime of penitence and self-mortification, which was promoted especially enthusiastically by Ruggieri.[64] Indeed, much to Ricci's distaste, some of the Jesuits' most ardent fans were Buddhist vegetarians, who clung erroneously to the view that the soul might transmigrate into an animal's body.[65]

*

If Ricci was frustrated by the nature and quality of the converts that the mission had thus far garnered, there were more pressing problems to be dealt with. From the very beginning of the Jesuits' stay in Zhaoqing, their residence was periodically stoned and the priests subjected to 'discourtesies and insults'. Rumours linking the missionaries to Portuguese plots abounded on the streets of the ancient city, and were especially virulent following episodes of coastal piracy. Moreover, the Tower of High Fortune, which – to modern Western eyes – looks so quintessentially oriental, was widely believed to have been commissioned by the foreign priests as a provocative statement of Western imperial power.[66] Macao was viewed with acute suspicion, and on more than one occasion Jesuits were accused of kidnapping Chinese boys in order to sell them as slaves to the Portuguese community. They were also charged with grilling the bodies of children, on account of the unfamiliar smell of roast pork that rose from the priests' spit.[67] Child abduction was a slur even more powerful and indicative of Chinese fears than the allegations of sexual misconduct that would surface in time.[68]

Sometimes the spur to attack the Jesuits came from on high. In October 1585, Ricci reported that the Wanli emperor had issued an edict expressly condemning the presence of foreign priests in China. The tone of the edict was inflammatory. The Jesuits were dubbed thieves and assassins, who had insinuated themselves into the heart of Guangdong province and would quickly spread throughout the empire. Impostors without licence to be in China, they were ordered to grow their hair and return to secular life. Meanwhile their churches were to be dismantled. Without hesitation, the Jesuits' friend Wang Pan instructed them to stop frequenting his palace and to remove the precious tablets that he had given to them from the door of the church. But this time the panic was short-lived. Apparently influenced by his consort, the Empress Wang, the Wanli emperor reversed his edict as quickly as he had issued it. Ricci commented that it was not only the 'queen' who had intervened, but the Queen of Heaven. Equilibrium was restored, and Wang Pan ordered his tablets to be put back.[69]

At other times, a groundswell of popular resentment

against the foreign priests broke out despite official efforts to contain it. During the years 1587–8, the Jesuits' standing in Zhaoqing seemed more precarious than ever before. Their house was repeatedly burgled, and malicious talk buzzed around them.[70] Particularly damaging to the Jesuits' reputation was the case of the Macanese convert named Martin who – when visiting the fathers in Zhaoqing – had conned a couple of local Christians into believing that the Jesuits had access to the secrets of alchemy. Martin had cheated his co-religionists of all their worldly goods, while he sought to convince them that he was on the point of discovering the Jesuits' methods of turning mercury into silver, and that he would disclose all. But when he could keep up the pretence no longer, he ran off to Canton, stealing the Jesuits' prism while he was about it. The magistrates of Zhaoqing hunted Martin down and subjected him to eighty lashes – he subsequently died in prison – but the two wronged Christians continued to nurse a vendetta against the Jesuits, whom they held responsible for their misfortunes. In the ensuing fallout of accusations and counter-accusations, it was alleged that Ruggieri had committed adultery with a woman living by the south gate of the city.[71]

Given the Jesuits' reliance on the protection of local authorities, their position was rendered even more insecure by the rotation of officials that characterised the Chinese administrative system. In 1588, their old friend and supporter Wang Pan was finally posted to a job in another province, and it was all change among the chief magistrates of the city.[72] Meanwhile the composition of the Jesuit house was also in flux. In November 1587, Ruggieri had returned to Macao, whence he would go back to Europe for good, and the Portuguese Duarte de Sande (Superior in charge of the Chinese mission from 1585 to 1597) arrived to take his place in Zhaoqing. The interpreters and servants of the Jesuit house were unimpressed by their new master, and relations deteriorated to such an extent that they posted notices on street corners claiming that Duarte did not have a licence to stay in the land, and calling for all the mandarins of the city to present a complaint against him if he did not leave within a few days.[73] The reasons for Duarte's unpopularity are not clear. In any case, his stay in Zhaoqing was comparatively brief, and he was replaced by another Portuguese, António de Almeida, the following year.

These were some of the tensions underpinning a dramatic attack that was launched against the Jesuits' house early in 1588. The pretext for this dated back to the floods that afflicted the city in October 1586. Two years on, in an attempt to prevent further inundations, the authorities of Zhaoqing issued a permit inviting local people to cut branches from barren trees to shore up the defences of the river. There were those who took this as a licence for theft and destruction, and a group turned up in the Jesuits' garden intent on pillage. Scared off the grounds by 'a black Kaffir' who was working for the Fathers, they resorted to stoning the residence from afar. But when the priests inside the house failed to respond they charged forward, making rough music in a furious assault, during which they smashed the windows, roof and doors of the building, and brought down the wall of the courtyard. Father Duarte left the house with an interpreter to inform the city magistrates. Ricci, meanwhile, beseeched the assailants to cause no further damage and to take what they wanted; but whenever he tried to approach them to speak, stones rained down on him and he feared for his life. Finally, recommending the house to the protection of God, Ricci went out into the garden, gathered a bundle of canes onto his back, and presented them to his attackers, inviting them to take any other materials that they needed. Overwhelmed by Ricci's cheek-turning, the Chinese gave up their game; shouting and beating on their basins like victors in battle, they returned to their homes.[74]

If the presence of the Jesuits on the outskirts of Zhaoqing was beginning to upset the local residents, it was also of new concern to the authorities in Canton, where a group of the oldest and most respected mandarins penned a petition calling for the foreigners to be expelled. These wise old men were, it seems, not immune to rumour, for they fervently believed that the Tower of High Fortune had been commissioned by the foreign priests and paid for by the Portuguese community in Macao. They deduced that the whole project must therefore be part of a Portuguese conspiracy to incite rebellion among the people of China.[75] According to their petition, the insidious plans of the Europeans were bolstered by bricks and mortar: 'They have built and put up houses on the ground which are several storeys high and they erect large monuments built one layer upon another, just like bees and ants.'[76] The Jesuits were surely spies, posted in Zhaoqing by the Portuguese in order to find out the secrets of the Chinese. In time, they would make alliances with local people of evil intent and would cause great harm to the empire, casting the Chinese, 'like fish and whales', into the sea.

Ricci transcribed and translated the accusations of the Cantonese elders verbatim, praising the 'elegance and order', the 'energy and lightness' with which they made their charges. It is typical of the Humanistically educated Jesuit that he should have been so impressed by the old men's command of language, despite the damaging inaccuracies of their accusations. The authorities of Zhaoqing dismissed the charges, not only because the claim about the Tower was, to anyone who had witnessed its construction, plainly false, but also because they resented the meddling of the Cantonese in the affairs of their city.

But Ricci might have guessed that this would not be the end of the hostilities. The Jesuits were about to fall victim to a new *dutang*, Liu Jiezhai, 'a cruel and ambitious man'.[77] An old adversary of the Jesuits, Tansiaohu, who had been responsible for overseeing the construction of the Tower of High Fortune, sought out Liu Jiezhai in Wuzhou where the *dutang* was staying.[78] Speaking to him about the Tower the people of Zhaoqing had built, and the temple that they had subsequently constructed in honour of their beloved former *lingxi dao*, Wang Pan, he sowed a seed in Liu Jiezhai's mind. Why should the *dutang* himself not have a temple dedicated to him? After all, one of his predecessors had enjoyed this honour. Moreover, Tansiaohu could recommend the ideal spot, just to the left of the Tower of High Fortune – the site of the Jesuit residence.

Liu Jiezhai liked the plan, and immediately dispatched to the *lingxi dao* a memorandum, informing him that

there had come from Macao a number of foreign priests, who had built a house on the banks of the great river, which was a thinly veiled front for giving advice to the Portuguese on everything that went on in China; and that the Fathers were people of great intelligence and employed various ruses in order to get the people to follow them. Consequently, by day and night, people flocked to their house to hear their sermons, never interrupting them. And the priests preached a law without name in China, to which effect every day they made use of new artifices; and in order to deceive the plebeian classes the better they discoursed upon all sorts of doctrine and books, and had erected in public a bell that chimed by itself. On account of which, he who had command over this province commanded the *lingxi dao* to undertake an investigation into all this, and to examine whether the charges were true or false. And if he discovered them to be true, then he should dispatch the Fathers immediately to Macao, or transfer them to the temple at Nanhuasi in the land of Shaozhou, a place where there were more than a thousand priests of idols.[79]

It fell to the deputy of the *lingxi dao* to inform the Jesuits of this new development, and although he acknowledged the falsity of the accusations, he insisted that – this time – there was nothing to be done but to accept the *dutang*'s will, and to leave the city.

Ricci was touched by the support of the mandarins of Zhaoqing: in attempting to resist the *dutang*'s orders, and to keep the Jesuits in the city, 'the magistrates demonstrated extraordinary love for us'. When they saw that nothing could be done to prevent their departure, the literati of the city petitioned the *dutang* to make appropriate financial compensation to the foreign priests. They put it to Liu Jiezhai that the priests had spent more than 600 ducats on building their house and church, and that – given that they had committed no wrong – it would be unjust not to make good their losses. The *dutang* offered a payment of 50 or 60 ducats. But this derisory sum Ricci proudly declined. He stated that the church belonged to God, and that he had no right to sell it. (This fundamental objection he followed up with the more practical, financial consideration that the building had cost more than 600 ducats to construct, and he was certainly not going to trade it in for 60.) In any case, Ricci resolved to take nothing, not least because by keeping a piece of property in Zhaoqing, the Jesuits would retain a pretext for returning.

Impatient with those officials who were standing in the way of the Jesuits' departure, the *dutang* had had enough of prevarication. In August 1589, he issued his final sentence and resolution on this matter, commanding the departure of the priests from Zhaoqing within three days.[80]

So the Jesuits took their leave, amid the farewells of tearful neophytes. And well the Christians of Zhaoqing might cry, for, abandoned by their pastors and without anyone to teach them the true doctrines of the holy faith, or to administer the sacraments to them, their salvation was – as the missionaries knew only too well – in jeopardy. The Fathers offered what consolation they could, sharing out their possessions and exhorting their followers to stay true to the faith and to stay out of trouble. They entrusted an image of the Saviour to one of the converts, proposing that the Christian community congregate on Sundays and feast days at his home, where they might speak of divine things and recommend themselves to God. The fragility of the Chinese mission was as clear as it had ever been.[81]

In a symbolic gesture, Ricci went for the last time back into the city centre of Zhaoqing, where he handed over a bunch of keys (a European innovation for which the Jesuits had won fame) to the deputy of the *lingxi dao*, and thanked him for all his kindness. Ricci again refused the offer of 60 ducats, but asked that the Jesuit house which had been constructed in honour of God should never be put to profane uses. The official issued the Jesuits with papers that testified to their good standing, and requested their safe conduct by boat to Macao. Ricci left the weeping Christians – 'like orphaned children' – with a final benediction, and embarked.[82]

When, in 1592, Ricci would come to review his years spent in Zhaoqing, his memories were bitter. In a letter to his old friend and colleague in Rome, Fabio de Fabii, he wrote:

To give even a partial account to Your Reverence of our sufferings at the hands of these people during the six or seven years that we were there would be to exceed the limits of this letter ... One year I was taken to the governor, accused of stealing children to send back to be sold in our lands; another year, my companion was accused of something even worse, although on both occasions our adversaries paid dearly for their false accusations, the first being whipped, the second dying whilst in prison. Many times we were suspected of being spies, not just by base folk, but by the oldest sages of the metropolis of Canton – allegations that we escaped with considerable difficulty. Defamatory notices were posted against us around the city; and our house was assaulted with volleys of stones, causing considerable damage both to our property and to our persons. Besides which, there were the many insults that we suffered on a daily basis, shouted out in the city squares, or on the streets, as we passed by. Take note that the devil treated us as his capital adversaries while he kept us in that house.[83]

Ricci's startlingly negative appraisal of the Jesuits' time in Zhaoqing emerged only retrospectively. Zhaoqing ended badly, and later accounts of the mission were written in the knowledge of that end. If we look at the seven surviving letters written by Ricci during the period of the Zhaoqing mission (all sent between 1584 and 1586) the tone is generally far more positive, stressing progress made in language and in conversions, the good relations that had been established with the literati of the city, the favourable impact of the Jesuits' scientific knowledge, and the successful publication of a Christian Catechism in Chinese. These features of the narrative are all present too in Ricci's *History*, but they are slotted into a more embittered narrative about their ill-treatment at the hands of the Chinese. Yet before hindsight had begun to jaundice his perception, certain key discourses about China had begun to take shape in Ricci's correspondence, and these would be elaborated in his later writings. Particularly significant are Ricci's views about Guangdong province, and his pronouncements on Chinese religion.

Ricci was convinced from an early stage that southern China was *not* the most fruitful field of mission, and that the Jesuits' fortunes lay in the north. In a letter written in September 1584 to a Spanish official, Giambattista Román, who had come to Macao from the Philippines, Ricci proclaimed that the province of Canton was 'the worst part of China'; two years later he told his friend Ludovico Maselli that Michele Ruggieri had headed north to Shaoxing, where 'the people are more inclined [to Christianity] than those of Canton'.[84] Ricci's desire to get beyond Guangdong province was partly based on history. Canton and its hinterland had, since the beginning of the sixteenth century, been the stage on which often hostile relations between China and Europe were played out. Portuguese merchants, pursuing trade and wealth, were not always models of diplomacy, and on occasion paid the price by spending time in Cantonese gaols. In this respect, the first Jesuits to enter mainland China benefited from their Italian identity. When Michele Ruggieri was warmly received in Canton in 1581, he remarked proudly that this was something that would never have been afforded to a Portuguese.[85] In 1584 he alluded to the aggressive reputation of the Iberian nations, writing to Acquaviva:

With these people one needs to proceed with great suavity, and not with indiscreet fervour. Otherwise, it would be very easy to close the door that God our Lord has opened to us, and I don't know when it would be opened again. I say this because the people are enemies of foreigners, and especially fearful of Christians, seeing themselves in these parts surrounded by Portuguese and Castilians whom they consider bellicose men.[86]

The Jesuits' suavity made the rumours about the Tower of High Fortune, and their own presumed involvement in a Portuguese plot, especially vexing. There was further trouble to come from the maverick Spanish Jesuit Alonso Sánchez, based in Manila, who in 1586 (six years after the annexation of Portugal by Philip II) wrote to his king proposing that the time was right for an invasion of China. He advised Philip that the job could be completed with 10–12,000 soldiers, adding that 'an effort should be made to have the troops so numerous, well equipped, trained and strategically handled that there will be no chance for resistance; and their mere presence and a demonstration will suffice to cause the Chinese to submit, with no great bloodshed'.[87] While Philip dismissed Sánchez's idea for the crackpot scheme that it was, it is easy to understand why Ricci and Ruggieri were keen to dissociate themselves from the Portuguese community at Macao, and to escape from the south, where anti-European sentiments were well-established. At the same time, the Jesuits mythologised Beijing as the centre of Chinese civilisation, and dreamed optimistically of converting the emperor, whose immense power would guarantee the salvation of the entire population. By the time that Ricci came to write his *History*, his loathing of the south was well developed:

the people of Canton, on account of living at the very end of the kingdom, at the mouth of the torrid zone, close to many neighbouring foreign kingdoms, and originally forming no part of China, are themselves foreigners; they are thus a rough people, with little civility, esteemed as such by the other superior and more noble provinces, from where the most important and grave magistrates of the land come.

Moreover, according to Ricci, the Cantonese were xenophobic in the extreme, on account of their susceptibility both to piracy and to land raids. For this reason, they hated the presence of the Portuguese in Macao, profitable as it doubtless was for the emperor, and for mandarins and merchants from other provinces. In short, the Cantonese were 'unbelievably contemptuous of all foreign kingdoms, and they call them by no other name than "foreign devils"'.[88]

Global politics provide a crucial context for understanding the relationship between the Jesuits and their Chinese neighbours in Zhaoqing during the 1580s. But it is also important to understand that relationship in terms of an encounter between two radically different religious outlooks. For whereas the Jesuits, who believed those in ignorance of the true faith to be destined to damnation, were committed to *conversion*, the Chinese, who considered their spiritual lives to be enriched by the *addition* of new devotional strands, took a syncretic approach to religion. Paradoxically, the only reason the foreign priests were accepted within Zhaoqing was that their cult was viewed as an enhancement to existing religious practices. And yet the Jesuits' true mission was, of course, to dismantle the 'idolatrous' traditions of their hosts.

The missionaries were wilfully slow to recognise just how profound this clash of intentions was. Rather than acknowledging the capacious and plural nature of Chinese religion, they preferred to characterise it as weak. In his first letter of 1584 to Giambattista Román, Ricci could not have put it more simply: 'In China, there exists no true religion.' The next year, he told his friend and confidant, Ludovico Maselli, that 'it is God's will that [the Chinese] are not at all attached to their sects'.[89] This view was plainly self-serving: if the Chinese were 'not at all attached to their sects', it would prove easy to detach them. That process of detachment would be ritually marked by the waters of baptism and the flames of burning idols.

By the end of the Zhaoqing mission, it was finally clear that the European priests were no mere 'adornment' to local religiosity; on the contrary, the Jesuit house and the Tower of High Fortune stood in conflict. And yet it is perhaps unsurprising that at the moment that the Jesuits asserted their model of conversion over syncretism, the toleration of the Zhaoqing officials began to wane. The following twenty years of Ricci's life would be devoted to fine-tuning the Jesuits' missionary tactics, seeking common ground wherever he could find it, sprinkling more Confucian wisdom into his ideological package and going quiet over the less assimilable features of Christian doctrine, such as the Virgin Birth and the Crucifixion, which he and Ruggieri had earlier publicised. His strategies did not result in speedy conversions: 'Don't ask me how many thousands of souls I have converted,' he admonished his friend Girolamo Benci in 1595, 'but only how many millions of men we have made hear for the first time that ancient news that in heaven there is only one God, the creator of the sky and the earth.'[90] This, one might think, was depressing news for Catholic priests, brought up to believe that the unbaptised would perish in hell. On the other hand, Ricci knew that if the Jesuits were expelled the Chinese would never be saved. And so, after Zhaoqing, the European priests were forced to retreat still further from the black-and-white truths of Christian theology, and to enter into the more plural world of Chinese belief. Small wonder that many have come to ask the question: who was converting whom?

2 Presents for the Emperor

In November 1588, as the fortunes of the Zhaoqing mission were reaching their nadir, Michele Ruggieri jostled amid a crowd of two hundred Portuguese merchants at the port of Macao. He was destined for Rome. In returning to Europe, the Jesuit was obeying the orders of his superior, Alessandro Valignano, the Jesuit Visitor in the Far East. But why, at this delicate point, was Valignano willing to risk the life of one of his most qualified missionaries on the perilous voyage home? The beginnings of an explanation might have been found in Ruggieri's luggage, for the Jesuit was not travelling light on the dangerously overburdened ship. We know that, besides the essentials for saying Mass, he took with him three Chinese garments and thirteen Chinese books – tasters of the civilisation from which he was departing.[1] He also carried with him several tablets inscribed with Chinese calligraphy. However, the most revealing item in his luggage was a handwritten document in Spanish, fifteen packed pages long, signed by Valignano. It was entitled, 'Memorandum of the things that need to be sent as a present from His Holiness to the King of China'.[2]

Destined for Rome, this manuscript, which now sits unremembered in the Jesuit archive, was the product of a decade's reflection and marked a crucial turning point in the China mission. Such a claim may seem grandiose: this was not, in any obvious sense, a policy document; still less was it a work of missionary theology. We might not go far wrong if we called it a shopping list. But it signalled clearly, in its length and precision, the belief that the Chinese elite could be wooed with *objects*, objects chosen, sourced and presented with the utmost care. Motivated by this conviction, Valignano, in consultation with Ruggieri and the other Jesuits in the field, had laboured over this wish list, itemising no fewer than twenty-one gifts for the Chinese emperor. The gifts were designed to function in complex and even contradictory ways. By their choices, the Jesuits aspired to impress the Chinese with the magnificence of European civilisation. The gifts would project the image of a sophisticated urban society, in which people enjoyed lavish clothes and furnishings, were surrounded by music and art, and reaped the benefits of highly developed technology. Equally, the gifts were designed to flatter the tastes and conventions of their hosts.

The hoard of gifts – were it ever to materialise from the paper list – would comprise a range of hybrid objects: Flemish locks adorned with Chinese characters; two hundred pieces of Venetian stained glass, bearing images of lions, serpents and dragons, fired in the workshops of Murano; belts and helmets 'of the sort that the Emperor of China is accustomed to wear', and an oriental folding screen. Alongside such mongrel items, the missionaries sought to commission more 'purely' European objects that would impress by means of their beauty and preciousness: three strings of coral, two mirrors, two decorative boxes and 'a reading desk richly decorated in stones of various colours, such as they are accustomed to have in Rome'. Some of the objects testified to the mutability of worth: Venetian glass triangles, for example, relatively cheap at home, were recognised to carry high value in the East. Some were not so much precious in themselves as for what they depicted: illustrated architecture books, picture histories of popes and emperors, and engraved images of Rome were chosen for their ability to conjure up a life beyond the reach of the Chinese. Amid flurries of scientific and luxury objects (including the clocks, glass and globes for which the Jesuits would become famous) were just two entries relating to items of explicit religious significance. The first demanded an illuminated manuscript copy of the New Testament, to be filched from an Italian monastery; the second called for paintings of Christ in Glory and the Assumption, and for images of the Madonna and Child. The question of how to represent Christianity in images and objects required particular care and continued to preoccupy the Jesuits throughout the history of their mission in China.

Valignano's document defies expectations. Of the many qualities we associate with sixteenth-century Jesuits (brilliance, resilience, heroism, learning, stubbornness, cunning, spirituality, sacrifice . . .), expertise in shopping does not usually feature. It is strange to imagine the conversation of this clutch of alpha males, gathered around a table in Macao, as they discussed what kind of cloth would best please the Chinese emperor. And yet here it is, the tenth entry on the list, which demands twenty-five pieces of brocade of the highest quality. Five of them are to be 'rich and lustrous', light in weight, including one of gold cloth, another of silver. Five more should bear the finest floral design, with 'golden flowers, such as they have in Italy'; these should be crimson, rose, white, green and yellow, all hues favoured by the Ming. Five are to be made of silk interwoven with gold (of the same colours, although the white might be changed for another, 'fresher' colour); a further five of the finest velvet (again in the same colours); and the final five of the finest cloth of diverse colours, including green and yellow.[3] All of which should be transported in a well-made gilded trunk, lined with satin of vermilion or yellow, and laid down in such a manner that they would not suffer from the long voyage. No less assured are these men when specifying an ebony handle for a mirror made of Venetian crystal or detailing the cameos that should adorn a belt.

But our surprise at this document is misplaced. As recent research has shown, sixteenth-century men, especially from the Italian elites, were active as consumers in the marketplace of luxury objects.[4] Inventories and wills from the same period show how exactitude and technical know-how could be flaunted in the description of household possessions. The Jesuits who were most significant in shaping the China mission at this time (Matteo Ricci, the son of an apothecary; Michele Ruggieri, whose father managed the estates of the important Orsini family in Puglia in the south of Italy, and the noble-born Alessandro Valignano) came from exactly the sorts of prosperous backgrounds that would have equipped them for a discussion of prestige commodities. Furthermore, their attachment to the merchant community of Macao had immersed them in the material worlds of east Asia. Armed with knowledge not only of the commodities prized in Europe, but also of the luxuries and artefacts esteemed by the Chinese, they were all well placed to act as brokers between East and West. Yet it was Michele Ruggieri who was chosen to co-ordinate this epic shopping trip, without which there could be no embassy to Beijing. This chapter of the story belongs in large part to him.

In the absence of proper investigation, the departure of the first Jesuit to enter mainland China has taken on the appearance of a demotion, confirming Matteo Ricci in his position as 'father of Chinese Christianity'. The downgrading of Ruggieri's role finds support in Ricci's *History* of the mission, in which the author casts himself unequivocally as the hero, and issues occasional digs at his older and supposedly less able colleague.[5] Ruggieri was certainly a less successful self-publicist, and his tendency to grumble about the trials of learning Chinese did his posthumous image no good at all. This negative reputation is well illustrated by the words of Vincent Cronin, Ricci's mid-twentieth-century biographer. According to Cronin, Valignano sent Ruggieri home because he

had come to the conclusion that the impetuous Southerner was unfitted for so difficult a mission field. After nine years he still had no fluency in the language; his two journeys had been almost disastrous failures; he was easily imposed on; he lacked the resolution and heroic qualities necessary to withstand constant opposition and disappointment.[6]

Cronin takes many liberties in this interpretation. In truth, we cannot know why Valignano chose Ruggieri to go to Rome, for we have scant record of the motives for the Visitor's decision. Nor does any correspondence survive between Ruggieri and his superior from this period. In 1587, Ruggieri returned to Macao, after two years of reconnoitring in southern China (the 'almost disastrous' journeys to which Cronin refers) and it was in Macao that he and Valignano must have met face to face to discuss the course of his vocation. It is fair to conclude that Valignano was not pleased by Ruggieri's close dealings with Alonso Sánchez – the maverick Spanish Jesuit whose aspirations to conquer China by force had appalled many within the order.[7] Furthermore, in a letter to Acquaviva, dated 23 November 1588, the Provincial commented on Ruggieri's poor pronunciation of Chinese, and referred more than once to the age of Ruggieri, judging him – at forty-five – to be 'old and weary'.[8] But it is equally true that Valignano was conscious of the gravity of the mission to Rome, and wanted to entrust it to someone with the maturity and authority to carry it through.

Whatever words passed their lips, it is unlikely that Valignano would have dismissed Ruggieri's achievements lightly. Elsewhere, he acknowledged his skills in reading and writing Chinese.[9] Ruggieri was, after all, the principal author of the first Catechism, and he had also written Chinese verses in the Confucian tradition. Moreover, it seems that 'the impetuous Southerner' had made many friends among the Chinese – he would later boast about how readily he had been accepted by them, and of his status as 'a citizen of China'.[10] In this respect, he contrasted favourably with the Portuguese priest Duarte de Sande, who took Ruggieri's place in Zhaoqing, and who was apparently so unpopular that he was forced to leave after only two years.

Valignano was absolutely committed to the idea of a papal embassy. And for that plan to become a reality, he required the mediation of a man of experience and articulacy, who could bear witness to the situation in China and whip up support for the nascent mission. Ruggieri's name was not the only one under discussion. In a brief letter of 30 September 1586, written in Portuguese (the surviving copy bears the name of no addressee), Matteo Ricci proposed that 'in order to carry forward, propagate and lend authority to this mission in the land of China', it was imperative to make arrangements with the Pope for a 'good present' to be sent to the Chinese Emperor.[11] A Jesuit should be back to Rome to negotiate with the Pope; Ricci suggested de Sande, who had arrived the year before. He might have reasoned that the newcomer could most readily be spared by the mission, while still qualifying as a first-hand witness. Valignano, on the other hand, probably thought better than to send a Portuguese Jesuit as his emissary to Rome, and opted instead for an Italian with good contacts back home, who was also the most senior missionary in the field.

In this light, Ruggieri's return to Europe appears less as a demotion than as a massive responsibility. This was certainly Ruggieri's own reading of the situation. In a long and unpublished autobiographical manuscript relating his experiences between 1577 and 1591, Ruggieri provides us with invaluable information about his own encounter with China, and about the process by which he himself became convinced of the need for an embassy to Beijing. In certain important respects, his account runs parallel to that of Ricci and suggests an almost simultaneous development of Peking-lust. But he also supplies a lively account of the mission prior to Ricci's arrival. Here he recalls how he established a language school in Macao, where young men from the mainland taught Chinese to priests in return for Portuguese lessons; and he offers his own narrative of the two journeys into the Chinese interior that he undertook during the years 1585–7, and of the experiences that precipitated his return to Europe.[12]

Ruggieri's story during these 'missing years' tells of an astonishingly bold exploration of the uncharted Chinese interior. Cutting all contacts with Macao, and with the Jesuit residence in Zhaoqing, the Italian priest – in company with a young Portuguese colleague, António de Almeida – went where no Western man had gone before. Stopping off at a number of cities, and staying for several months first in Zhejiang province, and – on his second trip – in a village in Huguang (a province encompassing modern-day Hubei and Hunan), Ruggieri learned a great deal about Chinese culture, and gained insights that undoubtedly fed into the document that he carried back with him to Rome. He also experienced institutionalised xenophobia at first hand, and discovered that it was impossible for a foreigner to reside in the Middle Kingdom without imperial support. There was no underestimating the role that gifts might play in gaining the Emperor's favour.

*

Ruggieri's winter 'peregrination' of 1585–6 lasted two months and took him over 900 miles across the south-east corner of China, from Canton to Shaoxing. Like so many of the Jesuits' best breaks, the journey owed its origins to an assured piece of networking. One day, the recently appointed Prefect of Zhaoqing, Wang Pan's successor Zheng Yilin, was paying a visit to the Jesuit residence when he proposed to Ruggieri that he might like to accompany him on his triennial trip to pay homage to the Emperor in Beijing. Ruggieri eagerly accepted the invitation. Writing to Claudio Acquaviva on 18 October 1585, a month before they set sail, he spoke excitedly of how smoothly God was steering the mission, of the ease with which they had acquired a licence to come somewhere near to the southern capital of Nanjing (or Nanking in the old-style transliteration) – a city he perceived as being 'very close to Beijing' (in reality, the two capitals were divided by about 600 miles) – and of his intention to establish a new Jesuit residence when he reached his destination.[13] The Prefect, however, was already beginning to wonder if he had overstepped the mark: having consulted with Wang Pan, and other officials, he presented the Jesuit with a licence to travel to Zhejiang and Huguang provinces, but made it clear that he should not enter the imperial capitals of Nanjing or Beijing.[14] Even so, Ruggieri had reason to thank God. Past ventures had shown that it was virtually impossible to travel without a Chinese escort. This time the Jesuits were being offered free transport and protection in a boat belonging to the merchant brother of Wang Pan, destined for his home town in Shaoxing in Zhejiang province. The brother's name is not recorded, but we do learn that this fortuitous contact was forged not in Zhaoqing but in the markets of Canton, where Ruggieri oversaw the swift sale of a large consignment of silk to Portuguese traders 'at a good price', thereby securing the patronage of the Shaoxing merchant. Ruggieri's enthusiasm for the adventure ahead of him must have been infectious, and Valignano did not hesitate to commit Almeida, newly arrived from India and speaking not one word of Chinese, to the expedition.

The Europeans, who departed Canton on 20 November, followed the route that had taken merchants and officials northwards since the construction in the eighth century of the Meiling Pass – an engineering miracle that linked the North river (or Bei Jiang) to the River Gan by means of a stone road, three yards wide, chiselled out of the Dayu Mountains.[15] The first phase of the journey was not without incident. On day three, the boat caught fire, setting light to the merchandise that was on board, as well as to the priests' chest, which contained everything that they needed (including money) for the voyage. Fortunately, the damage was less grave than was first feared; while the packing materials and storage boxes burned, their contents were salvaged. But the Jesuits – ever the victims of rumour and suspicion – were accused by some of having started the fire. After this setback, the journey continued, with Ruggieri and Almeida striving to keep a low profile, huddling below deck during the day and emerging only at night to stretch their legs. Consequently, Ruggieri had little to report on the first phase of the journey, other than vague impressions that the river was lined with prosperous towns and sumptuous temples, and that the woodland areas they passed by were rich in birds, goats, deer and other wildlife.[16] Not until they reached the end of the river, on 7 December, did they disembark. At the city of Meiling, they were greeted with open arms and generous hospitality, thanks to their association with the *lingxi dao*'s brother.

After a few days' respite, which offered an opportunity for the Jesuits to say Mass using their portable altar, they set off on the thirty-mile track over the Meiling or, literally, 'Plum' Pass, so called on account of the trees growing over its northern and southern faces. Ruggieri could not fail to be impressed by the well-made stone road, the summit of which was marked by a great gate whose inscription paid homage to the Tang Dynasty emperor who had been responsible for the construction of this 'smooth and easy' route across a 'harsh and exceedingly difficult' terrain. That day the rain fell lightly but persistently, and Ruggieri explained how he cheered his fellow travellers by composing improvised verses in Chinese describing the scenery and the gentle rain that soaked them. The Chinese were polite enough to praise him for 'the great perfection of his poetry'. The soggy Jesuit, spouting his verses in imperfect Chinese, must have made a curious sight for the throngs of merchants who used the pass on their journeys to and from Nanjing. For, as Ruggieri observed, the stone road was so heavy with trading traffic that it seemed like the middle of a busy European market. At either end of the pass, imperial slaves and officials attempted to facilitate trade and to keep law and order. In Ruggieri's view, such a spectacle of efficiency testified to the wealth and power of the Emperor.[17]

After the pass, the Jesuits continued their journey northwards by sedan chair. This was evidently a new experience for Ruggieri (in the 1590s, Ricci would become accustomed to being carried around) and it was discovered that the large European priest required four bearers, rather than the customary two. At Taihe, on the Gan river, the Jesuits spent two days attempting to rest, but were plagued by curious visitors. They had no time to eat, let alone to say Mass, and they resolved to leave quickly and to embark on the next stretch of their journey: fifteen days of river travel. As the priests passed by walled cities, they dreamed of establishing a network of 'beautiful residences' throughout the province, each one conveniently linked by river transport and easily accessible to the Superior.[18] Ruggieri's mood was buoyant; gates were literally being opened for the Jesuits, and he assured his readers that 'outside the province of Canton, foreigners are not feared'. Everyone, including the officials, 'treated the Fathers with much greater reverence than in Zhaoqing'.[19]

On Christmas Eve, they reached Nanchang, the largest city in Jiangxi province, in scale, at least, greater than Lisbon, although lacking in the 'superb palaces' of a European city. Nanchang stood to the south of Poyang Hu lake, a massive watery crossroads, and Ruggieri again marvelled that China should be blessed with 'so many rivers, functioning like wonderful streets, so beneficial to commerce'.[20] Here the fathers departed from the northern Nanjing route, instead turning eastwards against the flow of the river towards Shaoxing, where the brother of the *lingxi dao* was heading back to his family home. The wind was in their favour, and they soon arrived at Jingdezhen, the capital of Chinese porcelain production, and a site whose significance to the European imagination is today signalled by countless ceramics on display in Western art galleries. A nineteenth-century observer, John Henry Gray, Archdeacon of Hong Kong, describing the same journey, evoked the industrial beauty of the approach to Jingdezhen; he described the dense clouds of smoke arising from the furnaces, and a river bed 'literally strewed' with broken pieces of earthenware.[21] For Ruggieri, the experience was less aesthetic: with a worldly eye, he commented simply that higher-quality china could be bought more cheaply here than in Canton.

The two Jesuits and their escorts were nearing the end of their trip. Temperatures were dropping and the river was getting narrower. All the passengers were forced to disembark, and to reload their belongings and themselves onto a convoy of smaller vessels. Deep in Zhejiang province, a bridge built of boats (forty or fifty of them) marked the end of the navigable river, and, on disembarking, the Jesuits were invited to a feast at an 'idol temple'. Seeing an opportunity, the Fathers handed out copies of Ruggieri's Chinese Catechism, in the hope that the chapter dedicated to the condemnation of false idols would convince the people of their errors. Almeida was apparently struck by the similarity of a painted image of a woman stamping on a dragon and a moon to that of the Queen of Heaven, but Ruggieri disabused him by explaining that the woman was really the daughter of an emperor. Next, again making use of sedan chairs, the Jesuits' party continued towards the east coast for 25 miles until they reached Zhoushan, where they received a warm welcome. Here, Ruggieri reported on the incessant curiosity of the local people, who for the duration of the Jesuits' three-day stay 'did not stop asking questions about the things of our Europe'.[22] Such episodes fuelled Ruggieri's belief in the desire of the Chinese to discover more about the wonders of the Western world. From Zhoushan, the two European priests travelled once again by boat, on a river 'wider than the Po in Lombardy'. On 22 January, they passed the beautiful city of Hangzhou, though the fog was so thick that they could scarcely see anything beyond a few towers. Then, after one final change of boat and river, and an overnight trip by lantern light through the snow, they arrived at the house of the father of the *lingxi dao*, father also of the Jesuits' escort, in Shaoxing – a city surrounded by water that, with its network of canals, resembled Venice.[23]

Here, the Jesuits commenced a six-month stay, as guests of the *lingxi dao*'s father. Ruggieri was struck by the contrast with Canton: in the former, they had encountered imprisonment and beatings; here, they were greeted with 'banquets of honour and applause'.[24] They were given a comfortable house in a good location. The property comprised two apartments, a kitchen and garden; there was even an appropriate space in which to establish a chapel, where the priests celebrated Mass, 'much to the edification of the people who visited'. Above the altar, they placed an image of the Saviour, and the visiting literati bowed before it. Most gratifying of all, the *lingxi dao*'s father presented himself for conversion.[25] Manifesting great piety, the septuagenarian would every day prostrate himself before an image of the Madonna, reciting his rosary. The European priests soon attracted a reputation for healing, and their patron brought to them a young relative, a boy aged sixteen, who was thought to be possessed by the devil. The Jesuits concluded that he was a victim of the civil service exams who had gone crazy with too much studying, and Almeida set to work teaching him about God – apparently a successful antidote. Ruggieri also told of how he managed to win over the hostile Governor of the city, thanks to his ability to speak Chinese. His claims to linguistic proficiency were later expressly challenged by Ricci's allegation that 'it was impossible to achieve anything [in Shaoxing], since neither of the two Fathers knew Chinese'.[26] Ricci's competitive carping aside, it would seem as though Ruggieri's sojourn in Zhejiang province was, while it lasted, a successful one. News of the Jesuits' progress was celebrated throughout Europe, and Pope Sixtus V conceded to the Society of Jesus a plenary indulgence, intended to inspire universal prayers to God for the new Christianity of

China and Japan.[27]

Meanwhile, back in Shaoxing, the reputation of Ruggieri and Almeida appeared to go from strength to strength. The Governor sought the help of the priests in a matter of the utmost importance and sensitivity for any self-respecting literatus: he asked them to seek the intercession of the Madonna in his quest for a son and heir. The Christian prayers worked their magic, and a pregnancy was soon being celebrated. But no sooner had the good news broken than the Governor received word from Beijing that he must send all foreigners back to Canton. With great sadness, Ruggieri and Almeida turned tail. Their first peregrination beyond Canton had been anything but disastrous. But it was cut off in its prime.

A few months later, the restless Ruggieri set off on his second journey.[28] This time he had no Jesuit companion, though he did take with him two Chinese escorts – an interpreter (a Christian convert) and a language teacher (whose guidance on Chinese customs was invaluable). Ruggieri's intentions were clear: he went in order to find 'some convenient place, close to the courts of the King of China, and there to establish another residence of Fathers'. To this end, he asked the Governor and the *lingxi dao* for a licence to go travelling in the provinces of Guangxi and Huguang, 'the latter province being situated on the route that goes to the court of the King'.[29] Fifteen days after setting off by boat, he reached Guilin, situated on the west bank of the River Li. This was the metropolitan centre of Guangxi province and the seat of a viceroy, a city of 100,000 hearths. But what impressed Ruggieri most about the city was the presence of members of the imperial family. Ruggieri took note of the princely palaces, distinguished by the fact that they were painted red. According to custom, the occupants never left their residences, but all had their 'delights' brought within, and they were served by eunuchs, who also never went out. Ruggieri's companions were keen that he should obtain imperial hospitality during his stay, and the trio managed to procure ten days as the guests of a close relative of the Emperor, provided with beds and all things necessary, and subjected to an exhausting succession of banquets. Ruggieri complained that there was scarcely time to perform the sacrifice of Mass, and that he was forced to talk while he ate, such was the curiosity of the Chinese 'who wanted to know everything about our Europe'.[30] When Ruggieri was finally granted an audience with the Viceroy, he claimed that he was heading towards the province of Huguang; here he would visit and write an account of the province's greatest temple, which was a source of enormous revenue for the Emperor on account of the constant flow of visitors. Beneath this façade, Ruggieri was planning another route. As he acknowledged only to himself, he intended to cross Guangxi and Huguang provinces in order to establish future residences closer to the imperial court. For Ruggieri was by now of the firm opinion that without 'the express licence of the Emperor to preach the Gospel' the Jesuits 'would never achieve that which they sought, which was the conversion of the entire realm'.[31]

The Viceroy who had received Ruggieri with courtesy nevertheless dismissed the Jesuit, on the grounds that he would soon be leaving Guilin to take up a new post as governor of Guangdong province. But the Western priest now attracted the hospitality of another one of the city's resident royals, who – emulating the tradition of the Wanli emperor – would never show his face. 'A relative or nephew of the King of China', the Prince lived 'amid a grand estate, with mountains, valleys and hunting grounds, catering for every kind of leisure'. But because the Prince could not be seen, the

Jesuit was received by his majordomo, a eunuch, who treated him to a fine banquet.[32] Ruggieri was clearly impressed by the magnificence of the palace, and he was allowed to enter its 'last room', 'where the Prince was hidden in an apartment framed by the most beautiful painted screens, with slats so narrow that he could see out but others could not see in'. Ruggieri presented the majordomo with gifts and received others 'of far greater value and price' in exchange.[33]

Unfortunately, this imperial relative – keen though he seemed to have Ruggieri stay – could not persuade the authorities to allow it. Negotiations led to Ruggieri being escorted to a new residence, in Huguang province, which was devoid of urban comforts and princely contacts. Looking on the bright side, Ruggieri described his destination as 'a small but beautiful settlement of 300 households'. He stayed there for four months, until 'it was necessary' for him to return to Zhaoqing, on account of renewed suspicions regarding foreigners.[34]

It was the Governor of Zhaoqing who summoned Ruggieri back, and the same Governor now laid out the options available to the Jesuits with stark clarity. *Either* Ruggieri and Ricci could remain in the city 'as perpetual citizens', but forgoing any future efforts to bring in more Jesuits. *Or*, the priests should arrange to organise an embassy, complete 'with present', to Beijing.[35] Ruggieri had no difficulty in choosing. The first option must be declined, for soon enough the two founding Fathers of the Jesuit mission would be dead, and then the gateway to the China mission would be slammed shut. So it was that 'the Father Visitor was moved to send Father Ruggieri to Europe, to attempt to bring about this embassy from His Holiness for the good of the souls awaiting redemption and the precious blood of Christ'.[36]

*

Stepping onto the boat in Macao in November 1588, Ruggieri must have felt some pangs about leaving the country he had come to know more intimately than any other European alive. But he was far from being an unwilling exile. On the contrary, he considered himself to be implementing the most important phase of the mission to date. For Ruggieri was himself a seasoned advocate of diplomatic relations between the Pope and the Emperor. Two years previously, as he rested in Zhaoqing between his two arduous trips, Ruggieri had written to Acquaviva to urge him to persuade His Holiness to send 'some curiosities' from Europe to the imperial court. A number of the proposed gifts were to make it onto Valignano's list of 1588: strings of coral, an illuminated Bible, clocks of varying sizes. Others of Ruggieri's earlier suggestions were dropped, including the live ostrich, which would, he had judged, 'make a marvellous present for the King of China, for he greatly esteems its feathers; and a live animal or bird of the kind that is not found here would be very impressive'. Live animals – including, famously, the rhinoceros that was sent as a gift from India to the King of Portugal in 1515 – were to carry high credit in diplomatic exchanges of the sixteenth century.[37] This time, however, the Chinese Emperor would have to content himself with 'a box with five or six dozen feathers of various colours', probably garnered from the Jesuit mission in Mexico.

During his second trip into the Chinese interior, Ruggieri had gathered further evidence to bolster his ideas. Staying in princely palaces in Guilin, he had discovered the importance of 'contracambio', the exchange of gifts, as a mechanism for smoothing cross-cultural relations. Indeed, Ruggieri styled his encounters with members of the imperial family, hidden away behind the red façades of their residences, as a dress rehearsal for his projected visit to the imperial court. There is no doubt that Ruggieri was looking north, and was convinced that – once out of the unwelcoming zone of Canton – the Chinese were open to European influence. Everywhere that the Jesuit travelled, he was greeted by intense curiosity about Europe. At the same time, Ruggieri's travels had honed his own fascination with the material world inhabited by the Chinese. Whether following the trade routes in a sedan chair, weighing up the price of porcelain, visiting temples, or observing the developed infrastructure of a city, he had become familiar with a civilisation that was defined as much by technology as by belief, a civilisation in which objects were as meaningful as words.[38]

The quality and value of Chinese commodities was repeatedly noted in the reports of European visitors to the Middle Kingdom. In the first European book devoted exclusively to the subject of China, the *Tractado em que se côtam muito por estêso as cousas da China*, published in 1569–70, the Portuguese Dominican friar Gaspar da Cruz provided a lively discussion of the range of luxury goods that he had encountered in Canton. Like the Jesuits who would later settle in China, da Cruz was perfectly at home itemising and evaluating material goods. His account included sustained descriptions of 'the rich boots and shoes . . . covered with coloured silk, embroidered over with twisted thread of very fine work' that could be bought in the markets, and of the variety of bedsteads for sale, including one – 'a very rich one wrought with ivory, and of a sweet wood which they call cayolaque, and of sandalwood' – priced at an impressive 400 crowns. With an expert eye, he marvelled at the multitude of 'perfect workmen' – carpenters, metalworkers and ivory-carvers – to be found at their stalls producing an array of dainty boxes, ornate writing desks and tables, and of course the ubiquitous sedan chairs. Predictably, da Cruz reserved his most detailed descriptions for the empire's signature products, silk and porcelain. It was the price of the highest-quality Chinese textiles that most struck the friar: 'There are pieces of damask and taffeta among themselves so rich that they bring them not to us, because we cannot give for them what they are worth within the land.' His account of porcelain, by contrast, focused principally on the manufacturing processes. Da Cruz was keen to dispel the myths common 'among the Portugals who have not been in China, about where this porcelain is made, and touching the substance of which it is made, some saying of oystershells, others of dung rotten for a long time'. So he set out to explain, as numerous other European commentators would later attempt to do, the manner in which the soft white stone (or 'to be more precise . . . a hard clay') was beaten and ground and laid in cisterns of water, where it was stirred well, so that the 'cream' came to the top. It was from this cream that the finest porcelain was made, 'and so the lower the coarser; and of the dregs they make the coarsest and base, which the poor people of China do use'. Like Ruggieri, da Cruz was impressed by the wealth that trade had brought the empire: 'As the goods of China are very great and many, so the revenues which the King of China hath in every part of His Kingdom are very great.'[39]

Another friar, Martín de Rada – this time a Spaniard belonging to the Augustinian order, who visited Fujian province in 1575 as part of an envoy from the Philippines – went further in seeking to understand the values that lay behind Chinese attitudes to objects. Take, for example, his in-depth analysis of the meanings of the different hats worn by Chinese men:

The bonnets of the common people are round, and those of the gentry square like clergymen's birettas . . . The viceroys, governors, captains and ministers of justice when at home wear a bonnet like a bishop's small mitre with golden welts and embroidery. But when they go out in the streets or sit upon their thrones, they wear a kind of bonnet, the back half of which stands up nearly six inches and which moreover has, as it were, two wings or large ears sticking straight out at the sides. These bonnets are worn by all the ministers of justice, and captains and viceroys. However, if any one of these captains or justices goes to interview one of his superiors, then he does not wear such a bonnet, but takes along a state umbrella . . . The bonnets of the students are shaped like letter-carriers or caskets, highly gilded and polished. Those of their friars are shaped like mitres, but differently from the captains' described above; and they fashion something like rosettes out of the folds of the front part of these bonnets, so that by the form of the bonnet you can know who a person is and what office he has.[40]

De Rada recognised that luxury was a gauge of status, and in particular that the clothes of the Chinese were clear indicators of their position within the social hierarchy. He was also alert to the material props and trappings that accompanied a whole range of social rituals: the 'large canopied chairs' that carried elite men to their social engagements; the wide sleeves that were fundamental to Chinese 'compliments and civilities' ('they put their hands in their sleeves and clasping them together they lift them up as high as their breast'); the knee-pads which 'those who have to deal very often with a mandarin are wont to carry along' in order to facilitate the kowtow.

In common with other European travel writers who wrote about the East as 'outsiders', De Rada surveyed China with an ethnographic eye, alert to the conventions of everyday life – conventions that would have been far less visible to 'insiders' living within the culture.[41] But although such accounts focus on difference ('instead of doffing their bonnet, they put their hands in their sleeves'), they also point to underlying similarities uniting the two civilisations. A good example is the use of chopsticks, presented as at once an emblem of the 'otherness' of China and a sign of the sophistication and refinement that aligned the people with their European counterparts. The first Western account of the Chinese 'way of eating with two sticks' was written between 1512 and 1515 by the Portuguese apothecary Tomé Pires, then resident in Melaka.[42] His compatriot, Galeote Pereira, imprisoned between 1549 and 1552 for illegal trading off the south coast of China, took up the theme and drew parallels between the use of chopsticks and the use of forks:

They feed with two sticks, refraining from touching their meat with their hands, even as we do with forks, for the which respect, they less do need any tablecloths. Neither is the nation only civil at meat, but also in conversation, and in courtesy they seem to exceed all other.[43]

De Rada added the following admiring account:

They do not touch with their fingers anything that they are going to eat, but they pick up everything with two long little sticks. They are so expert in this, that they can take anything, however small, and carry it to their mouth, even if it is round, like plums and other such fruits.[44]

For both Pereira and de Rada, the cleanliness and delicacy of Chinese eating habits (so extreme that tablecloths and napkins were unnecessary) was an important mark of the civility of the nation. While chopsticks had been in use in China since antiquity, forks were a recent invention in the West. During a period of European history when the 'embarrassment thresholds' of the people were being raised, when a whole range of practices that had once been acceptable (urinating in public, wiping one's nose on one's hand, eating with one's fingers) were coming to be seen as disgusting (at least in elite circles), and when technological inventions (the water closet, the handkerchief, the fork) serviced and stoked these new sensibilities, travellers from the West were relieved to discover equivalent standards of behaviour among the Chinese.[45] Chopstick wielders and fork users, both aspiring to punctilious levels of cleanliness, could surely do business together.

Like the other travellers who dispatched reports from China, Jesuits acquired their initial training in the meanings of local objects in the markets of Macao and Canton. The Florentine adventurer Francesco Carletti, who had met Valignano in Japan, reminds us how closely the worlds of merchants and missionaries were intertwined in the East. He tells how, on disembarking 'secretly at midnight' in Macao without a licence, he went straight to the Jesuit college, where he left all his money in safekeeping, so that the city's authorities could not 'take it as confiscated'.[46] Carletti later expressed his gratitude to 'the Fathers of the Society of Jesus' for helping him to source a fine assortment of porcelain, 'the finest that it was possible to get'.[47] The acquisition of such local knowledge was by no means incidental to the missionary life. It was a professional obligation of the Jesuit abroad to discover and record details of his host culture, an obligation reflected in the letters and journals of Ruggieri and Ricci.[48]

Among Valignano's extensive writings on Japanese society was a short book on Japanese customs (penned in 1581) which included a chapter specifically dedicated to the subject of gift-giving.[49] The Jesuit Provincial was at once acutely aware of the need to take a gift when visiting the Japanese, and keen to limit excessive and expensive largesse on the part of the missionaries. He therefore offered detailed instructions on choosing the right presents and limiting them to the proper number of recipients. These include the stipulation that one should not create obligations where they do not already obtain and the advice that, in accordance with Japanese custom, gifts should ideally be determined by the place from which one has come. If, for example, one were coming from the port of Nagasaki the gift should be a *namban* or European piece; if Miyako, one should bring a present made in Miyako. There were further guidelines on ceremonial: gifts should be wrapped up in special kinds of paper and placed on a support or stand of fine cedar wood, so that they might be viewed by the receiver in the presence of the donor. Such fastidious attention to local custom is manifest in the document entrusted to Ruggieri by Valignano listing presents suitable for the Chinese Emperor.

Issuing instructions to the Pope's men from across the globe, Valignano emphasised that the 'overall harmony and appearance' of the gifts would matter as much to the Chinese as the gifts themselves. And, in describing the letters to be sent from the Pope to accompany the presents, he differentiated carefully between those addressed to the Emperor and those intended for his provincial governors. Whereas the former should be written in gold letters, richly illuminated with beautiful pictures (especially lions and serpents), tied with gold cords and sealed with a golden seal, for the latter it was not necessary to write in gold, and the illuminations could be far less grand, the cords made of silk thread and the seal of silver. Valignano had learned the lesson provided so fully by Martín de Rada in his discussion of Chinese headwear: magnificence must be tempered by due deference to social distinctions. In line with the strategy of accommodation for which the Jesuits were renowned, Valignano and his colleagues went out of their way to describe presents that would comply with the Emperor's sense of decorum. The detailed instructions accompanying the gift list reiterated on five separate occasions the need to consult with Father Ruggieri on matters of design and ornamentation.

But if the Jesuits aimed to soothe the Chinese with objects and motifs that they would recognise – hence the snakes and lions – they also viewed the present list as an all-important opportunity to vaunt the most impressive artefacts of European civilisation. In this respect, the list was as competitive as it was reassuring. Thus the twenty-five pieces of Italian brocade requested by Valignano were surely intended to evoke comparisons with the gilded cloth available in China. The terms on which that comparison might be extended are suggested by the account of Chinese cloth given by Francesco Carletti:

They weave those cloths of gold in very varied and beautiful and showy patterns, and instead of the silver and gold that go into them, they place there a certain thread of silvered and gilded paper which, cut very thin, they spin in the way that we make spun gold and silver. And instead of silk they use another thread that seems the same and has the same quality except that it must be protected from water and dust, because water will destroy it and dust tarnish it.[50]

Chinese cloth equalled its European counterpart on the surface but was inferior in its substance. Instead of gold thread, this cloth used paper, a technique that resulted in a fabric that was ostentatious but ephemeral.

Other items on the list deliberately introduced European inventions that were alien to Chinese culture. The locks and clocks that adorned the Jesuit buildings in Zhaoqing were impressive precisely because they were unfamiliar, and Valignano was keen that the Emperor be treated to the best examples of the genre. He also requested an organ and a harpsichord – objects that would not only pay testimony to the extraordinary skill of European craftsmen but would also convey a completely different kind of music to the Chinese. In his *History* of the mission, Ricci would later express his excitement at introducing keyboard and stringed instruments to the imperial court:

They have diverse and copious musical instruments, though they do not have organs, harpsichords, or clavichords. They only use strings made out of crude silk, and they are unaware of the possibility of using animal gut; but they temper their instruments as we do with the same consonance, although the music is entirely plain chant without the variety of voices – bass, alto, tenor – and singing of ours. And thus among them was never seen such consonance of voices, but they remain extremely content with theirs, thinking that in this world there is no other music. As a result of which they are stupefied by our organs and other instruments, that until now they had never seen.[51]

The instruments commissioned by Valignano suggest that the same desire to 'stupefy' lay behind the shopping list.

Three further gifts offered visual representations of European civilisation. Firstly, there were to be 'books of architecture', including fine engravings of the greatest and most beautiful European buildings. As Ricci would proclaim in his *History*, Chinese buildings – constructed without foundations – were 'inferior to ours', in terms of both their 'beauty and their strength'.[52] So the request for engravings was driven by the desire to impress on the Chinese the superiority of Western monuments. Secondly, Valignano demanded more books, beautifully illustrated, *not* with wars and martyrdoms, mind, nor with 'the mysteries of the passion of our Saviour Lord, which as yet are of little purpose to the Chinese', but with engravings of illustrious popes, kings and emperors, 'well illuminated with gold and other colours'. The Jesuits, in keeping with other European travellers to China in the sixteenth century, admired the centralisation and efficiency of imperial government. European claims to equality would have to be strenuously defended. Thirdly, Valignano called for engravings of Rome, ancient and modern, again 'richly illuminated' and preferably on parchment, in order to demonstrate to the Chinese the greatness of His Holiness and of the city in which he resided. 'And if it were possible to include some plates of prints depicting a solemn procession of His Holiness and of the Cardinals, Bishops, Prelates, etc., that would be a thing much esteemed [by the Chinese] for we have tried to give an understanding to the Chinese of the holy Catholic Church.' Representations of the open squares that lay at the heart of the ritual life of the European city would surprise the Chinese, since the urban topography favoured in the Middle Kingdom actively discouraged any form of mass assembly. In these gifts, the twin themes of civility and power were united. Although the images chosen by the Jesuits would offer the Chinese a very different vision of the ideal city, they nevertheless tapped into a shared devotion to order and authority.

One last aspect of European advancement was represented on Valignano's gift list: scientific knowledge, rendered concrete in the form of hour-glasses, mechanical clocks and globes mapping the heavens and the earth. We are talking here not merely about the Europeans' claims to technological superiority, but about their claims to understanding. The confusions and errors of Chinese science were a persistent topic of Ricci's writings. A typical pronouncement is found in a letter of 1595: 'They know nothing . . . They think that the earth is flat and square; that the sky is made of a single liquid, that is air, and many other absurd things.'[53] It was also Ricci's enduring belief that a scientific apostolate might win over the Chinese. As he wrote to his colleague Francesco Pasio in 1609, 'If we can teach them our sciences . . . it will be easy to persuade them to our holy law.'[54] The role of science in the China mission was ascendant throughout the life of Ricci. But in 1588 Valignano had already recognised the need for material exempla of the rightness and efficacy of European approaches to nature. Of course, at one level, clocks and globes, like coral and brocade, derived their cachet from their status as luxury objects, elegant, expensive to produce and possessed only by the social elite. But they were repositories also of a double knowledge, dependent, on the one hand, on an advanced mastery of astronomy and mechanics and, on the other, on a deep understanding of God's creation. The globes commissioned by Valignano – 'celestial and terrestrial' – recalled the opening sentence of Genesis: 'In the beginning, God made the heavens and the earth.' Representing the temporal dimension of the creation, they monitored the progress of night and day, which were in turn dictated by the movements of the heavens and the earth. Only by such indirect metaphors could the Jesuits' diplomacy hope to succeed.

When Ricci came to publish a new Catechism for the Chinese in 1605, he would stress the Creator God of the Old Testament, dwell hardly at all on the Incarnation, and omit the Crucifixion altogether. But if Ricci was later criticised for excising Christ from his Christian mission, here Valignano appears equally cautious. The predominantly secular tone of the gift list is striking; so too the insistence that the repertoire of visual imagery to be found on the presents confine itself to *cosas alegras* (happy things) and exclude representations of the Passion (Christ's suffering on the Cross). The list was not entirely worldly. Item 4 of Valignano's instructions demanded a fine manuscript copy of the New Testament, illuminated and on parchment, 'bound in crimson velvet' and 'richly embroidered with gold thread'. 'It will be easy for His Holiness to get one from a monastery of religious,' observed the Provincial. Failing this, a missal would do just as well; after all, he added, 'the Chinese will not be able to understand what is written'. Item 21 proposed some large oil paintings of religious subjects: an image of Christ in glory, surrounded with many angels, and of the Assumption of Our Lady, 'perfect and glorious' with baby in her arms, or alternatively of the Virgin and Child, 'surrounded by angels and very glorious'. The insistence that Mary bear the attribute of the baby Jesus even when depicted in the Assumption is unusual in Western iconography, and suggests the need to emphasise Mary's role as Mother of God lest she be mistaken for a god herself, as had happened in Zhaoqing. There could be no matter about which the Jesuits felt more certain than the truth of Christian teachings, and yet it was in this field that their claims had to be represented with the greatest delicacy.[55]

Although the Jesuits' choice of gifts was partly motivated by a desire to demonstrate the cultural superiority of the lands from which they came, they were by no means seeking to vanquish China with their claims to greater civilisation. On the contrary, the point of many of the presents was to suggest a comparability between Europe and China. Modern writers on the East–West encounter have frequently referred to the incommensurability of the two cultures, yet this document suggests something different. Far from being incommensurable, both parties were engaged in a non-stop game of comparison, measuring each other according to a wide range of criteria.[56]

The fact that East and West were weighed in the balance by Valignano's document is reflected in the tit-for-tat nature of the embassy that he was proposing. For, among his many achievements, Valignano is probably best remembered for having masterminded an earlier diplomatic mission: the visit of four Japanese youths to Europe in 1582–6. This round trip, accomplished by a quartet of teenage aristocrats from Nagasaki, converts schooled in Latin by the Jesuits, was extensively chronicled in Europe and gained the Society of Jesus much credit. In particular, the presents that they brought from the East for their hosts (the King of Spain, the Grand Duke of Tuscany, the Doge of Venice, and the Pope) were widely noted in contemporary reportage. These included a bamboo desk, examples of Japanese lacquerware and two suits of armour. But the present that attracted most attention was the folding screen or 'byobu' that the young legates gave to Gregory XIII just a week before the Pope expired.[57] A byobu was a folded screen, made of painted paper, light and portable, and in Japan an essential prop of every elite reception room. It was made of panels – two, four, six, or less commonly eight – on which images were designed to be 'read', like a handscroll, from right to left.[58] The screen depicted the magnificent palace at Azuchi, which was home to the great lord Oda Nobunaga, the most powerful man in Japan. Nobunaga had himself made a gift of the screen to Valignano, despite the fact that the Japanese Emperor had seen it and indicated that he would like to have it. The gift gained an additional mystique when, in 1582, Nobunaga was assassinated and his castle destroyed.

In planning the papal embassy to China, the Japanese delegation was clearly much in Valignano's mind. His shopping list contains several allusions to it, the most significant of which relates to the proposed gift (item II on the list) of a set of screens, 'panels made in the manner of a folding book, in the form that the Japanese knights brought His Holiness, which I gather now stand in the Gallery of Pope Gregory XIII of holy memory'. One might perceive a certain tactlessness on Valignano's part in this choice of gift. After all, Japan and China were ancient enemies, and the two nations stood poised on the brink of conflict at the very time that the Jesuit Visitor was drafting his instructions. In fact, Valignano's instincts were sure. For, perhaps contrary to one's expectations, the political isolationism of China was balanced by cultural openness. The elite consumers of China placed great store by exotica and were particularly fond of Japanese lacquerwork.[59] Of all the gifts, this one got the longest and most detailed description, as well it might, for Valignano was making a tall order of the craftsmen in service to the Pope. The Provincial required that the screens be of the same width and decorated in the same way as the Japanese exemplar. They should include representations of the twelve months of the year; of men, women, horses and diverse animals; and of landscapes, including rivers, churches, palaces and other important buildings, 'painted in oils by the best Roman artists'. In Valignano's opinion, the efforts of these artists would be rewarded: 'I believe that, of all the things that are presented to the King of China, this one will be among the most esteemed, and for this reason it is necessary to go to every effort to ensure that the screens are well made.'

As we have seen, the elites of late Ming China were deeply attentive to the meanings of things. Their care over objects was reflected in contemporary works of conduct literature. Wen Zhenheng's *Treatise on Superfluous Things* (1615–20), for example, included advice on cloth suitable for bed curtains, with varied prescriptions for summer and winter, and for men and women; there were also instructions on arranging flowers and planting blossom trees, on how to store calligraphy and paintings so as to prevent sun damage, and on shopping for antique furniture. As one art historian has commented, accounts like this one were characterised by their attention to detail, by their 'precision of colour, form, decoration and dimensions'.[60] But such a description, intended to indicate the particularity of late Ming consumer culture, captures perfectly the qualities of the shopping list drafted by European priests and carried across the seas to Rome by Michele Ruggieri. Despite the temptation to differentiate them, Europeans and Chinese of the early modern/late Ming eras were alike in bringing a passionate connoisseurship to their lives. On both sides, a 'high-spec' material culture was fuelled by a desire to encounter the exotic, the strange and the new – everything that stretched and exceeded the available vocabularies of description.

*

In the event, Michele Ruggieri's journey back to Rome proved to be a fraught affair. Even by the standards of sixteenth-century travel, the sea voyage was prolonged, unpleasant and full of danger. After an exhausting crossing of the South China Sea, the priest had to force his way through the crowds on the docks at Melaka to board a boat that was so heavily laden that the deck barely stood clear of the waves. Fifty of his five hundred or so companions were killed off by a deadly epidemic, caused – some speculated – by worms in the rice or poisoned water supplies.[61] Passing the Cape of Good Hope, Ruggieri and his fellow travellers saw macabre evidence of a recent storm that had destroyed another Portuguese ship with its six hundred passengers: the water was littered with floating bodies, broken timber and bundles of precious merchandise.[62] If Ruggieri was distressed by sickness, storms and broken boats, he was no less traumatised by the Protestant heretics (Dutch and English) who scouted the region in hopes of intercepting the Spanish treasure fleet on its voyage back from the New World. Their menacing presence was first encountered indirectly on the island of St Helena, where the ship stopped to re-provision, and where the disembarking Catholic passengers discovered that the chapel had been desecrated by English sailors. Worse was to come when Ruggieri learned – from the shouted taunts of English privateers harrying the Portuguese ships off the Azores – of the defeat of the Spanish Armada, the magnificent fleet of which he had heard rumours before he left the Far East.[63]

But Ruggieri's luck was about to turn. 'Giving thanks to God and to the Blessed Virgin', he arrived at Lisbon on 13 September 1589, after ten months at sea.[64] During the next few months, he would have many more reasons to thank God, as he lapped up the enthusiasm and curiosity of all he met and enjoyed opulent hospitality in the houses of the Portuguese aristocracy.[65] Clad in brand-new clothes and loaded with extensive funds by his patrons, Ruggieri set out just before Christmas to Madrid, where Philip of Spain was keen to give him an audience. Although the King was suffering from a high temperature and agonising gout, Ruggieri's presence immediately cheered up the ailing monarch, and the two men spent two hours chatting about China, while the 'Indian' servant whom Ruggieri had brought from the Far East paraded in native clothes, demonstrated the kowtow, and performed other gestures of Chinese courtesy. Philip's doctor, who had at first been concerned lest the Jesuit tire his patient, relented: 'Let us allow Father Ruggieri to stay with the King because while he is speaking with him His Majesty neither suffers the pains of gout nor has fever.'[66] After the inevitable presentation of oriental souvenirs to the King and his family (scented crowns of dried exotic plants for the Prince and Infanta, an inlaid box of cinnamon for the monarch), Ruggieri headed to Rome in company with a Spanish Jesuit, who Philip hoped would one day accompany the Italian back to China.

Ruggieri reached Italy in June 1590. The heat and the horse-riding (which he had not experienced for over a decade) made him ill, and he waited feverishly in and around Rome for an audience with the Pope.[67] Since Urban VII had died of malaria just thirteen days after he was elected in September 1590, Ruggieri's mission was further delayed. He and his Indian were finally summoned to meet Gregory XIV, whose pontificate would last less than a year. Gregory was renowned for his piety (he was a follower of both Carlo Borromeo and Philip Neri, bright stars in the galaxy of Counter-Reformation saints) and for his nervous tendency to giggle, including on the occasion of his coronation. Whether or not these characteristics manifested themselves to Ruggieri, the travelling Jesuit enjoyed 'loving conversation' with the Pope, and presented him with a description of China. There was a further invitation to dinner in the Vatican, where Ruggieri would have the opportunity to talk through the tablets, composed by Ricci in Chinese characters, on which was inscribed a message from the Pope to the Emperor. The negotiations appeared to be going well. But, just as the storms of international religious politics had interrupted his voyage home from China, so would they derail his project in Rome. For, preoccupied by the troubles caused by the claim of the Protestant Henri of Navarre to the throne of France, the rebellions and revolts convulsing the Spanish empire, and Elizabeth I's 'molestations' of

Philip II's treasure fleets, the Pope made no further solicitations regarding the matter of China.

For all the care that had gone into compiling it, the Jesuits' shopping list was to remain just a list. Ruggieri never returned to China, but passed the rest of his life in Italy, where he lectured to would-be missionaries and recorded aspects of his life and travels. There was to be no papal embassy to China until the disastrous envoy of 1705 when the Pope's representative, Bishop Maillard de Tournon, fell into deep disagreement with the Kangxi Emperor over the matter of papal supremacy. Kangxi's response was to expel anybody who refused to sign a paper recognising his authority in matters relating to religion and to imprison Maillard in Macao, where he died in 1707. For the Jesuits, caught between the Pope and the Emperor, this event spelled the beginning of the end of their mission. That is another story, amply documented and discussed. But the 1580s embassy-that-never-was deserves to be remembered too, and not just for its counter-factual suggestiveness. For, notwithstanding the failure of the envoy to get off the ground, the intense plans and negotiations, so thoroughly documented, tell us much about the centrality of material exchange to pre-modern diplomacy. Furthermore, they point to an area of shared cultural terrain between China and Europe: at both ends of the world, objects were the *sine qua non* of every relationship.

3 On Friendship

To have friends coming from distant places – is that not
delightful?

CONFUCIUS, *Analects*, 1:1

A famous writer of antiquity cut open a large pomegranate.
Someone asked him: 'What would you like to have, oh
scholar, of the same number as there are seeds?' He replied:
'Faithful friends.'

RICCI, *On Friendship*, 100

Following the departure for Europe of Ruggieri, intent on
persuading the papacy to send a diplomatic embassy to Beijing, Ricci embarked on a rather more hands-on attempt
to befriend the Chinese people. Having been expelled from
Zhaoqing by hostile literati in 1589, subjected to a violent
attack by local residents in Shaozhou in 1592, and forced
to leave Nanjing almost as soon as he had arrived in 1595,
Ricci might have begun to lose confidence in his campaign
of friendship. And yet, by the summer of 1595, now settled
in the city of Nanchang, he displayed a manic optimism.
Enthusing breathlessly about his new home, he described
the capital of Jiangxi province as a bustling city, 'twice the
size of Florence', and richly endowed with 'literati, nobility, beauty and perfection'.[1] The particular cachet of Nanchang derived from its curious demographic. According to
Ricci, one quarter or one fifth of the population was made
up of members of the Chinese imperial family. After the
succession, it was the requirement of all the emperor's sons
and anyone else who might conceivably have a claim to the

throne to go into exile. That Nanchang was a traditional destination for such imperial cast-offs seemed to Ricci to be a most promising characteristic.

Ricci's Nanchang letters are marked by constant allusions to his Chinese friends. Hard though it is to quantify friend-ship, it is surely significant that in a single letter to the head of the order, Claudio Acquaviva, dated 4 November 1595, Ricci made nine references to *'amicizia'*, and six more each to *'amici'* and *'amore'*.[2] When writing to a Portuguese col-league several months earlier, *'amisade'* and *'amigos'* appear with equal frequency.[3] This celebration of amity would find further expression in a book on the subject that Ricci compiled and published in the same year, and dedicated to Qian Zhai, one of his principal 'friends' and supporters in Nanchang, a member of the imperial family, known as the Prince of Jian'an.[4] The book was entitled simply *On Friend-ship*, and consisted of a hundred numbered adages relating to that topic, most of which were culled from Latin and Greek authors, in particular Plutarch, Aristotle, Cicero and Seneca, with occasional helpings from the Church Fathers Augustine and Ambrose. Given the paucity of European books Ricci had at his disposal in China, it is likely – as Ricci himself implied – that most of these were lodged in his memory from his schoolboy studies in the classics. Indeed, to the European reader, the compilation might have read as a rather conventional exercise in commonplacing. But, in China, it made a considerable impact, and a succes-sion of authorised and pirated editions proved very popular among its target readership of literati.

For a quaintly poetic account of why Ricci chose 'friend-ship' as the topic with which to inaugurate his Chinese pub-lishing career, we may turn to his preface. Here, the author explained how he had travelled 'by sea from the great West' and entered China, full of admiration for 'the noble virtues of the Son of the Sky of the Great Ming' (the Emperor) and 'the teachings passed down by the ancient kings'. After a period spent in Guangdong province, 'by the Mount of Plum Trees during diverse changes of the stars and of the snows', Ricci struck north for Nanjing, the southern capital.⁵ There, we know, he was unable to gain permission to stay but – skating over this fact – he tells us of how he headed back south-west down the Yangzi river to Nanchang, a place of 'singular beauty', populated by noble people enjoying a life of retirement or – as the Romans would have said – of *otium*. Ricci found this city of contemplation forcefully attractive: 'Being unable to separate myself from this place, I left the boat and took a house.'⁶ In Nanchang, Ricci found unparalleled hospitality, particularly at the hands of the Prince of Jian'an, 'who did not spurn me, but permitted me to pay him great homage, made me sit in the guest's place, offered me sweet wine and hosted a grand party for me'. According to Ricci, following this banquet, 'The Prince left his place, and came over to me, and taking my hands said to me: "When noble men of great virtue deign to pass through my land, I never fail to invite them, and treat them like friends, and honour them. The great West is a land of morality and justice; I would like to hear what is thought there of friendship."'⁷ Thus we are led to believe that it was at the request of his blue-blooded friend that Ricci composed a pamphlet on friendship, consisting of 'that which I had heard since I was a boy'.⁸

But what did 'friendship' mean to the Jesuits in China, and how were their efforts at making friends with the Chinese understood? Ricci's relationship with the Prince of Jian'an, as described in the preface to *On Friendship*, immediately alerts us to two central aspects of the Jesuits' real-life experience. The first was their dependence on patronage: without 'friends' in high places – and the Prince of Jian'an was a prime example – the missionaries could achieve nothing. The second was their immersion in male networks of intense sociability: the Jesuits quickly realised that only by giving and receiving hospitality would they gain the social acceptance that was a crucial condition of their mission. Life became an onerous regime of banqueting, of taking tea and wine, of conversation and disputation with the scholarly elites. In these two respects, friendship was strategic, functional and utilitarian, a definition that is well represented among the hundred adages published in 1595. Ricci cited the Roman dramatist Plautus unabashedly: 'Only the projects of those who have friends can prosper' (51). He recalled the wisdom of Aristotle when he proclaimed, 'The friend who does me no good is like the enemy who does me no ill' (23). And he echoed Cicero in his assertion that 'the reasons for friendship are reciprocal need and mutual help' (3).

With such counsel at the forefront of his mind, Ricci committed himself to a career of networking. The lifestyle was not entirely unfamiliar to him. Back home, Renaissance scholars were apt to praise the benefits of conviviality.[9] Western men did business together over wine and gossip. The great European universities were renowned as places of conversation and argument, not just of solitary study. The Jesuits themselves deliberately eschewed the normal constraints of a religious community (the monastic timetable, the habit) so as to facilitate their exchanges and relations with lay elites. And yet of course the precise customs and practices of Chinese male sociability were utterly distinct from anything that Ricci and his colleagues had experienced in Italy or Iberia.

The Portuguese Dominican friar, Gaspar da Cruz, who

spent a few weeks in Canton in 1556, was impressed by the appetite of local men for meeting, eating and drinking:

When any man meeteth any acquaintance of his that cometh from outside, or that he hath not seen him for some days, saluting one another, he asketh him presently if he hath dined, and if he answereth no, he carrieth him to one of these victualling-houses, and there they eat and drink privily, for there is great store of wine and better than in any place in India, which they make adulterated; and if he answereth that he hath dined already, he carrieth him to a victualling-house where they have only wine and shellfish, wherewith they drink, of which houses there are also many, and there doth he entertain him.[10]

There was no shortage of such houses along the outside of the city wall, including one street dedicated to the selling of 'dogs, cut in quarters, roasted, boiled and raw'.[11] But the hospitable urges of the Cantonese could also find vent in more refined milieux. Closer to the occasions that Ricci would later experience during his travels in south China was da Cruz's account of a private banquet, held in the house of a rich merchant:

The tables were set in three places of the house; for every guest invited there was a table and a chair very fair and gilt, or with silver, and every table had before it a cloth of damask down to the ground. On the tables was neither cloth nor napkins, as well because the tables were very fine, as because they eat so cleanly that they need none of these things. The fruit was set along the edges of the table, all set in order which was, roasted chestnuts and peeled, and nuts cracked and shelled, and sugar-canes clean and cut in slices, and the fruit we spoke of before called lichias, great and small, but they were dried. All the fruit was set in small heaps like turrets very well made, crossed between with certain small sticks very clean, whereby all the tables in a circle were very fairly adorned with these little turrets. Presently, after the fruit, all the services were placed in fine porcelain dishes, all very well dressed and neatly carved, and everything set in good order; and although the sets of dishes were set on top of the other, all were beautifully set; in such sort that he who sat at the table might eat what he would without any need of stirring or removing any of them.[12]

After providing a classic account of Chinese chopsticks, da Cruz goes on to comment on the peculiarities of drinking habits: 'They have also a very small porcelain cup gilt, which holdeth a mouthful of wine, and only for this is there a waiter at the table. They drink so little because at each mouthful of food they must take a sip of drink, and therefore the cup is so small.' What da Cruz does not make explicit in this passage was that such banquets were gender specific, the preserve of elite males, whose masculinity and status was in part defined by occasions of dedicated drunkenness. Despite the dainty vessels, the liquor was strong, and there was no attempt to disguise the fact that the purpose of alcoholic consumption was inebriation. A Chinese published collection of sixteenth-century anecdotes about the necessity of drinking included the entries: 'Drink takes you out of yourself' and 'Better to go 1000 days without a drink than to drink and not get drunk'. But – in keeping with da Cruz's account – this is not to suggest that drinking was yobbish or chaotic. In China, as the cultural historian Craig Clunas has revealed, the practices, traditions and material paraphernalia surrounding drinking were intricate and extensive and had evolved over centuries. When we pass by shelves of chinaware in a museum, we probably fail to realise how much of the surviving porcelain from the Ming era was used to store and serve alcoholic drinks (always taken warmed, whether fermented or distilled). The gold and silverware favoured by the rich has survived less commonly, given the temptation for later owners to melt it down.[13]

Il bevere et il parlare: drinking and talking. By 1592, in Shaozhou, Ricci already recognised the importance of these linked activities within his armoury of conversionary tactics.[14] In a new city, it was crucial for the Jesuits, borne in sedan chairs and carrying the customary visiting books, to set off on a round of visits to local literati. After the visits would come the feasts, 'so many that there were insufficient days' to fit them all in. Indeed it was perfectly common for a traveller from afar to be invited to four or five different dinner parties in one evening, in which case one would turn up, sit down, help oneself to something or other, and then go racing off to the next destination. A particular seasonal challenge for Ricci and his colleagues was how to accommodate their social calendar to the demands of Lenten fasting. Their solution was to skip lunch in recompense for an evening of feasting.[15] Adaptations of this kind were crucial to the success of the mission.

Thus it was that Ricci and his companions, roaming from one house to the next, developed their networking skills. Drinking *cha* with an influential mandarin in Shaozhou would result in Ricci being offered a long-awaited safe conduct northwards.[16] Attending a series of banquets hosted by a literatus in Nanjing would provide an opportunity for talking about God.[17] Making contact with a young man who had recently been appointed to the prestigious position of *chayuan*, Ricci thrilled at the thought that his new acquaintance had 'drunk wine with the Emperor'.[18] Determined to contract a friendship (*fazer amisade*) with a well-connected doctor in Nanchang, Ricci donned his visiting clothes, armed himself with a gift and presented himself at his house. How gratifying it was when the doctor immediately returned his visit, and issued an invitation to a banquet at which Ricci would acquire first-hand experience of those towers of fruit that had so impressed da Cruz, as well as rub shoulders with a pair of princes.[19] Ricci could scarcely be accused of trying to conceal his instrumental vision of friendship.

At the patronage game, Ricci was adept. He knew when to jump at an opportunity, and he also knew when to hold back. For example, when the Prince of Jian'an beseeched the Jesuit to come and take up residence in his palace, Ricci wriggled out of the invitation, for he rightly perceived the danger of giving himself up to one person at the expense of 'making friendships with many'.[20] He was also alert to the importance of distinguishing between true and false friends.[21] At least twenty-five of the hundred adages dealt expressly with the question of how to exercise caution in forging friendships: 'Before contracting a friendship it is necessary to observe; afterwards, it is necessary to trust' (7); 'Even the wise man deludes himself, believing himself to have more friends than he has in reality' (8); 'If I put my friend to the test only when times are good, I shall not be able to trust him' (14); 'The friend who is attracted by my fortune will certainly be sent packing by my disgrace' (83), etc. The wise words of Seneca, Cicero and Plutarch were frequently attested during the course of the China mission. Let down by a certain Zhu, an official in Nanjing, who had first shown support to Ricci and then dispatched him from the city, Matteo reflected drily on the infidelity of the Chinese:

And so ended the great friendship that we had established with this mandarin; from which we can understand how little faith it is possible to have in the word and promises of the Chinese ... After this occurrence, I was not only sad because I saw my hopes of remaining here dashed, but also very confused since I had plainly told all my friends and acquaintances that this mandarin was my friend, and that he was delighted to see me in Nanjing.[22]

Constancy – that ideal of stoic philosophy – was a value that defined Ricci's vision of friendship: a friend in need was a friend indeed.

The insistence on loyal, disinterested friendship was a thread that ran through Ricci's compilation. Especially appropriate to the Chinese culture of respectful visits and calling cards was the Aristotelian sentiment: 'He who in my prosperity visits when I invite him and in my disgrace visits without an invitation is a true friend' (64). The obverse was also true, and one had to be wary of friends who sought one out for profit: 'He who, in contracting friendship, seeks only his own interest and does not worry about benefiting his friend is a merchant, not a friend. – The common man contracts friendship as he loans money: he only calculates the profits' (28). This mercenary attitude to friendship perhaps brought to mind the money-grabbing merchants of Macao, a category of foreigner from which Ricci had many reasons for wishing to dissociate himself. And yet when the Jesuit author asserted in the ninth adage of his collection that 'the friend who gives a present to a friend, anticipating recompense, is not giving a present, but is no different from a vendor in the market', it is hard not to discern a whiff of hypocrisy. After all, the strategic presentation of gifts was fundamental to the Jesuit missionaries' way of proceeding in China. It was the same tactic that underpinned Ruggieri's return to Rome in order to garner gifts for the Emperor. The Jesuits *always* anticipated, or at least hoped for, recompense, if not of a material kind, certainly in terms of privileges, protection and freedom to continue their mission.

The classical authors whose writings underpinned Ricci's *On Friendship* devoted considerable efforts to negotiating the twin calls of disinterestedness and utility.[23] They recognised that certain friendships, such as those that linked patrons and clients, or cemented a political alliance, were need-based. Friendships of this kind, together with those relationships based on shared pleasure or congeniality, were dubbed 'ordinary' or 'common'. They were likely to be temporary, surviving only as long as need or pleasure prolonged them. By contrast, the 'true' or 'perfect' friendship had as its object not another person but the attainment of wisdom, goodness and beauty. This ideal gets a thorough airing in Ricci's compilation. First, the transitory nature of 'ordinary friendship' is suggested: 'When, in friendship, pleasure prevails over virtue, one cannot remain friends for long' (32). Then we are shown the other side of the coin: 'Lasting virtue is the best food for an eternal friendship. Everything, without exception, at length becomes boring to men; only virtue, the longer it lasts, the more it moves the feelings of men' (90). And yet utility – rather than being antithetical to virtue – could serve as its prop, for one could *both* prove one's virtue through usefulness to one's friends *and* enjoy moral betterment as a benefit of friendship. It is perhaps helpful to visualise classical models of friendship as a pyramid, in which *amicitia perfecta* ('perfect friendship') stood at the peak. Beneath it came all the other kinds of friendship: alliances based on shared pleasure and need, the natural affiliation of members of the same species to each another, and the social concord that individuals instinctively sought. According to this pyramidal structure, 'perfect friendship' was not disjoined from the lower levels of 'common' or 'ordinary friendship'; rather it encompassed all the parts – natural, social, political, pleasurable – within its wholeness.[24]

Confucian scholars had a different take on the utility of friendship. In common with the European tradition, they took care to condemn crass opportunism or profit in any human relationship. On the other hand, friendship was considered capable of serving useful ends for the family and society, and therein lay its justification. For according to Confucianism, there were five kinds of worthy relationship: that which bound father and son, ruler and minister, husband and wife, older and younger brother, and – finally – friends. Each of the other relationships was hierarchical, and except for the bond between husband and wife (although marriages were nearly always arranged), involuntary. Friendship, by contrast, 'the fifth relationship', was a bond that one entered into wilfully and which was relatively free of hierarchy. As such, it was considered potentially selfish, and destabilising to the fundamental structures of family and state. Friendship could, however, be tamed and rendered most useful when it was set to benefit the other four relationships: according to this model, the purpose of friends was to make one a better son, official, spouse or brother. Yet in the late Ming fascination with the self, friendship fulfilled another function, which would have been easily recognised by the Jesuits, and that was self-cultivation. Engaging in a relationship of amity was a dialectical process whereby one's more personal interactions with others led to greater personal reflection and thus a clearer understanding of one's self. Confucian writings stressed the possibilities for moral improvement inherent in friendship, and – like Seneca – counselled caution in selecting one's friends. Did Ricci know the Chinese maxim, 'He who touches vermilion will be reddened, while he who touches ink will be blackened'? Both metaphor and message are certainly echoed in the Jesuit's sixty-seventh adage: 'He who lives in a dyehouse, near the dyers and the colours, keeps his body clean with difficulty. He who makes friends with villains, always hearing and seeing their crimes, will certainly assume their ways and his heart will become blotted.'[25]

Friendship was therefore of public use in so far as it offered moral support to the pre-eminent relationships of family and state. 'From the emperor to the commoner, all need friends to succeed,' read one oft-quoted passage from a commentary to a poem in the *Book of Odes*.[26] The sentiment was soundly reiterated in Ricci's sixteenth adage: 'A man cannot accomplish everything alone; therefore the Lord of Heaven has enjoined men to friendship, in order that they lend each other reciprocal assistance. If this precept were removed from the world, humankind would be certainly lost.' Ricci likewise emphasised the importance of friendship to rulers, with a series of adages relating expressly to King Alexander (91–3), another citing Croesus (99) and yet another referring anonymously to an 'ancient king of the West' (97). But if, according to Chinese wisdom, friendship buttressed the other four relationships, it also borrowed status and respectability from the available models of subservience, filiality, marriage and fraternity. For Confucians at once endorsed the value and defused the danger of friendship by imposing on it the hierarchical structures of the other relationships. Thus friendship could stand in for fraternity: 'When at home, you have your brothers; when abroad, you have your friends', a maxim of particular relevance to the many Chinese merchants and officials – as well as the Jesuit missionaries – who travelled far from their families.[27] It could also be expressed by a ruler–minister analogy: 'If the ruler does not admonish his minister, then good government is lost. If the gentleman does not instruct his friend, then virtue is lost.' And it could even be contained within the model of conjugality: the famous friendship of two scholars from antiquity was, by Confucian logic, rendered harmless precisely because the men, who 'shared the same pillow', preserved the hierarchy of 'husband and wife'.[28]

'Unless one is a friend one cannot have the means to be a ruler or minister, father or son, husband or wife, elder brother or younger brother.'[29] So wrote Gu Xiancheng, a leading light of the Donglin Academy, an association of literati based in Wuxi in Jiangsu province (about 100 km north-west of Shanghai), which was renowned in the early seventeenth century for its critical reflections on contemporary society and politics. Gu's words were at first sight a classic justification of the functions of friendship in supporting the other relationships. Taken in context, however, his statement bore a far more radical message. For, thanks to the research of Joseph McDermott, we now know that Gu belonged to a group of outspoken intellectuals in the late Ming who were attempting to elevate friendship beyond its conventional status, and to advocate friendly counsel as a means of reforming the corrupt ways of imperial government. According to Gu, the value of friendship lay precisely in its absence of hierarchy, bestowing equal agency and responsibility on each party:

Each of the other four relations has only one part as the master, but with friendship both parties take charge. The rectitude of the ruler–minister relationship, the intimacy of the father–son, the distinction between husband and wife, and the hierarchical difference between an older and younger brother – they each have a sole subordinate. If one lectures and studies and tries to penetrate everything, one cannot speak of all the endless changing processes of nature to the ruler or the parents, or also to one's brothers, and even to one's wife and sons. Only with friends can one call things into question and talk in a relaxed way. The cloak of human feelings takes an endless variety of forms and shapes, and there are things about them one can only talk about to friends rather than to a ruler, father, wife and brothers.[30]

The political thrust of Gu's celebration of friendship was to insist on the need for greater equality between officials. His colleague and successor as leader of the Donglin movement, Gao Panlong, directed his discussion instead to the relationship between the emperor and factions. Rather than eradicating factions, an impossibility – he argued – since men stick together 'like glue', the emperor should concentrate on distinguishing between the partial, one-sided factions of petty men and the sincere factions of gentlemen; only by endorsing the latter would the emperor succeed in restoring order.[31] This admittedly elitist theme was taken up by later commentators, in the final decades of the Ming. Weary of weak government and the increasing domination of the Tianqi Emperor (1620–27) by his 80,000 eunuchs, the scholar Huang Daozhou called for a strong-willed ruler capable of developing friendships with officials. Huang's plea for the Emperor to find himself some good friends – a wise man to whom he can delegate responsibility, a counsellor whose suggestions he can trust and a companion with whom he can relax and enjoy himself – chimed with Ricci's account of his favourite Western ruler:

When King Alexander had not yet risen to the throne, he did not have a national treasury and gave generously to others all of the riches that he gained. The King of a hostile country, who was very rich and who was concerned only to fatten his treasury, scoffing at him said, 'Where is Your Majesty's treasure?' He replied, 'In the heart of my friends.' (93)[32]

It was within the late Ming context of this fresh and fervent reappraisal of friendship that Matteo Ricci's translated compilation of snippets from Aristotle's *Nicomachean Ethics*, Cicero's *De amicitia* and other Western favourites made such a splash.[33] It was certainly advantageous for the Jesuits to have arrived at a moment when Chinese scholars were exploring the value of close alliances between virtuous and learned men, as a complement (if not an alternative) to familial bonds. (The proficiency of Matteo Ricci and his friends at the former perhaps drew attention away from their deficiency in the latter.) And, in his choice of adages, Ricci discreetly chipped away at the presumed superiority of family over friendship:

The relationship between friends is more intimate than that between brothers; therefore friends call each other 'brothers' and the closest of brothers are 'friends'. (36)

Friendship surpasses kinship only in this respect: kin need not love reciprocally; friends must. In fact relations of kinship remain even without love between the kin; but if you take away mutual love between friends, how can the essence of friendship subsist? (50)

These claims carried a particular resonance for Ricci, not simply because he was a celibate male, who had denied himself the possibility of procreation and followed a vocation that took him far away from his natal family; but also because – as it happened – his friendships were passionate and his familial relations cool.

Of the fifty-five surviving letters of Matteo Ricci, only six were sent to members of his family. Three of these were addressed to his father, Giovanni Battista, and the first of the series, written from Shaozhou, on 12 November 1592, begins with a complaint:

According to my customary practice and duty, I have not failed these past years to send you my news and greetings, since I know that you are pleased to hear from such distant parts; but I have not received annual letters from home; ever since you wrote me a long and consequently pleasing account of the mercies that the Lord had shown you after my departure, I have received nothing more from either you or Antonio Maria.[34]

While Ricci's father and brother (Antonio Maria) were neglecting him, it had fallen to a colleague, Girolamo Costa, another Jesuit from Macerata, to inform Matteo of the death of his aunt Laria. Ricci went on to tell his father, somewhat pointedly, how – despite the fact that he had received this sad news while he was in bed, recovering from the injuries that he had sustained during the Shaozhou attack – he got up on the three subsequent days in order to say Masses on behalf of the aunt. This was as much as to say that he was aware of his family duties, even if his closest relatives were lacking in a comparable sense of obligation. But duty seemed to be the best that Matteo could muster; affection was certainly in short supply. Ricci persisted in a letter that was, by his standards, brief, touching on local news (fears of a Japanese attack, the quandary over the imperial inheritance), the state of the mission and the abundance of rhubarb in China, the last topic being one that he presumably thought would interest his pharmacist father. Ricci's letter ended in homiletic mode:

It is time to come close to God; for, as far as I can tell, *non longa tibi restat via* [you are approaching the end of your journey]; it is necessary to get ready to render your accounts of your past life. I know that one who has always lived with the fear of God, as you have done, will find it easy to give an account of everything; but, since this is a matter of the greatest importance, it is better to be too scrupulous than too lax in weighing up your affairs. *Est enim momentum unde pendet aeternitas* [For this is the moment on which eternity hangs].[35]

One might imagine that this was typical of Ricci's epistolary style; after all, he was a priest and missionary, whose professional obligation was the cure of souls. Far from it; the majority of his letters to his colleagues seem a great deal more relaxed, more natural, more effusive, and – even when dwelling on the most serious of spiritual matters – less portentous.

The carping continued. Ricci's second extant letter to his father, sent from Shaozhou one year later, still complained of the absence of contact from home (although this time Matteo conceded that the letters could have been lost at sea).[36] Only in the third and final letter, written many years later in Beijing in 1605 (consisting principally of a thumbnail sketch of the state of the mission, and virtually devoid of personal engagement) did Ricci report an improvement in correspondence, and note that 'in past years I have received your letters annually'.[37] Ricci's letters to his brother, Antonio Maria, also dwelt on the matter of poor communication: 'It is many years since I have received a letter from Your Reverence'; 'It is several years since I have received a letter from Your Reverence'. The two surviving letters, dated 1596 and 1608, echo each other depressingly.[38] Matteo's critical tone in 1596 is scarcely veiled, since he follows up his grumble about epistolary silence with a more specific charge: 'I heard the news of the death of my mother and father, and that you had received the position of canon, from Girolamo Costa' – the same Girolamo Costa who had kept Ricci up to date with the death of his aunt.[39] As it turned out, the rumour of Ricci's father's death was inaccurate; in any case there was no sign that Matteo was overcome with grief. On the other hand, Costa's information about Antonio Maria's recent election to the post of canon in the Cathedral of Macerata was spot on. Matteo was particularly peeved by his brother's silence on this matter, since he attributed Antonio Maria's success to his own interventions with members of the higher echelons of the Society of Jesus. (This was another coup for Ricci in the patronage game, this time exercised at long distance.) The occasion presented Matteo with further opportunity for sermonising:

With this position of canon, I think that you will be well provided for in temporal matters; I hope that it will also be of spiritual profit; because if, instead of doing good to the soul, it causes harm, you would do better to go out begging. Thus I recommend that you show gratitude to our Father General and to all members of our Company, both because it is the Company to which I belong, and also because of the good that you have received from it; since to be forgetful of benefits is a vice, and the father of many others.[40]

Curiously, Ricci's one hundred adages included nothing on gratitude, though here was no clearer indication of the obligations that one had to 'friends'.

Matteo's 1596 letter to Antonio Maria urged him to write with news of 'all our brothers and cousins and sisters', and in a fragment of correspondence – all that survives of a letter to another brother, Orazio, dated 1605 – he expressed the isolation of his missionary life in terms of distance from 'our dear father, mother, brothers and relatives'.[41] But these stilted displays of filial piety are undercut by the frostiness of his familial letters. To register Ricci's capacity for affection, one must turn instead to the loving missives that he sent to his friends back in Europe. One of the earliest of these was sent by Ricci in 1580 from Cochin, on the west coast of India, to his friend in Rome, Ludovico Maselli.[42] Ricci was only twenty-eight years old at the time; Maselli was fourteen years his senior. They had met at the Collegio Romano, where Ricci had been a student and Maselli the Director. But, despite these differences in age and status, the language of their friendship was that of intimacy and equality. And, as the beginning of Ricci's letter made clear, their links were closer than those of flesh and blood:

The peace of the Lord be always in our souls. Amen. It does not cause me such sadness, for thus I want to call it, to be far from my relations *secundem carnem* [of the flesh], although I *am* very carnal, so much as to be distant from Your Reverence whom I love more than my father. From which you can judge, Your Reverence, how welcome your letter was to me. I do not know what imaginings come to me sometimes, and I don't know why a certain sort of melancholy comes over me – though I think that it is a good thing, and it would concern me were it not to occur – thinking that my fathers and brothers, whom I loved and love so much, of that college where I was born and brought up, have forgotten about me, while I hold all of them so fresh in my memory.[43]

Here, Ricci demonstrated an emotional intensity entirely lacking from the letters to his father and brothers. Indeed, the substitution of friends for family prompted Ricci to go as far as to claim the Collegio Romano as the place of his birth and upbringing.

Three years later, now based in Zhaoqing, Ricci wrote again to Maselli (who had moved south to become Superior of the Neapolitan province). He concluded his letter: 'I would rather give Your Reverence this account by mouth than by letter . . . I cannot end without pouring forth many tears, as I remember Your Reverence, and that golden age when I was with you.'[44]

Maselli was not the only fond friend to elicit Ricci's tears. Reading the letters of Girolamo Costa had the same effect.[45] In a letter addressed to him from Shaozhou in 1594 (admittedly, at a low point in the mission), Ricci issued this lament:

Every time that I remember my dear friends and brothers in Europe, something which I do exceedingly often when I make my devotions, I feel a great hope come over me: that the Lord God must plan to give me some great consolation in the next life, since in this one he wished to deprive me of the sweet presence of so many saints.[46]

Ricci's epistolary friendships were tinged with grief. But they were also strengthened by remembrance and nostalgia. In all his most intimate letters, Ricci expressed the view that love would endure. Writing from Goa to Gian Pietro Maffei in Lisbon, he told his friend that he could sense his love, 'notwithstanding the great distance that physically separates us'. 'Distance has caused no forgetfulness in me,' he assured Martino de Fornari in 1583, the one writing from Macao, the other residing in Padua.[47] Or to Girolamo Benci, in Rome, from Ricci in Nanchang, 1595: 'I think that love grows in me, with the distance of countries.'[48] The importance of remembering old friends was also reiterated in Ricci's *On Friendship*: 'Since you have searched for friends for so long, and have found so few, which are so hard to keep, when they leave your view at least remember them in your heart!' (80), or – more poignantly – 'The pleasure of friendship with a good friend becomes more noticeable once one has lost it' (66).

The ultimate test of friendship was death. Ricci lost a succession of colleagues while in China. First, there was António de Almeida, the Portuguese Jesuit who died in 1591 in the sickly climate of Shaozhou, aged thirty-four. Ricci, who had tended the sick man throughout the night, recalled how he had spooned him mouthfuls of 'meat sauce and concentrated broth'. Two years later died Francesco de Petris, 'the only companion and refuge that I had in this desert'. Then there was João Barradas, a young Macanese Christian and would-be Jesuit, who perished in a terrifying shipwreck en route to Nanjing in May 1595. Ricci, who had himself survived the accident by grabbing hold of a writing desk which was floating outside of the boat, 'felt the loss of this good young man' with particular pain. Perhaps most traumatic of all was the loss of another Macanese, this time of Chinese blood, known by his Christian name of Francisco Martins, who was tortured to death in a Cantonese gaol in 1606. Ricci might have taken comfort from Seneca, whose thoughts on the death of friends appeared as number 15 of his compilation: 'I remember my dead friends without sadness, because when they were here I possessed them as though I might lose them; now they are dead I remember them as though they were yet alive.'

While Ricci recognised the functional qualities of friendship, as enacted through his own participation in clientage and networking, his relationships with his male colleagues often contained a far deeper, more instinctual, emotional dimension. *On Friendship* rejoices in the intimacy and shared feelings of friends: 'My friend is none other than half of myself; he is another version of myself. For this reason, I must consider my friend as myself' (1); 'Although my friend and I have two bodies, we share a heart' (2); 'If there was no friendship in the world, there would be no joy' (57). Yet, having traversed from the drinking houses of Canton to the deepest recesses of a man's soul, two important – and related – questions remain. Firstly, was the intense model of friendship between men, to which Ricci testifies so eloquently, compatible with virtue? Secondly, was it compatible with Ricci's dealings with the Chinese?

Ricci was, as he admitted to his friend Fabio de Fabii, a 'carnal' creature, at times, abounding in 'passions' that led him away from the path of virtue.[49] But it would be wrong to impose a hard line between the passionate and the virtuous friendship. According to a synthesis of classical and Christian ideas, in its most perfect form, the emotional energy of friendship could be channelled to virtuous ends. The union of souls meant the mutual reinforcement of virtue. 'Lasting virtue is the best food for an eternal friendship' (90).

Correction and criticism were central to Ricci's understanding of friendship: 'The true friend does not always follow his friend, nor does he always oppose him. When he is right, he listens; when he is wrong, he opposes. So speaking the truth is the duty proper to friendship' (19). For Ricci, the true friend was both teacher and doctor: 'Making a friendship is like curing a disease; if the doctor truly loves the sick person, he surely hates the illness' (20); 'The end of friendship is none other than this: if the friend is superior to me, I imitate and learn from him; if I am superior, I improve him. Learning and teaching, teaching and learning: each helps the other' (69). This was the ultimate end of the Jesuits' attempts to befriend the Chinese.

Ricci never evinced quite the levels of affection and intimacy towards his Chinese friends that characterised his relations with his closest Jesuit friends, especially those with whom he had grown up and studied in Macerata and Rome. He was easy enough conversing and disputing with Chinese scholars at banquets. He showed respect and gratitude to the literati who helped him, admiration and fondness for the converts he got to know. However, whether of joy or of grief, these exchanges were largely devoid of emotional outpourings. We can attribute this greater emotional distance to the inevitable barriers of language and culture that separated Ricci from these friends, and to the need to observe caution when interacting with a foreign people of vastly alien customs.[50] But with the ideal of the virtuous friendship, Ricci was assuredly on safe territory. Adapting an Aristotelian maxim to terms easily recognisable within Chinese culture, Ricci's eighteenth adage proclaimed, 'If the virtues and the ideals are alike, then the friendship will be firm – The ideogram "friend" is made from two ideograms meaning "like", signifying that the friend is me and I am him.' The cultural translatability of 'virtuous friendship' was further confirmed in the preface to the 1601 Beijing edition of Ricci's work, written by the literatus Feng Yingjing, who defined friendship in terms of 'a mutual engagement, mutual assistance, mutual correction, mutual perfecting . . . of which the ultimate aim is never to separate'.[51] His own friendship with Matteo Ricci had led him to conclude, 'I am increasingly convinced that the mentalities and teaching of the West and the East are identical.'[52]

The last reference to friends that occurs in Ricci's surviving letters comes in the 1608 letter to his brother, Antonio Maria Ricci. Perhaps unsurprisingly, given the psychology of that relationship, it is a negative comment: 'I have so many friends in so many places that they do not allow me to live.'[53] He went on to complain that he spent all day long sitting around answering questions from the curious. He would have done well to recall the fifty-sixth adage in his book on friendship:

God has given to man a pair of eyes, of ears, of hands, of feet, signifying that everything may be brought to a good end if two friends help one another reciprocally. In ancient script, the character 'friend' was made up of two hands which we could not do without; the character 'companion' was made up of 'wing and wing', that is two wings, without which the bird could not fly. Was it not perhaps in this way that the old sages thought about friends?

Tired though Ricci was by the end of his life, he could not deny that he had flown far on the wings of friendship.

4 Heavenly Knowledge

On the Feast of the Annunciation, 25 March 1605, the Jesuits celebrated one of their greatest triumphs to date: the baptism, at the Nanjing residence, of Qu Rukui, now known by his Christian name, 'Ignatius'.[1] Before receiving baptism, reported Ricci, Qu went down on his knees, and began 'with much spirit and devotion to beat the ground in front of him, which in this land is a sign of asking pardon'. He then recited a protestation of faith, in which he renounced his past life of sin, and his erroneous pursuit of false religion, and recalled his good fortune in meeting the Western priests. Displaying an impressive mastery of the tenets of Christian belief and practice, he presented himself to receive the waters of baptism 'that wash away all the filth of the past', pledged obedience to God, asked the Holy Spirit to guide him, and sought the intervention of the Virgin Mary. He ended his proclamation:

For this I beseech of the Queen, the Mother of God, that she deign to give me strength and to animate me from within, ensuring that my intentions are strong, firm, and without vacillation, and opening up to me the power of my soul, and making my spirit modest and pure; in order that my heart, thus illuminated, might hold truth and reason, and my mouth fill with holy words for me to spread and sow throughout China, so that everyone may know the holy law of God and be subjected to it.[2]

Qu's appeal to the Virgin resonated powerfully on this occasion, for his baptism took place on one of the major Marian festivals of the Catholic calendar: the celebration of Mary's conception of Jesus, nine months before Christmas.

Fifty-six years old and a native of Jiangsu province, Qu was a plum convert: a man of great intellect, charm and social standing, of whom the Jesuits were understandably proud. Ricci considered him 'among his oldest and greatest friends', and someone who had done much to enhance the missionaries' situation in China.[3] His position of influence was in large part bequeathed to him by his father, whose success in the civil service exams had been legendary. Qu's father had gone on to serve as President of the Ministry of Rites, in charge of state ceremonies, and was considered by some to have been the greatest literatus of his times.[4] So Qu was a catch, a promising example to counter Ricci's lament that the Jesuits had failed to convert anyone of any consequence.[5]

What had attracted this trophy neophyte with his eminent relatives and ready understanding of Christian theology to the font? Qu had first heard about the Jesuits in Zhaoqing in 1589, when he was undergoing some sort of mid-life crisis. According to Ricci, his father had died while Qu was still 'in the flower of his youth', and without the restraint of paternal authority, his life had begun to spin out of control. Despite his remarkable intelligence, he had never risen beyond the first level of the civil service exams. By the time Ricci met him, he had fallen into 'bad habits' and had blown most of his inheritance on failed alchemical experiments. Poverty had led him to travel around China, scrounging off friends and cashing in on his late father's credit. When Qu first sought out the Jesuits in Shaozhou, it was in the hope of being taught the secrets of alchemy. Ricci steered him instead towards a year's intensive study of mathematics.

European methods of arithmetic came first in Qu's curriculum. Ricci disparaged the inability of the Chinese to calculate without recourse to an abacus; from now on, Qu would do his sums with the assistance only of pen and paper. Next they proceeded to study the rudiments of astronomy. Ricci relied for his own knowledge of this subject on a commentary, written by his former maths teacher Christopher Clavius, on a thirteenth-century text by an Englishman called John Holywood, but remembered in scholarly circles as Giovanni Sacrobosco. Sacrobosco's *Sphaera* was the classic text on positional astronomy, seeking to plot the movements of the sun, moon, earth and planets within an imagined, rotating 'celestial sphere'. Although constructed as a commentary, Clavius's book was intended to be a pedagogical work, to which he appended his own rather conservative views on planetary theory and his observations on two eclipses that he had witnessed.[6] Finally, Ricci and his pupil embarked on a voyage through Euclidean geometry, which would result in Qu producing his own translation of Book One of the *Elements*.[7] All three aspects of Qu's course mirrored Ricci's own mathematical studies at the Collegio Romano, and in turn reflected the expertise of Clavius.[8] Nurtured in the cradle of the Collegio, the relationship between Ricci and Clavius had been a close one, and Ricci sought in some ways to re-create it through the Chinese pupil to whom he now referred as 'my disciple in mathematics'.

So the alchemist Qu Rukui first immersed himself in European mathematics, and then turned his attentions to Christian theology: a curious trajectory to the modern mind. The place of science in the Jesuit mission to China is of course well known. The image of Matteo Ricci, standing alongside his seventeenth-century successors Adam Schall and Ferdinand Verbiest, surrounded by globes, quadrants and armillary spheres, reminds us of Ricci's role in initiating a tradition whereby members of the Society of Jesus offered their scientific services to the Chinese.[9] At the start of the seventeenth century, Ricci would obtain the all-important permission to enter the city of Beijing because certain literati there hoped that he would be able to correct the Chinese calendar. Here in the East, by a remarkable coincidence, he followed in the footsteps of Clavius in the West, since his former tutor had in 1580 been appointed to the committee established by Pope Gregory XIII to preside over Europe's own calendar reform.[10] If reform of the calendar in Rome was, as one historian has claimed, 'symbolic of the Church's power to shape social reality', it was equally expressive of the power of the state in Beijing.[11] On both sides of the globe, as Ricci recognised, astronomical knowledge was highly politicised – a resource that could be drawn on but that needed to be kept under control. Therefore, in his letters back to Rome, Ricci pleaded not only for scientific books to be sent out to him but also for a Jesuit Father trained in astronomy (inseparable from astrology, in the early modern mindset) to join the mission. In 1605, Ricci sent this supplication to João Alvares, a high-ranking Portuguese Jesuit based in Rome:

I really want to beg something of Your Reverence that for many years now I have been requesting without response. One of the most useful things that could be sent from Rome to this court would be a Father or even a Brother who is a good astrologer. And the reason why I say an astrologer, rather than an expert in geometry, clocks and astrolabes, is because regarding these other things I myself know a good deal, and I have sufficient books; but the Chinese take little account of this, compared with the course and true position of the planets and the calculation of eclipses; in short, we need someone who could draw up ephemerides [astronomical tables] . . .

I say then that, if the mathematician of whom I spoke came here, we could turn our tables into Chinese script – I could do this easily – and set about emending the calendar. And this would give us a great reputation, and would open further the gates of China, and would enable us to stay here with greater security and freedom.[12]

Ricci was quite clear: the only way to secure the Jesuits' position in China was to assist the imperial regime with Western science.

But if Ricci has left us in no doubts about the trade-off between Western science and protection for the Jesuits at an official level, he was less explicit about the relationship between science and conversion at an individual level. What exactly did the Jesuits think they were achieving by teaching arithmetic or cartography to literati? What did the Chinese believe they had to gain by submitting themselves to Jesuit tuition? Was conversion to European scientific methods deemed by the Jesuits to be a prelude to conversion to the true faith? And how much conversion – of either religion or scientific learning – was occurring anyway? Contradictory beliefs evidently existed within the palimpsest of ideas accumulated by one such as Qu Rukui. When a recent editor of Ricci's letters dubs Qu a 'zealous and exemplary disciple', his impulse towards hagiography ignores the awkward facts that Qu's conversion was delayed by his reluctance to marry his concubine, and that he continued to practise alchemy long after his baptism.[13] The profile of the ideal convert and 'exemplary disciple' was dogged by attitudes that were unchristian and – according to European definitions – unscientific.

We shall come back to these awkward facts later. But first let us dig deeper into Ricci's writings to discover why he believed there was such a profound connection between Western scientific learning and true faith. In a chapter of the *History of the Introduction of Christianity to China* dedicated to science and the liberal arts, Ricci paid tribute to China's unique system of government. For, unlike any other nation in the world, here the ruling class owed its authority not to inherited privilege, wealth or favour, but to scholarship and intellectual agility, tested in the most rigorous and dispassionate fashion. In common with other Europeans who visited China, Ricci was fascinated by the examination system: the three-tier selection procedure whereby literati were centrally chosen to fulfil the duties of governance throughout the empire's provinces. Examinations for the first level of degree – the *xiucai* – were held biennially in every county; the selection of *juren* – the next and far more challenging level – occurred triennially in the provinces; the prestigious *jinshi* – the highest level of degree-holder – were also selected every three years, by examinations held in Beijing, the year after the *juren*.[14]

Ricci described in detail the halls that adorned each regional centre, purpose-built for the *juren* examinations: large palaces, surrounded by high walls, each containing four thousand cells, designed to ensure that no exam candidate would be able to see, let alone communicate with, any other.[15] Cheating was virtually impossible, but severely punished if detected. Awaiting entry to the examination hall, candidates unloosened the ties of their leggings, so that invigilators could more easily search inside their clothing to ensure that no books or writings were brought into the hall. Guards stood in watchtowers at each end of the building. Incarcerated within this monument to competition, the candidates, equipped only with two or three pens, ink and blank paper, embarked on a three-day marathon. There was provision for tea though, according to a contemporary critic of the system, nobody dared to avail himself of this, nor of the lavatory, for fear that his script would be stamped with a red mark, signalling the loss of a grade.[16] Throughout the empire, thousands of men – first-timers as well as retakers – would commence their first exam on the dot of nine o'clock; the next would start at twelve, and the last of the day would begin at three in the afternoon. At the end of which, candidates could level up the boards that constituted their desk and bench and place them together to form a bed. The pattern would then be repeated during the second and third days.

In each of the three-hour exams, the candidate was presented with a series of textual extracts, or accounts of notional situations to which he was supposed to respond.[17] These were supplied by the examiners who had travelled from Beijing to the different provincial examination centres, thereby ensuring a fair and equal challenge for the thousands of candidates across the land – an extraordinary feat of centralisation for any pre-modern state, let alone such a vast one as this. The first day of the *juren* exams was devoted to Confucian wisdom, and the candidate was asked to comment on three statements taken from the *Four Books* and four more from the *Five Doctrines*. All seven compositions were – according to Ricci – required to observe the rules of Chinese rhetoric, in order to attain the highest level of elegance and to make use of the most effective conceits. Perhaps most challenging of all, each composition was to be written in no more and no fewer than five hundred words. On the second day, candidates were asked to turn their attention to examples from ancient history, and to give their opinion on three episodes as if they were advising the emperor on how to act. The third day continued the focus on practical governance, with candidates being required to compose three essays detailing their responses to lawsuits of the kind that they might have to pass judgment on while in public office. One final measure was intended to guarantee the impartiality of the assessment system. Having made fair copies of their compositions in special notebooks – at the end of which candidates were required to write their own name, the names of their father, grandfather and great-grandfather, and their place of birth – and then having sealed the books with gum, so that no unauthorised person could peer into it, they handed over their notebooks to professional copyists, who would transcribe their work anonymously in red ink for perusal by the examiners.[18]

When the results of this complicated process were eventually released, they were publicly displayed on tables, ranking the successful candidates in order of merit. One need hardly wonder where the stressed-out victims of China's civil service exam system headed next. In Galeote Pereira's words, it was 'the Chinese fashion to end all their pleasures with eating and drinking'.[19]

Ricci was impressed: 'If it is not possible to say of this realm that the philosophers are kings, at least one can say with truth that the kings are governed by philosophers.'[20] This perception of Chinese government determined the central tenet of his mission strategy post-Zhaoqing: not only should he and his colleagues target the literati, as the most powerful element in society; they should also attempt to communicate with them as fellow intellectuals and high-fliers. Surveying the examination system, Ricci was clearly alert to the similarities and differences between it and the Jesuits' own background. The educational milieu with which they themselves were most familiar was also intense and highly competitive. At the Collegio Romano, Ricci and his colleagues had been used to a regime of tough study and challenging hurdles. The Jesuits adopted a Humanist framework for their schools and colleges, in which the study of theology was deferred to the end. At school, one studied 'grammar', a programme that immersed the child in the language of Latin, and to a lesser extent Greek; the kind of education that Ricci himself experienced between the ages of eight and sixteen at the newly established Jesuit school in Macerata. At college, one then progressed to the next stages in a Humanist education: two years of reading and studying the great works of classical poetry, history and – most important of all – rhetoric (for, after all, what did poetry and history teach if not eloquence and the means of expression?). There followed three years of philosophy, beginning with logic, and moving on to the Aristotelian works on natural philosophy and metaphysics, mathematics and astronomy. And finally – if one got that far – four years of theology.

The examinations presided over by the Jesuits were annual and public, based on a tradition of oral disputation. As in China, an examination was a daunting event, but it was an experience to be borne in front of a large audience, rather than in the solitude of a cubicle. The *Ratio Studiorum*, the compilation of guidelines for Jesuit education published in 1599, prescribed that philosophy exams be held publicly 'and from this examination, no matter how rigorously it is conducted, usually no Jesuits nor even, if possible, any of our day and boarding students should be excused'.[21] In other words, the transparency of the system was to be ensured by openness rather than seclusion. In the realm of literary studies, by contrast, compositions in prose and poetry were required, and here the procedures that occurred in closed camera were closer to a Chinese exam: 'The prefect himself, or another person whom he assigns to take his place, should supervise those who are writing. On the day set for taking the examination, after giving the signal, this person should give a theme, a brief one rather than a long one.'[22] It was then the duty of the prefect to distribute the work among the examiners, who would read the scripts and mark errors in the margin. But this was all just the prelude to another public performance: the 'viva voce' exam. According to the *Ratio Studiorum*, 'First, each should read out, if it seems good, part of his own composition. Then he should be told to correct his errors, and to give an account of them, indicating the rule that was broken. Later, something in the vernacular should be proposed to the grammar students for translation into Latin on the spot; and everyone should be asked about the rules and the material taught in each class. Finally, the examiners should require a brief commentary, if necessary, on some passage from the books taught in class.'[23] Success in such examinations was the necessary condition of continuing one's progress towards full membership of the Society of Jesus. Those who failed to flourish in their academic studies (whose Latin was not up to the grade, or who managed only a clumsy engagement with logic) were marked out for the lesser career of 'temporal coadjutor' in the order. They would be given sufficient training in moral theology to enable them to say Masses or hear confessions, but they would not venture into the study of casuistry and speculative theology, the high points of the Jesuit curriculum. As Ricci surveyed would-be literati, desperately studying for their exams, experiencing rejection or jubilant success, he doubtless identified with the cut and thrust of male careerism.

And yet the different emphases in the Chinese and European exam systems were significant. For, in comparison with the Europeans' celebration of oratory, exhibited in the near-cult status of Roman rhetoricians such as Cicero and Quintilian, the Chinese were far more impressed by the written word. In Ricci's analysis, 'Since antiquity, this nation made much more of writing well than of speaking well and all their rhetoric and eloquence consists of composition ... even those who live in the same city prefer to communicate by means of written notes.' This Ricci attributed – as a foreigner might – to the extreme difficulty of speaking Chinese:

Many of the letters have the same sound, even if they are represented by a different character, and each one signifies many things. For this reason, it is the most ambiguous language that one can find ... Even among eloquent people, literati, who pronounce the language well, the Chinese often ask one another to repeat a word, and to say how it is written; and, not having a pen to hand, they write the character with their finger using water, or make a sign in the air, or on their hand, since it is clearer to write than to speak.[24]

It is true that the use of homonyms to mean different things could confuse even a native speaker, but this was not the only reason why the art of oratory was never celebrated in China. Ricci might well have given another explanation for the demotion of oral communication in the Middle Kingdom; while the Chinese shared a common set of written characters, the spoken language was fragmented into radically different dialects. The official dialect of the Ming was that of Nanjing, the imperial capital from 1368 to 1421, yet in reality most government employees could neither speak nor understand it, and hence relied on written communications. Perhaps the largest consideration, however, lay with the political structures of this massive and authoritarian empire. Here there were no representative institutions, no senate nor parliament in which the members of the ruling elite were encouraged to voice their opinions. In the quest for order, debate was deemed counterproductive. Those who aspired to enter the imperial bureaucracy were trained to master the written word. Calligraphy, not eloquence, was the test of a man's moral fibre, and there was a general distrust of clever talk. As Confucius said, 'Fine words and an insinuating appearance are seldom associated with true virtue.'[25]

By contrast, the Jesuit schools and colleges prized oral communication. Following the so-called *modo parisiensis*, a method of pedagogy modelled on that followed at the University of Paris, Jesuit students were constantly drilled and questioned, in small groups and in front of a wider audience.[26] Plays and performances marked important events in the academic year, with students being called on to make orations, recite poetry and enter into public disputations on philosophy, theology and rhetoric. Schoolboys as young as eleven or twelve would be expected to stand in front of an audience and to declaim on subjects such as 'The Boy Jesus' or 'Good Government'. From reciting the Catechism to participating in an end-of-term drama, Jesuit students were encouraged to use their voices persuasively.[27]

For the vocal Jesuits who arrived in China, the absence of an emphasis on the spoken word was peculiar. Far more significant, however, was the Chinese deficiency in dialectic. Often considered the counterpart to rhetoric, dialectic – a term deriving from the Greek for controversy – was the technique that governed argument, and that advanced the truth by means of the to and fro of debate. According to such principles, in order to prove something, one had first to advance a premiss, and then line up the arguments for and against. By making one side of the argument more forceful than the other, one aspired to persuade. This was a skill that Jesuits would have had plenty of opportunity to practise in the interactive context of their oral examinations and disputations. It was also this method of argument that characterised the Aristotelian corpus that was the foundation of early modern European thinking.[28] Chinese science was thus, in Ricci's eyes, seriously impeded: 'They know nothing of dialectic; they speak and write not in a scientific manner, but in confusion, by means of various claims and discourses.'[29] Even in fields such as arithmetic and geometry, where the Chinese had acquired some knowledge, they lacked understanding. In the thirteenth century, Persian scholars had passed on to the Chinese certain mathematical tables, which they used without any awareness of the proofs on which the knowledge that they purveyed was based. In astronomy, Ricci commented contemptuously, 'they care nothing for the reasons of phenomena or occurrences but only seek to predict eclipses or planetary movements', using procedures that were, unsurprisingly, fraught with error.[30]

Ricci was inspired to disseminate the truths of Western science to Chinese audiences for two reasons. On the one hand, he was attracted by the committed intellectualism of the literati and by the pleasing familiarity of the elite male networks that he discovered. He felt an affinity with the men whom he met at drinking parties and in the academies of Nanchang – a sense of identification that was doubtless helped by his momentous decision in 1595 to assume the robes of a Confucian scholar. In such milieux, the literati sought out 'new conversations', and Ricci found that he could quite literally 'win the affection of this people' by speaking about mathematics.[31] On the other hand, he saw in the shortcomings of Chinese science an opportunity for demonstrating Western superiority, and for making himself and his colleagues indispensable in this foreign land.

Ricci was convinced that his tactics were working. In Nanchang, the crowds of visitors queuing up to meet the European priests were greater than they could deal with. In part, the people came to witness a novelty: they were entranced by the Jesuits' height, and by their bushy beards and large noses, all the more so given that the foreigners had learned both the language and the customs of China. Like Qu Rukui, they were also undoubtedly attracted by the rumour that the Jesuits were adepts at alchemy. But – again in common with Qu – they were equally impressed by Ricci's mathematical prowess. Ricci's letters betray a characteristic lack of modesty: 'To tell the truth, amongst them, I am a Ptolemy.'[32] 'If China were the whole world, there is no doubt that I could call myself the greatest mathematician and natural philosopher, for what they say amounts to a grain of rice, and it is a marvel how little they know, because all devote themselves to morality and elegance in speaking, or rather I should say in writing.' After cataloguing the errors of the Chinese – their ignorance of air, their belief in the five elements (fire, water, earth, metal, and wood), their manifold misapprehensions about eclipses – Ricci observed how impressed the literati were with the subtlety of his explanations, whether demonstrating 'a point of mathematics, or of philosophy, or of the matters of our faith'.[33] That the explanatory force of Western science could be transferred to the realm of Western religion was clearly another reason why Ricci was such a dogged proponent of Euclid and Ptolemy.

*

Aware of the power of Western knowledge, Ricci sought to disseminate it through the medium of print. In 1584, just a year after their arrival in Zhaoqing, Ricci and Ruggieri boldly published translations of the Ten Commandments, Paternoster, Ave Maria and Credo. In the same year, Ruggieri brought out his first attempt at a Chinese Catechism, and Ricci's *Mappamondo* found its way into a pirated printed edition. After a lull in writing and publication, when Ricci was striving both to master the written language and to gain a foothold in Chinese society, the Nanchang and Nanjing years proved to be productive.[34] Ricci compiled his sentences on *Friendship* in November 1595, and within a month or so a friend of his had found it a publisher. In 1596, he dashed off a treatise on *Memory* and, in 1599, compiled *Twenty-five Sayings* from the Greek Stoic philosopher, Epictetus. The next print publication was of a *Treatise on the Four Elements*, which came out in Nanjing in 1599. The last decade of Ricci's life was the period in which his attempts to publicise Western knowledge of the mathematical sciences bore the most fruit. There were three more editions of the *Mappamondo*, the publication in 1607 of the *Six Books of the Elements of Euclid*, and the 1609 edition of the *Isoperimetric Figures*, a further work of Greek-inspired geometry that focused on the area of different shapes with the same perimeter. In the meantime, Ricci was also busy translating a *Treatise on the Constellations*, produced with the help of a Chinese friend in 420 seven-line verses, and another theoretical book on geometrical measurements. The year 1605 saw the publication of Ricci's definitive work on Christian doctrine, *The True Meaning of the Lord of Heaven*, as well as the *Twenty-Five Sayings*, written six years earlier, while a second work propagating the wisdom of the Stoics, *Ten Discourses by a Paradoxical Man*, hit the press in 1609. The publication and re-issue of his works would continue after his death.

Ricci's enthusiasm for print stemmed from several factors. Firstly, as has been noted, the Chinese prized writing above speech. The publication of European texts therefore added to the Jesuits' status. Secondly, Ricci realised that – even where the Jesuits were free to travel and preach – their numbers were so paltry in such a massive country that they could only hope to make the tiniest dent on the Chinese consciousness. Print, by contrast, was capable of transporting European wisdom in a lasting form to a large number of readers. Thirdly, there was the infernal difficulty of communicating in Chinese, a problem that was, as we have seen, exacerbated by the different regional languages that prevailed. Ricci noted that whereas the spoken language of Chinese was radically different in the north and in the south, the written language was unified. With the help of his Chinese collaborators, Ricci could attempt to address the people clearly and accurately in writing; speech was, by comparison, a minefield.

The potential of Chinese print culture was exhilarating. In this population of nearly 200 million, Ricci observed that 'there are few who know nothing of books'.[35] Of course, he exaggerated literacy levels. But he was right to marvel at how cheaply and quickly Chinese books were produced; book purchasing was within the means of the great majority of ordinary urban workers at this time.[36] The extraordinary proliferation of print in sixteenth-century China occurred as a result of old technology and new men. The beauty of traditional woodblock printing was that it allowed total flexibility and minimal investment. The most important skill that underpinned the production of a Chinese book was the carving of wooden blocks. The carvers needed only a set of carving knives and tools. Once they had carved the blocks, the same men could print and sew the pages together. To produce a short work with a small print run, a publisher need only hire one or two woodcarvers. On the other hand, he could double his number of carvers in order to complete a book at double the speed. Not only was the equipment necessary for the production of books in China cheap; so were the raw materials, notably paper. Jiangxi province was the leading centre of the paper industry, where water-powered technology transformed bamboo into thin large sheets. In the city of Yanshan, in Jiangxi, there were thirty or more paper mills, each hiring between one and two thousand workers. But paper production took place in many provinces, notably Fujian, Anhui, Zhejiang, Guangdong, and Sichuan. The result was that, across China, paper was ubiquitous. It was used not only in the printing industry, but to create a variety of other commodities: paper boxes, paper canopies (for beds), rolls of paper for painting, paper flowers (that decorated virtually every house in Suzhou), pictures made out of paper threads (fashionable in Fujian), paper for cards and correspondence, and lavatory paper (renowned for its softness in the smart city of Hangzhou).[37]

Ricci could scarcely fail to be impressed by paper so cheap that you could wipe your arse on it. In Europe, where paper was made out of rag, which was in short supply, it was around three times as costly. Printing was also rendered more expensive in Europe by the triumph of Gutenberg. For while the development of movable type in Germany in the mid-fifteenth century has been heralded as one of the key episodes in the history of European civilisation, the financial outlay that the process required in some ways limited its impact. Given the investment that publishers had to make in sophisticated machinery (the printing press and the sets of metal type that went with it) and in highly skilled labourers, they were deterred from risk-taking. Movable type co-existed in China with woodblock printing, but – given the nature and number of the Chinese characters – was favoured mainly for official, large-scale publishing projects. In the realm of small-scale enterprise, woodblocks continued to flourish. The result was that, in contrast with their European equivalents, Chinese books, which were sold in shops, temple precincts, or by commercial travellers, were one of the most widely available and affordable commodities.[38]

So much for the success of old technology. What about the impact of new men? The late Ming period witnessed an unprecedented expansion in the numbers of both readers and writers. The massive growth in commercial publishing in the sixteenth and seventeenth centuries was underpinned by the development of a literary public sphere, in which new readers bought the works of new writers, and the dominance of print culture by the state-sponsored literary canon began to wane. The historian Kai-Wing Chow has drawn attention to the crucial role played by the examination system in this process. Obviously, the commitment of thousands of men to decades of exam-sitting fuelled a market in Confucian texts and commentaries. Then as now, men bought books in the desperate hope that they would help them to pass their exams. But, for the great majority of examination candidates, such investments were in vain. At every sitting, only a small proportion of examinees gained their degrees. Kai-Wing Chow has therefore shifted our gaze to the men who failed their exams, often repeatedly, and has argued that these highly educated, highly literate 'failures' formed a new class of literary professionals – writers, editors, compilers, commentators, critics, publishers and proofreaders – all of whom tried to scrape together a living in the publishing trade while preparing for the next set of exams. The new literary culture therefore existed in a delicate relationship with the examination system. It was both dependent on it and a reaction against it. Some authors challenged the authority of the official examiners, offering new readings of Confucian classics, new prose styles and a space for discussion and dissent. Others, by editing anthologies of exam essays, expressed their dissatisfaction with or criticism of the selection process. But, for the majority, their goal would remain a career in the civil service. When the next round of exams came along, they would be back in their cubicles, attempting to craft the 'right answer'.

It was from this deep pool of literary labour that new genres and styles of writing poured forth. The diversity of books available was dazzling. Alongside the manifold revision aids, there were mountain gazetteers, almanacs, encyclopedias, morality books, maths manuals, medical manuals, maps, etiquette manuals, how-to guides, travel guides, business guides, directories of prostitutes, erotic albums and pornographic novels. Everything, in short, that a member of the *shishang* – a hybrid term encompassing both *shi* (literati) and *shang* (businessmen) – could require. Of course, one could tell a similar story about printing in Europe, which was also enjoying rapid expansion and diversification. Indeed the parallels between China and Europe are striking, not least because – on both sides of the globe – print attained its ascendancy over scribal publication at the same moment (around the start of the sixteenth century), a development that in the European context is inexorably linked to the triumph of movable type, but which in China, as we have seen, was not. But there was one other glaring dissimilarity that marked out Chinese from European publishing, which was a fundamental condition of Ricci's entry into the field. Whereas European publishing was characterised by the most rigorous control, enacted through systems of licensing and censorship, in China there was precious little attempt to prevent or regulate publishing by the state.[39] Apart from calendars, works of divination and histories of the current dynasty, almost anything could be published by anyone. And while the main impetus for censorship in Europe derived from the desire to impose confessional uniformity, the Chinese authorities did not endorse a single religion. Confucians, Buddhists, Daoists . . . and Christians were free to print and distribute their teachings.

These were the extraordinary conditions that Ricci was determined to exploit. The Jesuits enjoyed their first major publishing success with the *Mappamondo*, printed initially in 1584 in an unauthorised version, frequently re-issued, and making use of the full range of Chinese tricks for marketing books (including the all-important dedications and endorsements from notable scholars). As we have seen, arriving in Shaozhou in 1589, Ricci gloated that his reputation preceded him, for everyone seemed to know that 'I was a great astronomer and cosmographer and that I knew how to draw the whole world, and that formerly in Zhaoqing they had published that which I had drawn'.[40] In 1605, Ricci told his father, 'The *Mappamondo* that I sent you two years ago has been reprinted more than ten times, and gives us great credit.'[41] And in 1608, he informed Acquaviva that 'above all it is the maps of the world and the books which we have published relating to our mathematics that . . . bring us great credit'.[42] Ricci's book *On Friendship* also commenced its publication history in a pirated edition. The account that he wrote from Nanchang in 1596 to Acquaviva, recording his dedication of the work to the Prince of Jian'an, illustrates how alert Ricci was to the conventions of Chinese publishing:

Last year as an exercise I wrote in Chinese letters some sayings *On Friendship*, chosen from the greatest of our books; and since they were by such diverse and eminent people, the literati of this land were more than astonished. In order to give the work authority I wrote a preface and dedicated it to that relation of the King who also bears the title of King. And so many literati asked me if they could see the work and transcribe it that I always had several copies prepared in order to show them and one of our closest friends transcribed the work himself and, returning to his home, in a city close to here, published it in my name, without saying anything to me; and although this made me sad, his good intentions were worthy of praise. Others also made printed books, which spoke well for us.[43]

Ricci's shrewd command of the techniques of authorisation and marketing reminds us of further similarities in the Chinese and European publishing trades. First he stressed the eminence of the writers and thinkers represented in the book; secondly, he provided a preface (in later editions, a second preface by a Chinese scholar was added); thirdly, he chose his dedicatee with care; and fourthly, he secured prepublication curiosity by engaging in manuscript circulation. His apparent dismay at the publication of his book without his permission might not have been profound. (After all, it absolved him from seeking the permission of his Jesuit superiors to print.)[44] This was surely a case where Ricci profited from the unregulated nature of Chinese publishing.

In the case of the *Paradoxes*, published in 1609, Ricci appeared to have established more decisive control over the dissemination of his work:

Many literati contributed many prefaces regarding these chapters . . . as it is customary to do in works that are being prepared for publication, from among which I chose two that were to be included in the Beijing edition, written by two of our friends at the emperor's college of literati [the Hanlin Academy] that are the most famous in the entire realm, one of which, besides the preface, wrote in rhyme a very talented and elegant summary or commentary on each of the chapters, that gives much authority to the work.[45]

Even here, however, the publication of the work soon took on a life of its own: 'Already we know that it has been republished in two or three other provinces.'[46] The chapter devoted to extolling the virtues of silence was so popular that a notable literatus 'wanted to print it by itself, as it seemed to him a worthy book in itself'. Ricci obligingly provided a preface for him to use.[47]

By the end of his life, Ricci's constant reiteration of the value of print was becoming somewhat monotonous: 'In China, one can achieve more with books, than with words';[48] 'They listen with great enthusiasm to the word of God, which is the source of much fruit; but we gain far more from the books that have been published in Chinese';[49] the Jesuits were, according to Ricci, known above all 'for the books that we produce, that are printed and reprinted in diverse provinces';[50] graduates came to visit Ricci and his colleagues, 'attracted by the fame of the books that we had published'.[51] True enough, the Jesuits' publishing exploits brought them a certain amount of fame and fortune, but this was rather more patchy than Ricci liked to admit.

The collection of adages on *Friendship* and the *Ten Discourses of a Paradoxical Man* seem to have appealed because of the resonances between Confucian and classical philosophy; Ricci cleverly tweaked the wisdom of the Greek and Roman philosophers, and drew particularly on the Stoic tradition to suggest a fundamental compatibility between European and Chinese ideas of morality. Other texts went down far less well. Ricci's *Western Art of Memory*, or *Xiguo jifa*, aimed at the market of exam candidates for whom memorisation was such a key skill, turned out to be of little practical use to the Chinese student. As the son of the Viceroy of Nanchang politely observed, 'These precepts are the true rule of memory, but it is necessary to have a very good memory in the first place in order to make use of them.'[52] Ricci himself saw the limits of the work's success: 'Although everyone admires its artifice, not all can be bothered to make use of it.'[53] This was a disappointment for Ricci, who in 1595 had astonished a group of scholars at a dinner party with his ability to memorise a series of more than four hundred Chinese characters that had been written down for him in random order. But the spectacle of Ricci's performance was lost in the written version, a lifeless document that rehearsed the medieval rules of memory, outdated even in a European context, originally devised for the benefit of clergymen attempting to memorise a sermon.

A more profound problem of the *Western Art of Memory* derived from the radically different natures of the Chinese and European languages. The attempt of Ricci and his medieval precursors to remember words as images was confusing in the Chinese context since the characters already worked as visual representations. In trying to help the Chinese remember the word for 'fisherman', for example, Ricci evoked the image of a fishing rod, but this distracted from the in-built mnemonic provided by the morphology of the Chinese character, incorporating both 'water' and 'fish'.[54] Other mnemonics broke the word down into its phonetic parts. In Italian, 'o che' ('or that') could be remembered by 'oche' (the word for 'geese'). 'Che' (the Italian for 'that') could thence be remembered as 'beheaded geese' ('oche' minus the first letter). If such techniques sound arduous in the European context, they were even less helpful to the Chinese, since the splitting up of words made little sense in a non-alphabetic language, where a single character could not be divided up in this way.[55]

The reception in 1605 of *The True Meaning of the Lord of Heaven*, the Catechism infused with Confucian learning that Ricci had drafted and redrafted over nearly a decade, must have given still greater cause for disillusionment. Ricci had high hopes of this work, and insisted that it be used henceforth in all the Jesuit residences across the empire. (Already in 1596, Ricci had ordered the destruction of the woodblocks from which Ruggieri's earlier Catechism had been printed.) The new version, which had required the invention of new vocabulary to express religious terms, was intended to be the definitive account of Christianity in China.[56] But although Ricci's letters from this time are full of optimistic statements, he says nothing to suggest that the Chinese were actually impressed by his work. Furthermore, evidence from the period following Ricci's death suggests that certain Chinese scholars reacted angrily to the Western priest's missionary tactics. In an undated propaganda piece, Huang Wendao, a scholar from Fuzhou province, complained that Ricci adapted his 'discourse' to the classics

in such a fashion that there appeared to be not much difference between what he was saying and the writings of Yao, Shun, Zhougong and Confucius. But in reality he was secretly developing his own doctrine. Rejecting Buddhism, criticising Daoism and denigrating Confucianism, he meanwhile harnessed Yao, Shun, Zhougong and Confucius as a means of conveying his own teaching.[57]

Another author, writing in the final years of the Ming dynasty, had even harsher words to describe the Jesuits' manipulation of the Chinese classics:

[The missionaries] invented the doctrine of the Master of Heaven, first learning the language and writing of China, then reading the Chinese books relating to the three doctrines [Confucianism, Buddhism and Daoism]. By borrowing from Buddhism, adding to Confucianism, inventing on all sides and much manipulation, they created this vicious doctrine in order to use it to upset the world, deceive people and undermine the foundations of our empire.[58]

Although these criticisms were not immediate, they point to the problems inherent in Ricci's methods of proselytising. In his attempt to take a place within the literary culture of Chinese scholars, he had got himself into deep water.

The unmitigated success among Ricci's publications was, by contrast, the *Mappamondo*: a predominantly *visual* representation, less impeded by the barriers of language that hampered 'intercultural understanding'.[59] Reprinted in ever larger and more lavish editions, the splendour of the map as a physical object won the respect of all who saw it. The same was true of the scientific instruments that Ricci carried around with him wherever he travelled. Were the 'mathematical instruments' that Ricci brought out to show the Prince of Jian'an in Nanchang in 1595 not more compelling than the books on arithmetic and geometry that he would subsequently publish in Beijing?[60] Had not the gift of clocks – not books – opened doors for the Jesuits, initially to Zhaoqing in 1583, and ultimately to Beijing in 1601?[61] And was it not the spectacle that these objects created rather than the superior knowledge on which they were founded that excited the Chinese?

The point was deftly made by Ricci himself following the presentation of the clock to the *dutang* in 1583, when he wrote that the Chinese 'marvel more to see a machine that moves by itself and sounds the hours, than at its skill at telling the time'.[62] Although in his policy statements about the mission, Ricci emphasised the power of written knowledge, he was keenly aware of the efficacy of objects. This was why he took so much care over the presentation of gifts. When the *dutang* of Nanchang provided Ricci with a permit to stay, the Jesuit reciprocated by having made for him a flat clock, mounted on stone, very beautifully crafted and large with bells, the hours and quarters marked, with Chinese letters, something that up until now they had never seen nor imagined ... and also a sphere and a terrestrial globe with Chinese characters.[63]

Ricci confidently asserted that these gifts would make the *dutang* 'very happy'. That such items were considered as much for their aesthetic value as for their scientific or technological brilliance was further indicated by their juxtaposition as exhibits or gifts alongside very different kinds of object. Clocks and mathematical instruments could thus stand cheek by jowl with religious images or silk slippers on a list of presents offered by Jesuits to local notables.[64]

Perhaps the most dazzling objects of persuasion at the Jesuits' disposal were their prisms. These were described in the records of the mission as 'triangular glasses from Venice', and were deemed by the Chinese to be 'precious stones' for their fantastic ability to project rays of coloured light.[65] At key moments, Ricci told how one of these mysterious stones had averted a diplomatic stand-off or changed the mind of an intransigent official, thereby permitting the Jesuits to continue with the progress of their mission.[66] This was partly due to what was – in Ricci's eyes – a misconceived belief in their value. In a narrative reminiscent of the story of how Manhattan was bought from the Indians for a few glass beads, Ricci revealed how a prism, worth only seven or eight *baiocchi*, was valued as highly as 500 ducats by the Chinese.[67] Ultimately, however, the power of the prism did not reside so much in its perceived monetary value, as in its ability to provoke wonder. 'Ecstatic, as if he was outside himself' was how Ricci described the reaction of one man.[68]

It is tempting to see the prisms – together with the clocks, the globes and the astrolabes – as further indications of the force of Ricci's scientific apostolate. According to such a vision, these objects appear in an ancillary role to print; they function to convince the Chinese of Western superiority. And yet we need to question our instinct to class the 'prism' (a word never used by the Jesuits) as a 'scientific' object or instrument; since antiquity, prisms had held no clear scientific significance and were not to do so until the later seventeenth century.[69] Furthermore, we need to pose a question persistently neglected in the historical literature on the mission: if these pieces of triangular glass were *not* valued in Europe for their scientific interest, then why did Ricci and his colleagues think to bring multiple examples of them to China?

During the Renaissance, glass-making underwent a technological revolution in western Europe, and the centre of its production was Italy. Some of the wonder of its manufacture was conveyed to a European audience in 1612, when the Florentine priest, Antonio Neri, published his treatise, *The Art of Glass*. He began his work – quoted here in the 1662 English edition – with a rapturous paean to the substance:

There is no doubt that Glass is one of the true fruits of the Art of fire, since that it is very much like to all sorts of minerals and midle minerals although it be a compound and made by Art. It hath fusion in the fire, and permanencie in it; likewise as the perfect and shining Metall of Gold, it is refined, and burnished, and made beautiful in the fire. It is manifest that it's use in drinking vessels, and other things profitable for mans service, is much more gentile, graceful, and noble then any Metall or whatsoever stone fit to make such works, and which besides the easiness and little charge wherewith it is made, may be wrought in all places; it is more delightful polite and sightly than any other material at this day known to the world.[70]

Neri went on to itemise the valuable functions served by glass 'in the service of distilling', in the making of medical instruments such as 'cupping-glasses, urinals' and equipment with which 'to draw womens-breasts', in the construction of spectacles and magnifying glasses, and in the ornamentation of 'Churches of God'.

In China, where the cult of porcelain reigned supreme, glass was less highly prized. The earliest vessels appearing in China were those brought from the Roman empire in the first centuries following Christ. Byzantine and, later, Arab craftsmen taught their trade to artisans in southern China, but not until the seventeenth and eighteenth centuries did large-scale glass-manufacturing begin to catch on. One might suppose, on the basis of this, an indifference to this European commodity.[71] But the Florentine merchant Francesco Carletti, visiting Macao and Canton at the end of the sixteenth century, perceived otherwise. Following on from his observation that the Chinese were generally uninterested in buying European goods, and preferred instead to trade for silver, he ventured an exception:

In my time they willingly purchased only glass objects, especially such as were in the shape of vases or plates with white stripes, as well as other sorts as long as they were not gilded, a thing that they do not like at all. They also bought lenses of all sorts, and especially coloured ones.[72]

Valignano was presumably aware of a Chinese appetite for Western glass, for on the list of presents for the Emperor that he drew up there appeared mirrors, prisms, stained glass and hour-glass clocks.

And yet by burying Ricci's prisms in a list of costly and beautiful luxury items we risk ignoring their significance. For while mirrors, stained glass and hour-glasses would fit readily into Neri's account of the *functions* of glass, prisms were apparently *use*-less. Two texts, published in 1565 and 1612 respectively, allow us to tease out further meanings of the prism in European context. The first, published in England by John Hall and entitled *A most excellent and learned woorke of chirurgerie*, was a commentary on the work of thirteenth-century surgeon Lanfranc of Milan.[73] But in a revealing passage regarding contemporary medical practice, Hall digressed to record an experience of Girolamo Cardano (1501–76), a physician and mathematician from Pavia in northern Italy.[74] The story focused on a Milanese noblewoman, who had fallen 'sycke of a whote or burnyng urine, with a continuall desyre to expell the same'. Consequently, the seven most famous physicians of the city, including Cardano, were convened to offer their diagnoses and prescriptions for cure of the afflicted woman. There follows a lively account of the assembled physicians, locked in disagreement about the cause of the illness: 'some estemed it to be a stone . . . an other an ulcer, other named it an harde tumor, . . . other sayde it was a Cancer'. And from out of the diagnostic chaos, a succession of grim and unsuccessful treatments are then inflicted on the poor woman:

And certainly she did not feigne hir grefe consyderynge that she drunke so many bitter medicines, with sufferyng so many fomentations and perfumes, permittyng also that secreate place to be seene, of so great a numbre of Phisitiens, beholding it by a glasse: observing also the diete so longe a tyme, sufferyng bloodlettyng, suffering the forsayde vessikes to be cutte, and the application and working of so many corrosives or burning medicins, which procured escares [scars], besydes Iron instrumentes and fyre.

Cardano looked on in sympathy and bemusement, as the hopeless remedies did nothing other than to increase the woman's pain. But just when everyone was running out of hope, 'there stepped forth to hir helpe, one Josephus Niger, a renowned professor of the Greke letters: who was of some suspected to be an inchanter, or worker in the wicked sciences', and who was tutor to the sick woman's ten-year-old son. Calling on the aid of the boy, the teacher of Greek was about to enjoy success where all the learned physicians of the city had failed:

This Joseph broughte with him a glasse of Cristall, in forme of a triangle, wherin he caused the childe to looke: who said that therin he sawe three foule and ougly spirites, standing on their feete before his mother, and when he had whispered other wordes in the childes eare, the childe saide that he sawe an other spirite on horseback, more high and great then the other .iii. with sceptour threforked, or of three prickes, who bounde the other three spirites, one after an other, and being so bounde, he hid them under his saddel: which done, he delivered his glasse to be kepte.

And the denouement of the story:

This woman having some perswasion by this arte doth fall on sleape, hir grefe, hir burninge, and hir apetite to make water doth cease, the rosiall colour came again in hir face, hir flesh was restored unto a good liking: so that anon after she conceived: and thus was she well and perfectly healed.

And so the triangular glass had its uses after all, as a device that could help to summon supernatural power so as to restore rosy cheeks to one on the brink of death and to chase away the devil. The reference to the crystal was a rarity, but the use of objects such as saints' relics and holy water as props to miraculous healings was familiar enough in the sickrooms of Catholic Europe.[75]

The second text post-dates Ricci but suggests, at least, that the events witnessed by Cardano were not unique and that the prism would continue to be used to manipulate evil spirits. It comes from a work published by the French Dominican Inquisitor Sébastien Michaelis, who had presided over one of the most remarkable possession cases of the seventeenth century, which took place in an Ursuline convent in Aix-en-Provence in 1610, and prefigured the more famous 1634 episode of the 'nuns of Loudun'.[76] Two years after the events, Michaelis came to write up the tale, which focused on a young noble nun, named Madeleine Domandols de la Palud, whose body had become inhabited by the demon, Beelzebub:

The same day the Lord Arch-bishop of *Aix* his Almner did bring a certaine instrument of glasses made triangle wise, and none of the assembly did understand for what purpose that instrument served. Where-upon *Belzebub* [who spoke through Madeleine] being asked what it was, he readily made answere, It is an optick glasse to make a man see that which is not: which saying of his was found agreeable unto truth, for it caused men to see Woods, Castels and Arches in the aire of all manner of colours and other things of the like nature.

This is the preface to a classic baroque scene of exorcism, in which Michaelis describes how Beelzebub 'did take on and yell very hideously'.

From these two texts we learn that prisms were associated with healing and exorcism, with the conjuring up of apparitions and with the battle against demons. Although the documents are scarcely clear about how the prism was supposed to function in these contexts, we can be left in little doubt that it was an object of no ordinary significance, considered – by some – to have supernatural properties.

Already imbued with mystical qualities in Europe, the prism took on a new life in China. The Jesuits were, as has already been said, assumed by many to be practising alchemy. Watched jealously by Daoist practitioners of 'the art of Change', the Western priests' 'precious stones' were deemed to be the tools of their success. So it was that in 1587 a prism was stolen by Martin, alchemist and neophyte, no doubt attracted to Christianity in the first place because of his misconceptions about the Jesuits' abilities.

Ricci was contemptuous of the Chinese obsession with alchemy, and lamented the fact that he and his colleagues were falsely believed to be capable of making *argento bono* (good silver) out of *argento vivo* (mercury).[77] In Book I of his *History*, he included a section on 'the madness of alchemy' as part of a chapter on 'the reprovable customs of the Chinese'.[78] But for all that Ricci publicly tried to discourage the futile pursuit of alchemy, he acknowledged that many of his supporters came to him because they hoped to learn the secrets of the art. Moreover, Chinese (and indeed European) beliefs about alchemy were far more sophisticated than Ricci liked to admit, and attracted support from many among the educated elite.[79] Its object was not simply that of turning base metal into gold, but rather to discover why transformations of matter occurred, and to learn how to bring about and control that change. The immense range of feats that might be achieved in the Chinese conception of alchemy is suggested by the fourth-century writings of Ge Hung:

As for the art of Change, there is nothing it cannot accomplish. The body of man can naturally be seen, but there are means to make it invisible; ghosts and spirits are naturally invisible yet there are means whereby they can be caused to appear . . . Water and fire, which are in the heavens, may be obtained by the burning-mirror and the dew-mirror. Lead which is white can be turned into a red substance. This red substance can again be whitened to lead. Clouds, rain, frost, and snow, which are all the *qi* of Heaven and Earth, can be duplicated exactly and without any difference, by chemical substances.

On both sides of the globe, alchemy was also closely related to the newer discipline of chemistry, and the experiments that took place using fire found a respectable place in many established laboratories.[80] Such experiments were not dissimilar from the account of the firing of glass, described by Neri and quoted above. That the marvels of glass production were allied in early minds with the secrets of alchemy is further suggested by the fact that Neri, that eloquent apologist for glass manufacturing, was also dedicated to the 'art of change'.

But there was one serious sticking point that divided East–West perceptions of alchemy. The overriding objective of Daoist practitioners of the art was to create an elixir of life. This was the desire of Qu Rukui, the prestigious Christian convert whom we encountered at the start of this chapter, and of this the Jesuits could scarcely approve. Christianity was, after all, a religion in which death played an important part. To the European priests, it seemed that Qu's fear of death was pathological, to be cured only by dedicated practice of the *Spiritual Exercises* of Qu's namesake, Ignatius Loyola.[81] And yet when Ricci craved the support of Qu in 1598, what gift did the Jesuit offer his 'disciple'?

Among the other things that [Ricci] gave to him as a present was a triangular glass, that he had greatly desired and wanted to buy in Canton, and he was very happy with this gift. And he immediately commissioned a silver box with golden locks on both sides, that gave it great authority; but much more did a very elegant composition that he made above it, claiming that it was a piece of the material of the sky.[82]

It was another propaganda coup for Ricci and his colleagues. The fact that this glimmering triangle of European glass should be considered 'a piece of the sky', at the very time that the Jesuits were seeking to accommodate the Chinese veneration of the heavens to the Christian belief in the Lord of Heaven, was a fortuitous embellishment to the gift's significance.

The story of Qu's prism caught the imagination, not least because the proto-neophyte's loyalty was proven when he refused to sell the prism for '500 ducats', since he did not want any future owner to beat the Jesuits in their aspiration of bestowing one of the glass triangles on the Emperor himself.[83] And yet it also pointed to the profound tensions in Ricci's own account of the mission. The model disciple of mathematics had been bought off with a tool of alchemy.

ABOVE Soviet military map of Cambridge, 1:10,000 (1989).

BELOW Portrait of Matteo Ricci (1610) by You Wenhui, also known as Emmanuele Pereira.

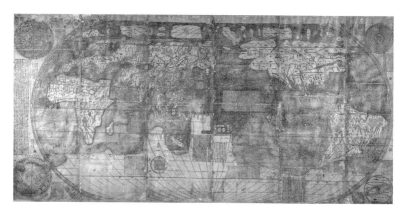

ABOVE Mappamondo by Matteo Ricci; this edition was published posthumously in 1644.

LEFT Tower of High Fortune, Zhaoqing: the pagoda that neighboured the Jesuits' first residence in mainland China.

BELOW Chinese visitors to the Zhaoqing residence were impressed by the Jesuits' elaborately locking doors. This sixteenth-century Flemish lock gives a sense of the kind of highly ornate object which the Jesuits envisaged as an appropriate gift for the Emperor.

This *byōbu* from early seventeenth-century Japan is an example of a 'Namban' screen that depicts the arrival of a Portuguese ship at Nagasaki. The screen satirizes the strangeness of the Europeans, especially their enormous breeches and pointed noses. On the far right may be seen a group of Jesuits wearing black. The existence of such screens portraying foreigners may have encouraged the Jesuits in their view that the Pope should commission a European screen as a gift for the Emperor.

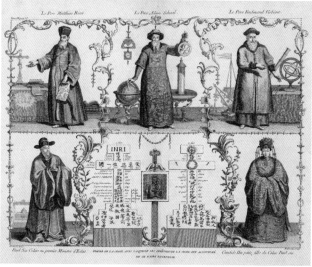

ABOVE Ming wine jar from Jingdezhen (1567–1572). Much of the porcelain from the Ming era that we see in museums was used to store and serve alcoholic drinks.

BELOW Eighteenth-century engraving in which Ricci is pictured alongside his successors, Adam Schall and Ferdinand Verbiest, both of whom directed the Beijing Observatory. In the bottom half of the engraving, the Jesuits' most eminent convert Xu Guangqi is depicted with his daughter.

ABOVE Portrait of a civil official (1600–1644). The subject is recognisable as a literatus on account of his two-winged black hat, belt, and robe with golden phoenix insignia. On the table behind him lie his writing tools.

BELOW Eunuchs lighting fire crackers on an imperial barge; detail from a Ming handscroll, more than thirty metres long.

ABOVE Ex-voto from Tolentino (1582). A man is shown kneeling before the bed of his sick wife, as he prays for her recovery to the Virgin and Child and to Saint Nicholas.

BELOW The Basilica of the Holy House at Loreto in the Italian Marches, close to where Ricci grew up.

ABOVE Peter reaches out to Christ in the 'Apostle in the Waves'. From *Master Cheng's Garden of Ink-Cakes* or the *Chengshi moyuan* (1606).

BELOW The appearance of Christ, after the Resurrection, to his disciples while they are fishing in the Sea of Galilee. From Jerome Nadal, *The Annotations and Meditations on the Gospels* (1593). Ricci probably adapted a similar engraving to illustrate the story of Peter being rescued by Christ, above.

ABOVE Christopher Plantin's Polyglot Bible (1569–72). The sophisticated fonts that were used in the printing of the Hebrew, Chaldaic, Greek and Latin texts would doubtless have appealed to a Chinese viewer, well-versed in the arts of calligraphy.

BELOW Ricci's grave, in the Jesuit cemetery, Beijing.

5 Jesuits and Eunuchs

When the operation is about to take place, the candidate or victim – as the case may be – is placed on a *kang* in a sitting – or rather, reclining position. One man supports him round the waist, while two others separate his legs and hold them down firmly, to prevent any movement on his part. The operating 'knifer' then stands in front of the man – with his knife in his hand – and enquires if he will ever repent. If the man at the last moment demurs in the slightest, the 'knifer' will not perform the operation, but if he still expresses his willingness, with one sweep of the knife he is made a eunuch.

The operation is performed in this manner: white ligatures or bandages are bound tightly round the lower part of the belly and the upper parts of the thighs, to prevent too much haemorrhage. The parts about to be operated on are then bathed three times with hot pepper-water, the intended eunuch being in the reclining position as previously described. When the parts have been sufficiently bathed, the *whole* – both testicles and penis – are cut off as closely as possible with a small curved knife, something in the shape of a sickle. The emasculation being effected, a pewter needle or spigot is carefully thrust into the main orifice at the root of the penis; the wound is then covered with paper saturated in cold water and is carefully bound up. After the wound is dressed the patient is made to walk about the room, supported by two of the 'knifers', for two or three hours, when he is allowed to lie down.

The patient is not allowed to drink anything for three days, during which time he often suffers great agony, not only from thirst, but from intense pain, and from the impossibility of relieving nature during that period.

At the end of three days the bandage is taken off, the spigot is pulled out, and the sufferer obtains relief in the copious flow

of urine which spurts out like a fountain. If this takes place sat-
isfactorily, the patient is considered out of danger and congratulated on it; but if the unfortunate wretch cannot make water he is
doomed to a death of agony, for the passages have become swollen
and nothing can save him.[1]

This graphic account comes not from the pen of a sixteenth-century Jesuit, but from that of a nineteenth-century
British soldier and administrator in the employ of the Chinese Maritime Customs, George Carter Stent. Published
in Shanghai in 1877, Stent's was the first comprehensive
study of the Chinese palace eunuchs and of the traditional
methods of castration. In the manner typical of a Victorian
amateur scholar, he was not punctilious about revealing his
sources, but we know that he was an exceptionally fluent
speaker of Mandarin, and we may infer – from his reference
to an 'informant' – that he had access to at least one person
with direct knowledge of the procedures that he described.
His evidence is in any case convincingly detailed, ranging
from the exchange of fees, through the excision, recovery,
convalescence and side-effects, to the so-called 'high promotion' of the eunuch's 'precious' relic, set in a 'pint measure'
on a high shelf, and treasured with the utmost care until
such time as it would be reunited with the owner on his
death and burial. Stent's account remains valuable today,
not only for the rare factual insights that it supplies but also
for its focus on the grim physical reality of castration. For
as he himself suggests, the standard manner of describing
eunuchs is so vague 'that one is almost tempted to believe
that eunuchs exist only in the Arabian Night's Entertainments and other eastern tales, or in the imaginations of
the writers, rather than actually belonging to and forming
no inconsiderable part of the human race'.[2] While more
recent scholars have further demystified Chinese eunuchs

by providing a wealth of concrete detail regarding their social and political functions, they have been curiously inattentive to the overwhelming significance of their genital mutilation.[3]

At the time that Stent wrote, that not 'inconsiderable part of the human race' numbered, in China, around two thousand. It had declined sharply from its high point at the end of the Ming dynasty, when the emperor had enjoyed the service of one hundred thousand castrated men.[4] The Jesuits arrived in China at the very moment when the expanding numbers and powers of eunuchs were becoming the object of fierce debate. Ever keen to align himself with the literati – those who earned their positions and their authority from scholarship rather than from the surgeon's knife – Matteo Ricci was a staunch opponent of the eunuchs, and inveighed against the inhumane practice of castrating boys to serve the emperor. The custom, Ricci correctly noted, had originated as a kind of double punishment, by which particularly worthless wrong-doers were subjected first to castration and then to a life of perpetual servitude in the palace of the king. But seeing how, by this means, criminal reprobates came in time to wield considerable powers, others sought to emulate them by presenting themselves voluntarily for castration and service at the imperial court. Beset as usual by the pangs of intellectual and social snobbery, Ricci complained at the extent to which this practice had come to dominate palace life under the Wanli Emperor:

One can say that this Kingdom is now governed by eunuchs, ten thousand of whom live in the palace. And, moreover, they all come from plebeian stock, they are poor and unlettered, and brought up in perpetual servitude. They are the most stolid and base people in this kingdom, who – when it comes to any grave matter – are utterly impotent and inept. From which one can easily gather what kind of upbringing the ruler of this great empire will have, reared among eunuchs and women devoid of any nobility.[5]

According to Ricci, literati looked on helplessly at the acts of cruelty and injustice committed by the eunuchs, unable to resist them, whether by force or by providing good counsel, since the Emperor had ears only for castrati.

Ricci did not encounter eunuchs directly until 1598, when he bought passage on a boat carrying fruit up the crowded imperial canal to Beijing. The canal served to link the southern and northern capitals, and to carry goods from the economic heartland of China around Nanjing to the political centre. A series of canals running north–south had connected the east–west flowing rivers since the fifth century, but not until the early fifteenth century were these waterways overhauled and extended to form a massive artery, running from Hangzhou to Beijing, and measuring 1,800 kilometres.[6] Designed as the principal means whereby rice was taken as tribute from the provinces to the capital, by the sixteenth century the imperial canal was carrying a far wider variety of taxable goods northwards. Ricci noted barges full of fruit, fish, clothes, pieces of silk, tea and leafy vegetables travelling in flotillas of eight or ten, depending on the nature and volume of the commodity. The transportation of perishable goods obviously posed problems, especially since the canal was principally used in the summer months to avoid the winter freeze. Ricci was impressed at the system whereby cities situated alongside the canal were required to supply the boats with ice, which was stored underground in copious quantities.[7]

From the late fifteenth century, the collection of taxes was the preserve of the eunuchs. Hence the boats that carried not just food and fabrics but also gold leaf from Zhejiang, sandalwood from Shandong, sand from Hejian, and many other materials to the capital were captained and staffed by castrati. It was to the captains that civil passengers seeking transport needed to address themselves. And it was by this means, and at considerable expense, that Matteo Ricci, his Italian companion Lazzaro Cattaneo, and two lay brothers found themselves accommodated among a cargo of sour and juicy fruits a little like cherries, en route to Beijing. At first the captain, 'as barbaric as eunuchs are wont to be', sought to cheat the Jesuits by denying that he had already received half the payment in advance, demanding immediate payment of the full amount, and threatening to throw the Jesuits with their luggage onto the bank of the canal.[8] Calling on his contacts, Ricci forced the eunuch to stand down over the matter of the payment. For the rest of the voyage, the Jesuits disdained to enter into conversation with the captain, and declined to give him the present that they had apparently intended for him. Ricci's account of this first encounter established the stereotype of the grasping and capricious eunuch that was to recur throughout his writings. But it also proclaimed a frostiness on the part of the Jesuits that they would be unable to maintain in future exchanges. Like it or not, the eunuchs were powerful, and if Ricci hoped for the ear of the Emperor, he would be reliant on their mediation.

On arrival in Beijing, Ricci's attitude had melted a little. Thanks to the patronage of the influential literatus Wang Zhongming, whom the Jesuits had first met in Shaozhou, and who had come to Beijing in order to take up the job of Minister of Rites, they received a warm welcome from a eunuch close to the Emperor; the fact that he deigned to go down on his knees before the foreigners seemed to Ricci to be a very good sign. Through the eunuch's interventions, the European priests were optimistic that they might gain the opportunity to bring Valignano's long-gestated plan to fruition, and to present the Emperor with the gifts that they had been hoarding for over a decade. By this point, the accumulation of presents destined for the Emperor included a clock, an *ancona* or altarpiece of the Saviour, a harpsichord, two of the (by now obligatory) triangular glasses and a second, Spanish altarpiece of the Madonna; the last had split into its three constituent boards, which was less disastrous than the Jesuits might have imagined, since the Chinese took it to be a sign of the painting's exceptionally antique status. The eunuch was impressed with the objects, though he expressed disappointment that the priests had nothing to say about alchemy and proclaimed that if they had been able to tell the Emperor how to turn mercury sulphate into silver this would have been the greatest gift of all. Seeing that the Jesuits remained silent on this subject, the eunuch announced that, in any case, circumstances prevented him from taking up their cause with the Emperor, since following the invasion of Korea by the Japanese, and the related threat to China, the sovereign would not wish to hear of the presence of other foreigners. As Ricci commented in his *History*, the Chinese were incapable of telling one foreign nation from another.[9] But, in Ricci's view, it was the Jesuits' failure to supply the eunuch with alchemical secrets, rather than the Korean war, that was the real reason for the eunuch's withdrawal of support. The stereotype of the avaricious and untrustworthy castrato was reinforced.

The Jesuits stayed for a month in the northern capital, before conceding defeat and heading back south to Nanjing. It was early in 1599, therefore, that Ricci experienced his third significant run-in with eunuchs, at the court of the southern capital. Here resided thousands of castrati, headed by the famous 'Commandant of Nanjing', whose job it was, among other things, to run the massive imperial palace.

Ricci lost no time in seeking an audience with the then Commandant, Feng Bao, whom he judged to be extremely old, and 'conforming to the style of eunuchs, lacking in courtesy'. The castrated courtiers might have come to the same conclusion about the Jesuit, since he refused point blank to go down on his knees before Feng, saying that 'he was no man to abase himself before a eunuch'. Ricci was saved from the worst consequences of his rudeness, since the Commandant was deaf, and kept by his side a servant who repeated in a loud voice everything that the foreign priest said. The servant was wise enough to slot in courtesies where they were lacking, and the Commandant was duly satisfied by Ricci's address. Then there followed an exchange of gifts. Apparently, Feng Bao gave generously to the Jesuits, but was clear that he hoped for a prism in exchange. When Ricci explained that they could not part with those gifts intended for the Emperor, the Commandant claimed mischievously that the Emperor already owned far more impressive examples and would be unmoved by the undersized prisms brought by the Jesuits. There the all-important courtesies came to an abrupt end: Ricci and Feng Bao were never to speak to each other again.

There is undeniably something puerile about such exchanges, reported in Ricci's hand. The castrati are represented as desperate to assert their authority over the foreign priests; the Jesuits cannot conceal their contempt for the eunuchs. Both parties jockey for honour in a manner which looks set to unbalance what is already a fragile relationship. But there was more at stake in these quarrels than may at first be evident, and the tensions played out between Matteo Ricci and Feng Bao belonged to a far broader political context. The invasion of Korea in 1592 constituted the first concrete step taken by Hideyoshi Toyotomi, the ruler of

Japan, in his plan to establish an east Asian empire. There was no doubt that the conquest of China was his ultimate objective. And it was thanks to extensive military support from China that Korea was in the end able to drive the Japanese out. However, the invasion did not end until the death of Hideyoshi in 1598, and the six-year war presented a drain on Chinese resources.[10] In order to boost the imperial coffers, the Wanli Emperor introduced new taxes, and revived the imperial mines, both policies that he determined should be enacted by eunuchs.[11] Castrated men were therefore recruited in vastly inflated numbers during this period, and were an increasingly visible presence in the provinces as well as at court.[12] The association of eunuchs with the exaction of taxes of course did nothing to enhance their popularity, and in 1598 Ricci perceived the people of China to be on the verge of rebellion: 'These eunuchs, who are for the most part an idiotic, barbaric, arrogant people, devoid of conscience and of shame, carried out these offices with such cruelty that, in a brief time, one saw the whole of China in revolt and in an even worse state than it had previously been on account of the Korean war.'[13] The cause of this widespread disaffection was not only the 'cruelty' of the eunuchs themselves but also the scoundrels and conmen – 'the dregs' of Chinese society – who assisted the eunuchs by stealing and committing crimes whenever the opportunity arose. 'On account of such thieving,' claimed Ricci, less than a tenth of the revenues raised ever made it into the Emperor's treasury. In a long section of his *History* dedicated to the subject, Ricci explained how castrati were ruining China. House-owners were compelled to pay eunuchs large sums of money to prevent them from destroying their homes in pursuit of buried silver. City authorities also bribed eunuchs in order to keep them away. Magistrates attempted to curtail the power of the castrati, but received no support from the Emperor, who was determined that they should continue in their revenue-raising campaign. Such was Wanli's loyalty to the eunuchs that anybody who resisted them risked being thrown into gaol. According to Ricci, the result was that the eunuchs got more insolent by the day, and killed and stole from the poor with abandon.

Exaggerated, prejudiced and rhetorical as Ricci's account surely was, he was nevertheless remarkably attuned to current affairs. The Korean war did indeed create a fiscal crisis in China; the proliferation of eunuchs around this time not only resulted from Wanli's policy, but from the destitution of peasants forced off their land on account of inflation and taxation, and driven to seek castration. But where Ricci really had his finger on the pulse was in his realisation that the Chinese loved to hate the eunuchs. The roots of this hatred were ancient. The earliest known chronicles spoke of the treachery of the castrati, while the Book of Odes, the classic collection of Chinese poetry dating in parts from 1000 BC, included this proclamation:

> Not heaven but women and eunuchs
> Bring misfortunes to mankind.
> Wives and those without balls
> Bleat with similar voices.[14]

By the beginning of the seventeenth century, at the time that Ricci was writing his *History*, contempt for the eunuchs had gained a political significance, and a discourse was taking shape that presented the decline of the Ming in terms of the lascivious conduct and insolent power of the eunuchs.[15] Their arch-enemies were the literati, those who had struggled through the punishing examination system in order to attain their authority, and who bitterly resented the usurpation of their power by eunuchs whom they perceived to be a lesser species. By heaping his own condemnations on the castrati, Ricci hoped to identify himself and his colleagues more closely with the mandarin class.

In 1596, the eunuch Ma Tang was appointed Collector of Taxes at Linqing and Tianjin. In May 1599, he had attracted such popular loathing that a revolt broke out against him; his palace was set on fire and thirty-seven of his underlings were killed. The following summer, Ricci himself arrived in Linqing, in the hope of making his final journey northwards to the capital, and the curtains opened on a final set-piece contest between the Jesuit and the eunuch. That this encounter should have been staged on Ma Tang's boat was especially appropriate. The eunuchs were, after all, renowned at this time for their tyrannical control of the imperial canal, and Ma Tang's opulent vessel, which was fit for a king – carved and gilded on the outside, incorporating multiple chambers, halls and loggias – provided a persuasive locale for the display of his greed and corruption.[16] It was to Ma Tang's golden barge that Ricci was obliged to bring the Emperor's presents, and there they were laid out very prettily in the large hall. The eunuch professed great admiration for the European objects, and even troubled to go down on his knees before the images of the Saviour and of the Madonna. But, despite the goodwill shown by Ma Tang, Ricci 'did not trust eunuchs and still less this one who had such an evil reputation'.[17] With his customary grace, the Jesuit therefore explained to Ma Tang that he had no need of his help, since in Beijing he already had many friends, including top-level mandarins, who could assist him. At this the eunuch laughed, claiming that no mandarins outside the palace had the power that he himself enjoyed within, and that if he issued a memo to the Emperor, he would be sent a reply within two days, whereas to the literati the Emperor would take far longer to reply (if he bothered at all).

Ma Tang held the upper hand. Much as Ricci wanted to ignore and despise him, he was in no position to reject patronage. The Jesuits therefore found themselves once again beholden to a eunuch, and – in the coming weeks – on the receiving end of some rather exceptional eunuch hospitality. What can Ricci have made of a banquet, at the palace of Ma Tang, that was followed by spectacular entertainments – games, plays, conjuring tricks and acrobatics – the like of which he had never before seen? When the Flemish Jesuit Nicholas Trigault published Ricci's *History* of the mission in 1615, he took care to describe the performers as 'parasites', but Ricci's original version is noticeably lacking in the pejorative language that we might expect from him. Indeed, he sounds genuinely excited in his accounts of the juggler tossing three large knives, two palms long, into the air; or the man standing on his shoulders throwing and catching a large earthenware pot with his feet; or the dumb-show performed by men dressed up as giants. The *pièce de résistance* was, in Ricci's eyes, the spectacle of a boy who having danced gracefully for his audience then put his hands on the ground and by sleight of hand appeared to pull out from between his thighs another boy, made of plaster, who (standing on his hands) repeated the dance that the real boy had just performed with his feet. At the end of the show, the two boys fell to the ground and pretended to wrestle so convincingly that both of them appeared to be alive.[18] Ricci's contempt for the eunuchs and their lifestyle was not as cast-iron as he liked to suggest.

However, as an intermediary at the imperial court, Ma Tang left something to be desired, the Emperor tending either to ignore or to reject his overtures. Much against

Ricci's will, the eunuch insisted on the Emperor's presents being transferred to his own palace. Meanwhile, the Jesuits were placed virtually under house arrest in a temple outside Tianjin. On the basis of a rumour that Ricci was still hiding 'precious stones' that he was reluctant to give to the Emperor, the Jesuits' possessions were searched. Triumphantly, the eunuchs pulled out a crucifix, carved in wood and painted with blood that seemed to be real. The 'cruel' Ma Tang assumed that he had discovered the equivalent of a voodoo doll, and began to scream, 'Here is the fetish that you have made in order to kill our emperor.' Ricci, unable to explain the mysteries of Christ's Passion in such unpropitious circumstances, stumbled. Recovering, he managed to explain that the figure was 'a great saint from our land, who had wanted to suffer for us the pains of the cross; for this reason, we paint and sculpt him in this manner in order to keep him always in front of our eyes'.[19] But this answer by no means satisfied the Jesuits' adversaries, whose suspicion only increased on discovering several more crucifixes among the foreigners' possessions. Next, the eunuchs got their blasphemous and corrupting hands on further holy objects – two reliquaries and the priests' chalice (made, of course, of silver, the most precious metal in China). Although Ricci was eventually successful in negotiating the return of these pieces, his relationship with Ma Tang was at its lowest ebb. Corruption and cruelty the Jesuits had come to expect from the eunuchs; but the desecration of such holy objects was a crime in an altogether different league.

Castrati continued to feature in Ricci's narrative. When the Jesuits were eventually permitted to enter Beijing in January 1601 – seemingly on the whim of the Emperor himself – they remained under the close watch of eunuchs, including agents of Ma Tang.[20] Following the long-awaited presentation of European gifts to the Emperor (an event exclusively managed by the eunuchs on behalf of the Jesuits), the priests met regularly with the castrati to instruct them in clock maintenance and in playing and tuning the harpsichord. Given the infamous seclusion of the Wanli Emperor, all communications had to be mediated by his emasculated servants. Indeed, since the early fifteenth century, when the Yongle Emperor had moved his court from Nanjing to Beijing, eunuchs had constituted a human buffer between the Chinese ruler and his people. The palace, completed in 1420, occupied an area of a quarter of a square mile, and was gorgeously landscaped with pines, cypresses, rare flowers, artificial hills, statues and pavilions. This 'Forbidden City', a pleasure-ground for the emperor's entertainment, including of course the harem, was staffed by eunuchs. But it was in the 'Imperial City', an area of about three square miles, surrounding the emperor's palace, that the majority of the Beijing eunuchs – probably double Ricci's estimate of ten thousand at the time of his arrival – lived and worked.[21]

By the beginning of the sixteenth century, castrati were organised into twenty-four directorates, bureaux and departments. The most important of these was the Directorate of Ceremonial. As the name suggested, this was in charge of various aspects of imperial protocol, including the cutting of the hair of princes at the age of one month old – part of the ritual preparation of potential heirs to the throne – and the monitoring of pregnancies among the emperor's wives. This required the eunuchs to record details of the women's menstrual cycles, and instances of morning sickness and miscarriage, although there is no evidence for the claims of the Japanese historian Mitamura for the eunuchs' direct and highly ritualised involvement in managing the emperor's nocturnal affairs.[22] Overseeing matters relating to the emperor's wives

and children was just one small part of the tasks accorded
to the Directorate, which was effectively the administrative
nerve centre of the Ming government, processing all communications among the various eunuch departments of the
capital, and co-ordinating policies between central and provincial government. Second in importance to the Directorate of Ceremonial, and the largest eunuch department, in
terms of personnel and office space, was the Directorate of
Palace Servants. This was in charge of palace construction,
including mansions for princes and imperial mausolea outside the capital. It also ran numerous warehouses for rice,
salt, ice and other necessities.[23] The eunuch agency in charge
of the Imperial Stables hired 2,000 new palace guards in 1581,
a testimony to Wanli's love of horses and soldiers.[24] Besides
the emperor's guards, this department was responsible for
nine stables of elephants, a horse-racing track, circus arena,
three breeding and fodder farms (producing rice, beans, and
straw for the horses), the production of saddles and horse-
shoes, and the care of the emperor's cats.[25]

The Directorate of Palace Foods, working closely with the
Directorate of the Palace Kitchens, fed the entire personnel of the Imperial City, with the exception of the emperor
and his family, whose refreshments were the responsibility
of a special group of eunuchs, and whose cravings for cakes
and confectionery were serviced by a dedicated bakery.
The rest of the population of the palace–city complex con-
sumed 210,000 piculs of rice, 100,000 jars of wine, and 70
tons of salt each year.[26] The bulk of these staples came from
tributes from the provinces. But the eunuchs employed by
the Palace Foods department also ran several farms, providing beef, lamb, fish, flour, oil, soy sauce, vegetables and
other produce. Besides feeding the personnel of the Imperial City, the Kitchens were also charged with catering for

special occasions, at which time the two Directorates could hire as many as 6,300 extra cooks.[27] Separate bureaux saw to the production of wine, vinegar and noodles and to the acquisition of fruit, vegetables and tea.[28] A Directorate of Imperial Farms – among its other duties – supplied exotic animals and birds, including deer, elk, turtles and cranes to the Imperial Academy of Medicine. Here, four to six royal physicians worked with some thirty to fifty eunuch herbalists, who refined an infinite variety of remedies using popular ingredients such as ginger, liquorice, lilac, milkwort, yam root, peony, almonds and dates, as well as rarities including pomegranate peel, sulphur, deer penis, elk horn and bear paw. Among the eunuchs' most celebrated recipes were elixir pills and aphrodisiacs. Ironically, the castrati were especially renowned for producing pills capable of enhancing virility.

Many other departments, staffed by castrated artisans, were responsible for furnishing the court with the essentials and inessentials of life in the Imperial City. There were also separate departments for the manufacture of headgear and garments, and for dyeing clothes and fabrics. The Palace Carpentry Directorate commanded a team of skilled craftsmen, responsible for making palace screens and other forms of interior decoration, lamps and lanterns, furniture of all kinds in hardwood and bamboo, artificial flowers, sandals, wooden toys, chess sets, playing cards, combs, ivory and lacquerware, dishes, cups, fans, buckets and canes. The office also employed a dozen weavers to process woollen yarns sent from central Asia, and to make high-quality carpets. Finally, it was responsible for providing paper and other writing materials for the offices in the palace. Lavatory paper, however, was the responsibility of a separate department, the Baochaosi, situated just outside the Imperial City, and producing an annual yield of literally millions of sheets, generally from two to three feet in width. Its factory housed seventy-two ovens, and every month it processed tonnes of straw, shredded wood, lime and plant oil. Each sheet was stamped with a red mark, and loaded in piles onto a wheelbarrow. The paper was then distributed to every room in the Forbidden Palace and to lavatory facilities throughout the Imperial City. But this was not the source of the paper used to wipe the ruler's bottom; his was a thinner, softer paper from Hangzhou, and was manufactured by the Palace Servants Directorate. A further department, known as the Bathhouse, was dedicated to matters of personal hygiene, and bore responsibility for providing washing water and soaps to the palace women and high-ranking eunuchs.[29]

The Armaments Bureau manufactured weapons and ammunition for the palace guards, and was in charge of making cannonballs. It also operated a smaller factory just outside the palace wall, where eunuchs produced hardware tools, such as keys, locks, hammers, needles, screwdrivers and scissors. The Silverware Bureau was in charge of two mints, one for the production of gold and silver jewellery, the other for silver coinage. Eunuchs also manned the Imperial Treasury, where precious metals and stones, jewellery, valuable fabrics and copious quantities of tax monies were stored.

Further services were provided by eunuchs in the Palace Custodians Directorate, charged with cleaning the numerous halls and pavilions in and outside the Forbidden City. For many eunuchs, their life would not rise beyond the tedium of polishing copperware and sweeping the immense courtyards.[30] Then there was the Directorate of Entourage Guards, who carried the imperial sedans and were always ready with canopies, fans, and umbrellas to protect the emperor and his family from the heat and rain. It was their particular duty to attend hunts, since they were required to carry bows and arrows, wine and snacks, as well as boxes of presents, in case the emperor should feel like making impromptu awards to any of his companions.[31] The Fire and Water Department, meanwhile, provided firewood for cooking and fuel for heat, light and sacrificial burning. They were also responsible for dredging moats, repairing wells, and for clearing the Imperial City of waste. The two elements intrinsic to their work were brought together in their preparations for Chinese New Year, when they were required to fill every gigantic copper cauldron and every available pail and bucket with water, lest the fireworks get out of control. However, entertainments were the remit of a separate department, employing over two hundred actors, musicians, puppetmasters and dancers, dedicated to amusing the emperor and his family.[32]

Finally, the eunuchs played an important role in religion in the Imperial City. The Directorate of Imperial Temples was responsible for temple maintenance and for the manufacture of incense sticks.[33] They were often put in charge of construction projects for new temples, and the wealthy among them engaged in considerable personal patronage. Many eunuchs were committed Buddhists, and given their inability to reproduce (though some had sired families before deciding to undergo the operation) had a greater investment in the afterlife than in the devotions of filial piety.[34] In the temples of the Imperial City, some functioned as Buddhist monks, while others were followers of Lamaism and donned the hats of Tibetan monks. Eunuchs were also sometimes trained, at the emperor's behest, to perform Daoist rites of exorcism. The thin line between religion and science was made apparent in the Terrace of the Spirits, where eunuchs trained in astronomy were required to report good and bad omens to their Director. Studying holy hymns and scriptures, to aid them in their planetary prognostications, these eunuchs were also responsible for monitoring the famous clepsydra or water clock. Day and night, more than ten eunuchs sat and watched the water dripping through a small orifice into a container, and measured the hours according to the progress made by a float on the water. At the end of every hour, eunuchs from the Directorate of Palace Custodians would bring the hour tablet – a bar, about a foot long, painted in green and inscribed in gold – to the Heavenly Purity Palace and would exchange it, as in a relay race, for another. Eunuchs were therefore responsible for announcing the times of the day to the Imperial City, and as such were to be involved with the Jesuits in relation to their gift of a mechanical clock.

But while, in practice, the Jesuits continued to brush shoulders with eunuchs on a day-to-day basis, they were also engaged in an ideological war against them. Ricci made much of his support for the literatus Feng Yingjing, the supreme criminal justice for the province of Huguang, who was renowned for standing up against the villainy of the eunuchs in his region. A favourite with the Jesuits for his combined opposition to Buddhism and to eunuchs, it was the latter that was to win him the status of a popular hero; according to Ricci, people put up pictures of the literatus on the walls of their houses, and venerated his image 'as if he were a saint'. Feng was to pay for his principles: summoned to Beijing in 1601, he was dismissed from his office, viciously beaten and imprisoned in a tiny cell. Ricci, who had met Feng previously during his stays in Nanchang and Nanjing, immediately went to visit the disgraced official, and remained in communication with him during the three years of his imprisonment.[35] During the same years, Feng would reward the Jesuit's support by undertaking to have published various of Ricci's works, including *On Friendship*, to which he appended what one can only assume to have been a heartfelt preface, *The True Meaning of the Lord of Heaven* and the *Twenty-five Sayings*. Patronage from a literatus of Feng Yingjing's status, even a disgraced one, was exactly what the Jesuits had striven for. Ricci's rejection of eunuchs had, as he had hoped, cemented his identification with the literati.

In his important study of Chinese eunuchs, Shih-Shan Henry Tsai has attempted to rehabilitate the reputation of the emperor's castrated servants in the face of centuries of adverse propaganda. It is thanks to his research that we now know the great diversity and significance of the tasks undertaken by thousands of eunuchs in the period of the late Ming. Furthermore, Tsai has alerted us to what he calls the 'dualism' on which the Chinese system of governance operated, whereby eunuchs and literati acted as each other's checks and balances.[36] During the period in which Ricci wrote, castrati played a crucial role in the administration of the largest single state in the world. Lest we are tempted to take Ricci's account at face value, we must realise that he borrowed and manipulated discourses and stereotypes from contemporary political debate to serve his own purposes. His was anything but a dispassionate analysis.

*

In 1608, when Ricci started to write his *History* of the China mission, the political circumstances were certainly ripe for a full-blooded attack on eunuchs. These were not, however, the only species of Chinese men for whom Ricci evinced his contempt. The passage in which the Jesuit referred to the castrati as 'stolid and base' formed part of a larger chapter entitled 'reprovable customs of the Chinese' belonging to the first book of his *History*. Here, eunuchs were positioned within a terrain of depravity that included polygamy, whoredom, sodomy, pederasty, infanticide, suicide, drunkenness and alchemy. In the section dedicated to sexual sin, Ricci complained that vice prevailed in this people, characterised by 'effeminacy' and 'incontinence'. He claimed that Chinese men were so 'enervated' by their excessive sexual activity with concubines and whores (of whom there were said to be forty thousand on the streets of Beijing alone), let alone with servicing their multiple wives, that they lost their reproductive powers. His theory perhaps owed something to the fact that he and his colleagues were several times called on by high-ranking officials seeking fertility treatments. But there was worse to come. According to Ricci, the true 'misery of this people' was revealed in the predilection of the men for homosexual acts, which they practised without incurring any censure of the law, or even shame. In Beijing, boys publicly comported themselves as prostitutes, dressed very 'charmingly and dolled up in rouge'.[37]

The womanliness of Chinese men was a recurring theme. Ricci could scarcely contain his contempt for their beards, made up of only 'eight or nine hairs', and he ridiculed his male hosts for spending two hours in the morning just in combing their hair and putting their clothes on. He was at first equally unimpressed by the lack of aggression displayed by Chinese men, whom he dubbed '*femminucce*' or 'sissies' since they perceived no dishonour in running away from attack.[38] This last view, first put forward in an early letter of 1584 to Giambattista Román, Ricci would come to revise. When he wrote his *History*, over two decades later, he included this analysis of Chinese passivity:

Nobody carries arms in the city, unless they are soldiers going to muster, or those accompanying the most important mandarins. Likewise, nobody keeps weapons at home, with the exception of a scimitar, owned by some to take with them on their travels in order to offer protection against assassins . . . And just as among us it is a fine thing to see an armed man, among them it is considered bad, and they are fearful to see such a horrible thing.

He went on to praise the Chinese for avoiding the factions, tumults, and blood feuds that characterised European life, and marvelled at the fact that – in China – 'to flee, and to refuse to wound another man, is considered to be the most honourable course of action'.[39] Ricci's reappraisal of the Chinese eschewal of violent revenge suggests a development over the years of his relativist stance. It may also reflect an increased desire to perceive Christian values – in this case, turning the other cheek – as naturally present in this pagan land. But whatever the underlying agenda of Ricci's comments, they reveal an unceasing fascination with the defining characteristics of Chinese masculinity.

Earlier Western travellers to China had been similarly preoccupied with Eastern perceptions of what it meant to be male. Like Ricci, they were quick to perceive sexual incontinence as a defining feature, were troubled by the prevalence of what the Dominican friar Gaspar da Cruz termed the 'accursed sin', 'unnatural vice' and 'filthy abomination' (i.e. male homosexuality), and were equally struck by the Chinese disinclination to fight.[40] The Jesuits therefore contributed to an orientalising trope about the effeminacy of Chinese men. However, they did not invent the incidence of male prostitution on the streets of Chinese cities, and there is considerable external evidence to suggest that sexual relations between men, at least in elite society, were tolerated to a degree that would have amazed Europeans at this time.

Chinese authors commented on the widespread practice of pederasty during the late Ming. According to the Fujian writer, Xie Zhaozhe (1567–1624), 'Nowadays, from Jiangnan and Zhejiang to Beijing and Shanxi, there is none that does not know of this fondness.'[41] Indeed, it is likely that Ricci's description of boy entertainers, at a party hosted by the eunuch Ma Tang, gave accurate witness to the fashion for young male prostitutes, often acquired as orphans or victims of famine by entrepreneurs, and trained in singing, dancing and acrobatics. At elite parties, they would show off their bodies in elaborate acts, after which they would be available to guests for fondling and sex.[42]

Fortunately, Chinese culture offered more sober models of masculine propriety for the Jesuits to draw on, including a Confucian ideal of fatherly virtue that gelled well with the expectations of Christian missionaries. For, in China, the structures of patriarchy – literally, rule by the fathers – were firmly entrenched. The Chinese perceived their homeland as a *guojia*, a 'state-family', in which the state was consciously modelled on the principles of family organisation. The hierarchy and mutual devotion implicit in the five relationships were thus played out in their ultimate form in the relationship between the emperor and his people. According to this formulation, sons, encouraged since childhood to filial piety, could aspire in adulthood to become faithful literati and capable ministers by transforming their devotion to their parents into loyalty to the emperor. In turn, the emperor's management of his own family served as the basis for his running of the state.[43] Strong fathers, dutiful sons and subservient women were the ideals on which Chinese society was founded.[44]

In Ricci's otherwise full ethnographic survey of China, which constituted the first book of his *History*, he had very little to say about the place of women. He did, however, pause to voice his approval of the custom of footbinding (thereby distinguishing himself from the Protestant missionaries of the nineteenth century), and remarked that 'this was surely the invention of some wise man, in order to prevent women going out and about and to keep them at home, as was fitting'.[45] And in his letter to Giambattista Román of 1584, which was to some extent a first draft for Book One of the *History*, he commented that 'noble women, on the rare occasions that they leave their houses, go about covered in small sedan chairs carried by four men; such is their honesty that they cannot be seen by anyone'.[46] Other European writers also noted the seclusion of Chinese women, Gaspar da Cruz claiming that, in Canton, women – save for 'some light huswives and base women' – kept themselves so 'close' that they were invisible to the outsider.[47] By and large, the submissive state of Chinese women did not present European observers with any difficulties.

Filial piety was potentially more problematic, since it motivated the Chinese to worship their ancestors. This was the very point that was to lead a subsequent generation of Jesuits into intense controversy, since their accommodationist approach was seen by some to result in the endorsement of a heretical practice. Ricci's account of the deference manifested by the Chinese towards their parents, however, could provoke little criticism. And when he referred to the unsurpassed 'obedience' of sons to their fathers, there is no doubt but that he meant his readers to consider this a virtue.[48] In Europe, as in China, a strong ideology of patriarchy prevailed in which authorities ranging from the absolute monarch to the city councillor fashioned their rule as 'paternal'.[49] Still more significantly, the Christian God was of course frequently represented in his paternal guise. Ricci was therefore able to invoke the ideal of filial piety in his exhortation to the Chinese people to show deference to the Lord of Heaven:

The creator of heaven, earth, and all things is the father also the supreme sovereign of all. If mankind does not reverence Him and serve Him it will lack both father and sovereign, and this is to be totally disloyal and altogether lacking in filial piety. Can one be virtuous at all if one is disloyal and is lacking in filial piety?[50]

The Chinese vision of patriarchy was, therefore, easily assimilable by the Jesuits, as were the strict hierarchies of age and gender that characterised society in the Middle Kingdom. These were surely reassuring indications of the civility and order of China that harmonised rather than clashed with European values.

It is of course unsurprising that the Jesuits, having surveyed the models of masculinity available, sought to fashion themselves according to the Confucian ideal of the literatus, the emperor's mediator between the institutions of the state and the family, and the official channel through which paternal authority flowed. But, in donning the robes of a Confucian scholar in 1595, Ricci could not efface the difficulties that this re-identification in fact triggered. In particular, he was burdened with the vexing business of how to explain his own celibacy to a people whose whole culture, belief system and institutions revolved around the ideal of the family. That this matter pressed heavily on his consciousness is suggested by the fact that he devoted the majority of the eighth and final chapter of his Catechism, *The True Meaning of the Lord of Heaven*, to a defence of clerical celibacy. The Catechism was constructed as a dialogue and Ricci's statements were interspersed by a question or a challenge from a fictional 'Chinese scholar'. So the initial perplexity of the Chinese at the Jesuit's rejection of married life, and his eventual turn towards the ideal of celibacy – 'It is truly fitting that a man should not marry for the sake of studying the Way' – find dramatic expression.[51]

In accounting for the Catholic stance on celibacy, Ricci went straight to the top, and sought to explain why it was that the Pope (whom the Jesuits had described, inaccurately but compellingly, as the highest authority in Europe, a sort of counterpart to the Chinese emperor) did not marry. The argument was simple: 'Because he is free of all family ties he is able to devote himself solely to the public good, and since he has no children, he regards the numberless people as his sons and daughters, and exerts all his mind and energies in the guidance of the masses.'[52] According to this classic argument, familiar to all in the Catholic world, the celibate was better able to act as father to the masses than one encumbered by his own blood family. Ricci's arguments for the celibacy of his own order were, however, plural and wide-ranging. Firstly, there was the 'test' provided by chastity, which Ricci concurred was difficult in the extreme, and a means of demonstrating true virtue. Secondly, there was the diversity of mankind, and Ricci's belief that 'the people of a nation ought not to be condemned to uniformity'. Instead, Ricci argued for a division of labour among God's servants: marriage was not something to be eliminated, but nor was it the only vocation available to men. In particular, 'the offering of sacrifice to the Sovereign on High demands men who are devoted to nothing else and who are pure in body'. Thirdly, and here Ricci departed from the classic defence of celibacy to adduce an argument perhaps especially persuasive in the context of China's demography, he warned against reproduction *per se*:

The troubles of today are not due to the smallness of the population, but to the fact that the population has grown large without a corresponding growth in virtue. To plan to have many children and to be ignorant of how to instruct them is merely to increase the animal population.[53]

Hence, members of the Society of Jesus chose an 'even more public-spirited' route; by 'curtailing the birth of children', they urgently pursued 'the Way', and were able to offer spiritual succour to those unfortunates – no doubt the result of their parents' uncontrolled procreation – who had fallen into a life of sin. From a contemporary vantage point, it is surprising to hear the Jesuit addressing the issue of family planning.

Ricci then started over, offering eight more compelling reasons for the merits of *not* marrying, in response to the Chinese scholar's continued bafflement. This time, the Jesuit began with the mundanity of parenting: 'A father cannot avoid thinking about trade and commerce.' Given the demographic considerations to which Ricci had already alluded, the quest for wealth and for food had become ever more consuming. This focus on the material was hard to combine with the spiritual life: 'The most important thing in the cultivation of virtue is to despise wealth and goods.' How could a Jesuit persuade others to scorn material wealth if he himself was engaged in pursuing it? Secondly, Ricci argued for the opposition of passion and morality; only by chastity, he claimed, could one thoroughly understand the 'subtlest truths of morality'. Thirdly, in the same way that 'cold medicine is applied to those suffering from feverishness, and hot medicine to those with cold ailments', celibacy was the only true cure for lust.[54] Fourthly, the renunciation of marriage, parenthood and sexuality was the means by which Jesuits sought to achieve self-mastery. Ricci's fifth argument took further the theme of single-mindedness and discipline with reference to the surprising metaphor of the battle horse:

An expert in the rearing of horses who comes across good horses like piebalds and chestnuts which can travel a thousand *li* in a day will rear them with all care so that they may be prepared for the front line of battle. Fearful lest they be immersed in sexual activity he removes them from the herd and denies them any contact with the opposite sex. The holy religion of the Lord of Heaven also seeks out men of valour who will be able to travel to the remotest corner of the earth in order to explain the principles of the Way ... Do you want to weaken their resolve by means of the pleasures of sexuality; and do you wish to refrain from supporting them in their heroic attempts to subdue evil habits stemming from the passions?[55]

So Ricci and his colleagues likened themselves to champion steeds, whose strength depended on their being kept free from the distractions of the passions. Sex was weakening; celibacy gave men strength. Argument number six situated man's craving for food and sex within his 'lower nature', the part indistinguishable from beasts. What distinguished humans from beasts was 'the cultivation of the way', man's most righteous calling. The seventh argument was based on the need for members of the Society of Jesus to be mobile – to travel the world, unrestricted by the shackles of marriage and family. Finally, argument number eight claimed that men should relinquish sexual desire, since the chaste life would bring them closer to God: 'The angels are devoid of sexual desire, and the nature of a chaste person approximates to that of the angels because, although his body is here on earth he is similar to those who live in Heaven.'[56]

Ricci's arguments were well honed. They were mostly to be found in the traditional theology of the Catholic Church, and had recently been rehearsed by priests and polemicists throughout Europe in the context of the Protestant Reformation, and in response to Luther's claims that marriage, not celibacy, was the highest calling. But Ricci was fully aware that the Chinese objection to celibacy had a different origin. It was to the claims of filial piety that he must now turn. Hence the question placed in the mouth of the 'Chinese scholar': 'But in our canonical writings there is the statement: "There are three things which mark a man as being unfilial, and the greatest of these is to have no progeny." What have you to say about that?' Ricci fell back on the arguments typical of a Humanist scholar. He went back to the sources – '*ad fontes*' as one trained in Latinate learning would have said – and sought to demonstrate that Confucius himself had never made such a claim. The condemnation of celibacy must therefore have crept into later, less authoritative writings. In particular, Ricci blamed Mencius, the most famous of Confucius's interpreters, who had been a pupil of Confucius's own grandson:

My view . . . is that the words you have quoted were not handed down from the Sage, but were uttered by Mencius. It may be that he received a faulty statement in the [oral] transmission [of the Sage's teachings], or perhaps he was using these words to explain the significance of the emperor Shun taking a wife without reporting the fact, and that others employed deliberately misleading terminology . . . In *The Great Learning*, the *Mean*, and the *Analects of Confucius* Confucius discusses filial piety in great detail. Why is it, then, that he, his disciples and his grandson all fail to make any mention of regulations concerning this most unfilial piece of human contact? Why was it not until the time of Mencius that such a doctrine was first recorded?[57]

To his arguments based on textual criticism, Ricci added more practical objections to the Chinese insistence that doctrine of filial piety required men to reproduce:

If it really were the case that a lack of progeny represents an unfilial attitude then every son ought to devote himself from morning to night to the task of begetting children in order to ensure the existence of later generations. He should not interrupt his task even for a day. But does this not mean leading a man into bondage to sex?[58]

Furthermore, a man who was the most prolific reproducer might be the slackest citizen, siring many sons but keeping them all in his home town and never doing a single decent thing with his life: 'Can such a man be called filial?' Ricci next tackled the issue of infertility: 'There are those who seek sons but never have them; but how can there be anyone who seeks to be filial and yet fails to be so?' Europeans, claimed Ricci, had a clear notion of what it meant to be unfilial: 'causing one's parents to do wrong, murdering one's parents, robbing one's parents of their wealth'. Could the Chinese really claim that a failure to produce progeny 'represented a lack of filial piety and an act, moreover, more grave than the three mentioned above'?[59]

But, of course, the root of the problem lay in the Chinese innocence of divine truth. For, in the absence of belief in salvation, the Chinese clung wretchedly to the rites surrounding the dead body, and deluded themselves into thinking that this was all that remained of the person. Therein lay the obsession with producing children. Ricci offered, in his mind, a more optimistic Christian perspective on death:

To believe that once a person has died he is completely dissolved and that nothing of him remains is truly to assert that a man has no posterity. If I serve the Lord on High in this present life and hope that for all generations to come I shall continue to serve Him, how can I have any anxiety over a lack of progeny? After I die my spirit will be preserved in its entirety and will be even more fresh and healthy. Whether the empty body I leave behind is buried by sons or by friends, it will rot away. What other choice is there?[60]

The true faith would render obsolete the Chinese obsession with producing heirs.

For all Ricci's defensiveness over the issue of celibacy, there is little evidence that the Chinese were as bothered about the Jesuits' non-married status as he feared. True enough, Confucius's proclamation in the *Analects* that, 'while his father and mother are alive, a son should not go on distant journeys', might have left Ricci feeling somewhat uncomfortable.[61] However, it was more likely to be Ricci's unfilial desertion of his own parents rather than his lack of wife and progeny that incurred the disapproval of those he met. Certainly, in the torrent of anti-Christian writings that poured off the presses in the decades following Ricci's death, celibacy was not the issue that critics focused on.[62] After all, China had its own caste of celibate clergy in the form of Buddhist monks and nuns. Opting out of society in order to devote one's life to the pursuit of the Way was a very familiar concept. But it was perhaps the very proximity of the Jesuits' position to that of the Buddhists that made Ricci squirm.[63] On entering China, the Jesuits had of course styled themselves as Buddhist monks. But already in 1589, during a visit to the South Flower temple at Nanhua, twenty miles from Shaozhou, Ricci evinced great distaste for the monastic life practised there. Many of the monks kept wives and children; others distinguished themselves as thieves and assassins.[64] Indeed, such was the 'dissolution' of the monastery that – according to Ricci – the monks assumed that he and his colleague Almeida had been sent by their superiors to reform the house. Getting out as soon as possible, the Jesuits sped back to Shaozhou, and told officials there that 'they could not remain in that place of Nanhua, since it was far from the literati and the mandarins of the city, with whom they had always previously lived'. Furthermore, 'the people of Nanhua were of evil reputation, and it was scarcely safe to live in their midst'. The authorities in Shaozhou were, at first, bemused by the Jesuits' hostility. Surely the European priests were no different from the monks at Nanhua?[65]

By the time that Ricci came to write his *History* of the mission, he had developed an advanced contempt for the species of Buddhist monk with which – as he rightly feared – he and his colleagues might be confused:

These ministers are, and are considered to be, the lowest and most vicious people in China, both on account of their origin, since they are all the sons of base and poor people, sold in their childhood by their parents to old bonzes, and on account of the ignorance and poor education that characterises their masters. And hence they know nothing of literature nor civility . . . And, while they do not have wives, they are little concerned with guarding their chastity, even though they keep their dealings with women as well hidden as they are able.[66]

Ricci's attack on Buddhist monks was powerfully reminiscent of a tradition of anti-clerical writing in Europe with which the Jesuit would have been all too familiar. Since the Middle Ages, writers such as the Italian Giovanni Boccaccio and the English Geoffrey Chaucer had made their reputations by spinning yarns about dishonest, whoring priests; more recently, the baton had been taken up by Protestant pamphleteers producing scathing parodies of the dissolute lives of Catholic celibates. For Ricci and his colleagues, celibacy was a touchy issue. The Jesuits' change of clothes in 1595 was thus an urgent requirement. For, given their lack of wives and their devotional obligations (reciting the Office, attending church), it was almost inevitable that they would be taken for Buddhist monks, laying themselves open to the most unwanted kinds of criticism.[67]

Just as in his assessment of Chinese religion Ricci first identified the three principal branches of belief, Confucian, Buddhist, and Daoist, clung to the first (the adherents of which he was sure he could do business with), and determined to lop off the second and third, in his evaluation of Chinese masculinities, he adopted a similar approach. Sketching a spectrum of male roles that ranged from louche eunuchs and unchaste monks, through sodomites and fornicators, culminating in the solid patriarch of literatus status, Ricci threw in his lot with the last. But in late Ming China, as in early modern Europe, there was no safe place for a man to stand. Despite the prevalence of patriarchy as an ideology and an institutional principle, the realities of male existence were always fraught with anxiety. As has already been discussed, those who aspired to be literati faced colossal stress in the form of the examination system.[68] And even those who made it to the top continued to exist in a highly competitive and unstable world of promotions and demotions, successes and disappointments. The internal contradictions of patriarchy were perhaps suggested by the continual requirement placed on literati to travel (thereby causing them to break the Confucian dictate to stay at home) and their related tendency to engage in polygamy. Small wonder that Ming doctors commonly diagnosed the condition of *yu* or 'emotional stasis' among their male patients.[69] Buddhist monks similarly fell foul of the expectations heaped on Chinese men, and attracted criticisms for their abandonment of family life and even for their shaven heads, since a strict interpretation of filial piety demanded the return of one's body, hair and skin intact to one's ancestors.[70] The vulnerability of eunuchs was perhaps more obvious. Their smooth, puffy faces and high voices attracted mockery; so too their reputation for bedwetting. And in allowing for the removal of their reproductive organs, they laid themselves open to the most vitriolic accusations of unfiliality.[71]

Effeminate, incontinent, and impotent, eunuchs provided a flashpoint for the anxieties of both Jesuits and their Chinese hosts. In the language of Freud, one could interpret these fears as 'castration anxiety', the male anxiety developing from boyhood that one will lose one's penis and, more symbolically, one's power. For European men living in the early modern period, it has been pointed out that the terror of castration was more real than imaginary, since – from the late sixteenth century – an epidemic of syphilis rendered the surgical removal of the penis a not uncommon recourse.[72] Furthermore, male singers who had been castrated before puberty were common in European courts and cathedrals, especially in Rome, from the mid-sixteenth century, and were famous for their vocal range and ethereal tones. (By the eighteenth century, four thousand boys were castrated each year in Italy in the service of this particular aesthetic fetish.)[73] This is not to say that Ricci and his colleagues reached for their crotches every time they encountered a eunuch. Neither the Jesuits nor the literati can have felt their own members to have been directly threatened. But the conspicuousness of eunuchs in Chinese society and the prevalence of debates over filiality intensified anxieties over what it was to be male. Ricci's writings are profoundly coloured by these uncertainties.

6 The True Meaning of the Lord of Heaven

A Christian woman was nine months pregnant when her baby died within her belly. Her female neighbours applied various remedies proportionate to the gravity of the situation, but began to despair of the health of the woman, since they knew full well from experience that when a baby dies in such a manner, the mother never survives. The husband, distressed and afflicted on account of his double loss, made recourse to Our Saviour, whose image he had in his house, saying: 'You, Lord, know that with all my power I try to observe your law, and go out of my way to help those [missionaries] seeking to negotiate with my patron' (a mandarin of great importance) 'and, equally, I know that, if you want, you can deliver my wife from death; I pray you to grant this to me, so that my daughters are not abandoned, and if you do this, I promise you I shall not be ungrateful.' Following the prayer of the good man, the dead baby was immediately born, leaving the mother alive and healthy; a notable marvel to everyone who heard or saw it.[1]

This miraculous tale emanated from the southern Chinese city of Nanchang. It forms part of a letter sent by Matteo Ricci from Beijing to Claudio Acquaviva in Rome in October 1607: a round-up of the last two years' events in the four Jesuit mission stations of Shaozhou, Nanchang, Nanjing and Beijing. The story of how God intervened to save a Chinese Christian woman from certain death by effecting the expulsion of her dead baby is one of twelve miracles narrated by Ricci in his letter. These in turn make up half of a larger cluster of around two dozen stories signalling the providential course of the mission in the final five years of Ricci's life.

Before exploring this miraculous turn in the fortunes of the Jesuit mission, it is worth pausing to consider how profoundly out of place is the appearance of the Nanchang woman as she bursts into the narrative of Ricci and his friends. There are several ways in which this tale defies our expectations. Whereas we are used to seeing the Jesuits as highly cerebral creatures, here they devote their attentions to matters not of the mind, but of the body. In contrast to their usual insistence on the power of books to persuade by reason, here they bear witness to the supernatural power of an image. Perhaps most surprising of all, however, is the unavoidably female focus of the tableau evoked by Ricci. Hitherto, the Jesuits' tale has been one of highly educated and ambitious European males attempting to impress highly educated and ambitious Chinese males. When Ricci and his colleagues were not rubbing shoulders with literati, they were sparring with eunuchs and Buddhist priests or communicating with other members of their all-male Society. Ricci's voluminous correspondence was similarly male-oriented: of the fifty-five surviving letters, not one addressed a female. Apart from passing references to the evils of polygamy and prostitution and very occasional mention of a mandarin's wife, women are virtually absent from Ricci's account of his time in China. And yet here is our Jesuit missionary steering us away from the salons of literati and into the emotionally charged locale of a gynaecological crisis.

The Nanchang miracle points to the tensions that were at the heart of the China mission. It also draws attention to a profound mismatch between the Jesuits' stated aims and the reality of their contact with a small but significant number of converts. This in turn reflects a warping of the historical record. There is no escaping the barrage of information, scripted by Ricci and his colleagues, regarding their evolving plans and strategies. By contrast, the story of the two thousand or so women and men who chose to adopt Christianity during Ricci's lifetime is scarcely visible.

A year before his death, Ricci wrote a long letter to the Vice-Provincial in East Asia, Francesco Pasio.[2] The tone of the letter is urgent and serious, and there is no doubt that he was writing for the benefit of posterity. Drawing on his own extensive experience, he presented in some detail his vision of the future of the mission in the form of eight coherently argued points. Given that the letter sums up the conclusions of nearly thirty years' reflection on the question of how to convert the Chinese, it is worth quoting at some length. Ricci emphasised first and foremost the hard-won status the Jesuits enjoyed as virtuous men and as literati, 'the two things that here are most highly esteemed', and stressed the need to preserve that identification.[3] Next, he argued for the role of 'reason' in converting the literati (the number-one target of the mission): 'In this kingdom . . . sciences and opinions founded on reason are greatly prized . . . And consequently it seems that it will be easy to persuade the principal men of the kingdom of the things of our holy faith, confirmed with so much evidence of reason, and when the most learned men agree with us, it will be easy to convert the rest.'[4] For Ricci, the optimal medium of evangelisation was print – the subject of his third point – which he celebrated for its ability to convey an accurate and lasting message: 'Books spread more easily, they speak to more people and they continuously voice their truths in a more considered fashion and with more precision than that which is spoken with the mouth.'[5] More recently, historians of the book have questioned that confidence in the fixity of early modern printed texts (which were as apt to proliferate errors as to ensure precision); given Ricci's experience of the confusions that could be generated by Christian writings in Chinese context, he perhaps should have known better.[6] But Ricci retained an unshakeable faith in the power of the printed word. In his fourth point, the Jesuit turned to another abiding belief of his: the importance of Western science in appealing to the Chinese. Though worn out, and nearing the end of his life, Ricci was as ebullient as ever regarding this aspect of his apostolate: 'The Chinese have a wonderful intelligence, natural and acute . . . From which, if we could teach our sciences, not only would they have great success among these eminent men, but it would also be a means of introducing them easily to our holy law and they would never forget such a great benefit.' Given how impressed the Chinese had been with the mathematics taught to them by the European priests, how much more would they value knowledge of 'more abstruse matters, such as physics, metaphysics, theology and the supernatural'?[7] Or so Ricci dreamed.

Having enumerated the wonderful things that the Western priests had to offer the Chinese, Ricci moved on to describe those aspects of Chinese culture that the Jesuits must strive to assimilate. The fifth point reassuringly found the Chinese since ancient times to be a people inclined to piety and to natural law (in truth, less deluded in matters of faith than 'our own Egyptians, Greeks and Romans').[8] Number six sought to capitalise on the extraordinary power and stability of the Chinese empire, proposing that if only the Emperor could be persuaded to convert, the whole population would follow.[9] In the seventh point, Ricci exhorted his successors to learn Chinese (a skill that had already won the Jesuits the accolades of doctors and saints).[10] Most controversially, point eight insisted on the need to accommodate Confucianism. On the other hand, Buddhism and

Daoism could be dispensed with since they were idolatrous, and were – according to Ricci – continually impugned by the all-important literati.[11]

The letter to Pasio shows Ricci's mission strategy at its most well formulated and cogent. This was a thoroughly elitist programme that targeted the imperial court, the ruling class of literati, and the highly educated, and that was powered by reason, books and science. Here, Valignano's policy of accommodation was reiterated in its most sophisticated Riccian form. In China, the crème de la crème of the order was to dedicate itself to studying the language and to mastering the texts and values of Confucianism. Accommodation was, however, by no means to be indiscriminate. Jesuit missionaries must devote themselves to only the purest and most ancient writings of the sage. They must shun not only Buddhism and Daoism, but also the later accretions of Confucian writers and any whiff of syncretism.[12] Given Ricci's skills as a rhetorician and publicist, it is no surprise that his own version of events has dictated his posthumous image, as a scholar and scientist kitted out in the clothes of a Confucian literatus. The Jesuit mission to China is remembered as a triumph of Humanist learning, eloquence and cultural synthesis.

These were precisely the characteristics that marked Ricci's most ambitious publication: a Chinese Catechism entitled *The True Meaning of the Lord of Heaven*. First published in Beijing in an edition of two hundred copies in 1603, and re-issued in Canton in 1605 and Hangzhou in 1607, the Catechism was the product of many years' study and reflection. True to his own principles, the Jesuit had devoted himself not only to attaining a level of competence in the Chinese language that would enable him to express the fundamentals of Christian belief in clear and elegant fashion but also to mastering the Confucian philosophy that underpinned Chinese government and society. It was not the Jesuits' first attempt at producing a Chinese Catechism. Ricci had already co-operated with Michele Ruggieri in 1584 on an earlier work, written in questions and answers, entitled *The True Record of the Lord of Heaven*. But Ricci had come to despise the Buddhist terminology adopted in the first Catechism, and – by 1594 – had arranged for the destruction of the woodblocks with which it had been printed. From 1591, he immersed himself in the Confucian classics, and produced a full Latin translation of the famous *Four Books*. During the year 1594–5, he turned his attentions to the *Six Classics*, selecting quotations from it as he read. Around the same time, Ricci and his colleagues ditched the clothes of Buddhist priests, and began to dress as Confucian scholars. Inhabiting this new identity, Ricci wrote a first draft of the *True Meaning* in 1595–6, then sent it off to be scrutinised and if needs be censored by the Bishop of Japan, resident in Macao, Don Luis Cerqueira, as well as the Jesuit Visitor, Alessandro Valignano, and the head of the China mission, Duarte de Sande. The feedback process turned out to be a drawn-out one, not on account of what Ricci had written but because of painfully slow communications. Duarte de Sande intended to hand over the manuscript to Ricci at Nanchang in 1598. Unfortunately, by the time that de Sande arrived, Ricci had headed north. De Sande then fell ill, dying in July 1599, and the corrected proofs did not get to Ricci in Beijing until 1601.[13] The text that eventually emerged from this process was an extremely clever exercise in persuasion that depended, nevertheless, on deft misrepresentations of both the Christian faith and the religion of the Chinese.

Framed as a dialogue between a 'Western scholar' and a 'Chinese scholar', the *Lord of Heaven* attempted to convince its readership of five main tenets: first, of the existence of a single, personal, all-powerful creator; second, of the immortality of the soul; third, of the separateness and potential for agency of humans (in opposition to the view that all phenomena of the world are united in one organic entity); fourth, of the existence of Heaven and Hell (in opposition to the idea of reincarnation); and fifth, of the capacity of humans for good or evil, notwithstanding the fundamental goodness of human nature, and the commitment necessary for the cultivation of virtue. This summary of the arguments suggests a dry and unyielding text; the reality was far more readable. Drawing on the traditional arguments of Catholic theology – especially the thirteenth-century writings of Thomas Aquinas – Ricci made extensive use of vivid analogies in order to persuade his readers of the truth of these Christian positions. Thus Ricci's arguments for what in contemporary parlance we might call intelligent design are supported by a mountain of colourful examples:

If we observe birds and animals we find them to be basically stupid. Nevertheless, when they are hungry they know how to seek for food, and when thirsty, they know how to search for water. Afraid of arrows they flee into the blue depths of the sky, and alarmed by traps they hide in hills and marshes. Some eject food from their mouths and some kneel to suck, all for the purpose of self-preservation and rearing the young. They ward off evil and turn to that which is beneficial. In this they are no different from intelligent beings. There must be a Supreme Lord who secretly instructs them for them to be able to behave in this fashion. For example, if I see thousands upon thousands of arrows fly by me and each hits a target, even though I may not have seen a bow drawn, yet I recognise the fact that there must be skilled bowmen firing the arrows for them not to miss the target.[14]

From birds and arrows, he jumps to buildings:

If we look at a mansion we find that it is provided with doors in front to facilitate exit and entry. Behind are gardens in which are planted flowers and fruit trees. A hall is built centrally for the reception of guests, and rooms are placed to the left and to the right to serve as sleeping quarters. Columns are implanted below to support the beams in the roof, and thatch is placed above to keep out wind and rain. When all these things have been ordered harmoniously the master of the house can dwell securely within it. But if such a building is to be brought to completion, it must be built by a skilled artisan.[15]

Unsurprisingly, in the light of his mnemonic techniques, Ricci was skilful at invoking visual images in order to enliven and render memorable his arguments.

Equally dexterous were Ricci's appropriations of Chinese values to bolster the Christian cause. In a brilliant manoeuvre, the Jesuit tweaked Aristotelian theories of causation in order to imbue his claims for a Creator God with the concerns of a Chinese audience committed to ancestor worship:

When we come to discuss the manner whereby all things propagate themselves, we find that they are born from the womb, from eggs, or grow from seeds, and that none creates itself. Since wombs, eggs and seeds are themselves things, we must ask what first produced them so that they in turn could produce other things. We must trace every kind of thing back to its first ancestor; and since nothing is capable of producing itself, there must be Someone who is both original and unique who is the creator of every kind of thing and object. It is this One whom we term Lord of Heaven.

Not contented with his manipulation of the cult of ancestors in service to Christian theology, Ricci then laid claim to another ideological commonplace of the Chinese – the sole and undivided authority of the emperor over his people:

The things in this world are exceedingly numerous, and if there were no supreme lord to keep and maintain order among them, they would inevitably disperse and be destroyed. It is like a musical performance: even though the musicians might wish to make music, without a maestro, there would be no music. Therefore, each family has but one head, and each nation has but one sovereign. Should there be two, a nation will find itself in a state of anarchy. A man has only one body; a body has only one head. If it had two heads the man would be a freak. We know, therefore, that although there are many kinds of spiritual beings in the universe, there is only one Lord of Heaven who is the first creator of heaven and earth, mankind and all phenomena and who constantly controls and sustains them.[16]

The existence of a single God was as obvious as the need for monarchy.

The *Lord of Heaven* was a document of its times, belonging to a moment of profound debate and realignment in both European and Chinese contexts. The genre of the Catechism had first emerged in the early Christian Church – appropriately enough – as a mode of conversion, and an essential part of the instruction deemed necessary prior to baptism. It had flourished anew in the late Middle Ages, when the sacramental focus shifted from baptism to penance, and when Catechism was prescribed as a probe to the sinful conscience and as the required prelude to confession. In the era of Reformation and Counter-Reformation, Catechism took on renewed purpose in the battle for souls.[17] Luther and Calvin both contributed to the genre, and the Jesuits were soon renowned for their authorship of popular Catholic Catechisms. In particular, Peter Canisius (later canonised) was credited for turning back the tides of Protestantism in Germany with his so-called 'Small Catechism', first published in 1558, and revised, reprinted and translated innumerable times in the coming century. Ricci would have almost certainly been familiar with Canisius's work. In 1565, Juan de Polanco, Secretary to the Society of Jesus, reported in a circular letter that the Jesuits had had 3,000 copies of Canisius's Catechism printed on the presses of the Collegio Romano.[18] It is perhaps unsurprising, therefore, that Ricci's own Catechism – although produced thousands of miles away from the conflicts of the Reformation – should have been inflected with certain polemical views.

Thus the chapter on 'Motivation, Reward, and Punishment' is driven not only by the need to convince the Chinese of the existence of Heaven and Hell; it is also a reaffirmation of the Catholic doctrines of salvation and free will:

There is not a man who does not provide against the future and who does not consider things before they arise. The farmer ploughs and sows in spring, hoping for a harvest in the autumn. The pine tree grows for a hundred years before it produces any seeds, and yet men plant them . . . In his youth a scholar will labour diligently over his books so that his learning will be broad and penetrating and he will eventually be able to support his king and be of benefit to his nation.[19]

All these examples, carefully chosen for their accessibility to Chinese ears, were simultaneously designed to demonstrate the fallibility of Protestant teachings on predestination. Attempting to dispel the notion (horrific to a Catholic) of man's inability to earn God's favour, Ricci insists on the fundamental impulse to invest in one's future. Just as an examinee will labour over his books in the hope of one day gaining an important post in the administration of his country, so must mortals struggle to achieve good works in this world in order to attain salvation in the next.

The *Lord of Heaven* was equally attuned to contemporary debates in China, and the incipient protests of those literati who would soon be united within the so-called Donglin

Academy provide a crucial context for understanding Ricci's own vociferous condemnation of syncretism.[20] For on top of the positive messages of creation and salvation, brought to the Chinese by Ricci's Catechism, the whole text is over-laid with criticism of Buddhism, Daoism and – still worse – those ill-considered tendencies towards religious hybridity that threatened to muddy the clear waters of Confucianism. In the second chapter of the *Lord of Heaven*, Ricci set about dispelling 'heterodoxy' – as he straightforwardly called anything but the ancient doctrines of Confucianism – by means of reason. In this, he was confident that he carried the opinion of 'the superior men' of China with him. But while, in Ricci's view, Confucian books expressed a consist-ent animosity towards Buddhism and Daoism as barbarian and heretical, never before had anyone systematically tried to demonstrate the falsehood of their teachings (or so he claimed).[21] Ricci attempted therefore to lay bare the essential incompatibility of Buddhist and Daoist beliefs with those of Confucius, and argued that the 'nothing' of the Daoists and the 'voidness' of the Buddhists could in no way be fudged with the 'existence' and 'sincerity' of the Confucians.[22] As Ricci went on to claim, 'In the world of opposites there are no greater distinctions than those between emptiness and fullness and between existence and non-existence.' Not all Chinese scholars would have agreed with his bold procla-mations. Since the early sixteenth century, Wang Yangming (1472–1529) and his followers had introduced concepts and criteria from Daoist and Buddhist sources into their lec-tures and writings on Confucian works. But from the end of the century, there was a backlash against Buddhist idola-try and the syncretic trend, and intellectual practitioners of fusion were increasingly parodied as 'mad Zen'.[23] This was the bandwagon of criticism on which Ricci hoped to jump.

Within the internal world of Ricci's dialogue, the Chinese scholar was bowled over by the Westerner's arguments:

Your profound doctrine satisfies the ear and intoxicates the mind. I thought about it all night long and quite forgot to go to sleep.[24]

Perspicacious Teacher, in your discussion of the origin of things you have not only reached reality, but you have also clarified terminology ... I am ashamed that we Confucian scholars have not been able to see clearly the important matters in life ...[25]

Now that I have heard your brilliant exposition, any doubts that I had in the past have all been dispelled.[26]

But the voice of the Chinese scholar in Ricci's catechism found rare echo among the literati with whom the Jesuits actually conversed.

*

The figure who stands as the embodiment of the ideal convert, the 'Chinese scholar' of Ricci's dreams, is the Shanghai boy made good, Xu Guangqi (1562–1633): 'a grand literatus of Chinese letters and science, with a beautiful intellect and great natural virtue'.[27] Ricci was right to be proud, for Xu was immensely successful. He passed the *jinshi* exam in 1604, and subsequently became a member of the elite Hanlin Academy in Beijing. His ascent up the slippery pole of political power ended in his appointment to the post of Grand Secretary of the empire. Moreover, he was a committed intellectual and an avid publisher of new ideas. Xu was extremely receptive to European learning, and in particular to the Western concept of proof. He worked at Ricci's side translating works of Western science – notably Euclid's *Elements* – into Chinese. Following Ricci's death, Xu carved out a niche for the Jesuits in leading a reform of astronomical practice at the imperial court. True enough, in his own land, he was most renowned for his treatise on agriculture and for his renovation of the Chinese army, neither of which were obviously influenced by Western knowledge. Nevertheless, there was no doubting his friendship towards the Jesuits, and he was just the kind of friend that they sought. Finally, Xu Guangqi was a confirmed opponent of Buddhism and insisted – like Ricci – on a return to the pure and uncorrupted Confucian doctrines of the first three dynasties. Xu was baptised a Christian in 1603 and, assuming the classic name of the convert, was henceforth referred to by the Jesuits as 'dottor Paolo'.

Also fitting snugly into the Jesuits' mould was Li Zhizao (1565–1612), baptised in Beijing in 1610 just two months before Ricci's death. Li's relationship with Ricci derived from their shared love of learning. They first met in Beijing in 1601 when Li – having nurtured a keen interest in cartography since his youth – was impressed by Ricci's map of the world. The two men would later collaborate on several of Ricci's 'translations', particularly during the period 1606–8, when Li had time to kill, having been disgraced at court and forced to retire to his home town of Hangzhou in Zhejiang province. On the basis of what he had learned from Ricci, Li composed Chinese versions of Clavius's works on *Arithmetic*, the *Sphere* and *Astrolabe*, and the *Isopometric Figures* (the last produced during the space of ten days in 1608).[28] Won over by its anti-Buddhist stance, Li wrote a preface to the new edition of Ricci's *The True Meaning of the Lord of Heaven* in 1607. Despite his attraction to Christianity, Li's baptism was delayed on account of a 'certain impediment':

He is very well instructed in matters of our Holy Faith and stood ready to be baptised if the Fathers had not discovered the impediment of polygamy, which he promises to rid from his house. But he holds our Holy Religion to be true and thus he preaches and exhorts others to adopt it, as if he were a Christian. Already many members of his household have received holy baptism, and they are among the best Christians of all.[29]

Quite how the problem of the concubine was resolved (and whether or not there were children at stake) is undocumented, though we know that Li would later advise another would-be convert to abandon his concubine.[30] Back in Beijing, in 1610, Li became very sick and, since he was far from his family, Ricci nursed him day and night over a number of weeks. When the illness threatened to take Li's life, Ricci urged him to accept the faith. He was baptised, taking the name of 'Leone' and donating 100 taels of silver to the Church in Beijing. While Li soon recovered from his sickness, Ricci was dead by May of that year.[31]

Xu and Li – together with Yang Tingyun (1557–1627), another literatus convert from Hangzhou, baptised shortly after Ricci's death – have become known as the 'Three Pillars of Christianity in China'.[32] Their conversions not only brought the Jesuits influence in high places; they also constituted a propaganda coup, to be broadcast throughout China and Europe. Unsurprisingly, Xu, Li and Yang are given full hagiographical coverage in Ricci's *History*, and are ostentatiously paraded in later Jesuit accounts of the mission. But their prominence in the historical record should not blind us to their numerical insignificance in terms of the Jesuits' chalkboard of converts.

Of the two thousand Chinese baptised during Ricci's lifetime, only a tiny handful matched the profile of Xu Guangqi and Li Zhizao. The Jesuits were acutely aware of their failings in this respect. In 1586, writing from Zhaoqing, Ricci complained that although there had been forty baptisms, 'we have not yet converted to Christianity a single person of serious consequence' (with the possible exception of the elderly father of a local magistrate); this despite the fact that Ricci had made numerous friends and contacts among the local literati.[33] Instead of the learned Confucians sought out by Ricci (whose moral premises could, he believed, be readily assimilated in a Christian context), the majority of the Jesuits' converts were uneducated people heavily freighted with the 'idolatrous' customs of Buddhism. This irked Ricci, who always stressed that, according to his tripartite categorisation of Chinese religion into Buddhism, Daoism and Confucianism, the last was the one that the Jesuits should aim to accommodate. Indeed, the *Lord of Heaven* was founded on what has been termed a 'dualistic paradigm', which – beyond vague criticism – had little to say about Daoism, and which pitted Confucianism against Buddhism. According to this model, a purified Confucian version of 'theological legitimacy' was distilled from and juxtaposed against its opposite – what one sinologist has referred to as a 'dystopian vision of spiritual dissolution and chaos' in the form of Buddhist practices and beliefs.[34] This dualism is reflected in Ricci's recycling of the classical terms 'Pythagoreans' and 'Epicureans' to describe Buddhists and Confucians.[35]

In the fifth chapter of the *Lord of Heaven*, Ricci offers a comprehensive condemnation of 'followers of Pythagoras'. Firstly, he writes off their belief in reincarnation, on the grounds that if one had been a bird or a beast in a former life, one really ought to be able to remember one's prior existence.[36] Next, he asserts that it is 'obvious' that animals have a different kind of soul from humans, and that the attempts of Buddhists to claim that 'the souls of birds and beasts are intelligent just as men's are' is simply 'too irrational for words'. On the other hand, he maintains that 'there is no evidence' for the Buddhist belief that human souls are transformed into animals.[37] This rejection of reincarnation then leads him into an attack on vegetarians, who scruple to take the life of animals 'lest the oxen and horses they slaughter are later incarnations of their parents', and yet – quite inconsistently – are willing to subject the same beasts to hard labour in the fields.[38] What way was that to treat one's ancestors? Buddhist dietary principles were in any case found by Ricci to be illogical in their execution, since 'we find that they only refrain from killing living creatures when they fast and abstain on the first and fifteenth of the month' (though, in reality, the Jesuit knew of several Chinese vegetarians who were far stricter in their habits). According to Ricci, this was 'like a person who kills people daily and devours their flesh, but who then, wishing to join the camp of the compassionate, says: "I shall refrain from killing and eating people on the first and fifteenth of the month."' Furthermore, it was clear to the Jesuit that God had made animals for the comfort and use of humans:

Birds and animals have feathers, fur, and hides which can be used to make winter clothing and shoes; they have ivory tusks from which can be made wonderful utensils or which can be used as marvellous medicines to cure sickness. Then, there are some animals with excellent flavours which can serve to nurture both old and young. Why should we not select what we want from among them and make use of them? If the Lord of Heaven does not permit men to kill animals for food, has he not endowed them with excellent flavours to no avail?[39]

Added to the failure to distinguish between men and beasts, the Buddhists were also guilty of making a false distinction between animals and plants. In Ricci's view, if they objected to eating animal flesh, then they should also abstain from consuming fruit and vegetables:

You say that grass and trees have no blood because you are only aware of red blood. You do not know whether what is white or green might not after all be blood . . . Why must it always be red? If you try to observe prawns, crabs, and the like in water, you will find that many of them do not have red blood, yet Buddhists refrain from eating them. Some vegetables, on the other hand, do have red liquid within them, yet Buddhists do not prohibit the eating of them. Why should [the Buddhists] assign such importance to the blood of animals and pay so little heed to the blood of grass and trees?[40]

Ricci's arguments against Buddhist doctrines and in particular their dietary laws are among the weakest in the Catechism. His repeated reliance on 'common sense' – despite his advanced awareness that what is deemed 'obvious' in one culture may seem improbable in another – suggests a determination to talk away the opposition rather than to engage it in rational debate. After all, elsewhere in *The Lord of Heaven*, when defending Christian doctrines, Ricci often resorted to notions of wonder, invisibility and inexplicability: 'If it were easy for man to understand Him He would not be the Lord of Heaven.'[41]

Whatever the quality of Ricci's arguments, there is no doubting the passion with which he hated a Buddhist vegetarian. This was unfortunate to say the least, as one realises when one considers the identities of those who converted to Christianity.[42] Take 'Gioseppe', a prosperous merchant in Shaozhou, who presided over a household of thirty to forty people, and who was baptised in 1591; renowned among his own community for his saintliness, he ate 'neither meat nor fish nor eggs nor anything similar, but subsisted on leaves and vegetables and other things of the kind'. Gioseppe possessed some regrettable misapprehensions about Christianity, and his conversion led him to behave in ways that the Jesuits could scarcely condone:

He was persuaded that becoming a Christian meant leaving the world and adopting the hermit's life, relinquishing the things of this world, as he has done, leaving his wife and all the traffic of his house, and only attending to matters of his [spiritual] health.[43]

Gioseppe was not alone among the neophytes in his extreme and – in the eyes of the Jesuits – misguided approach to religion. Writing from Zhaoqing in 1585, in one of his earliest pronouncements on the nature of the Chinese converts, Ricci noted that there had thus far been twelve baptisms, the majority of whom were 'men of penitence, who fast in the manner of the Chinese, that is who eat neither meat nor fish'.[44] Later accounts of conversion were accompanied by descriptions of the ritual destruction of images, and confirmed that the neophytes came from the ranks not of the literati but of those idolatrous Buddhists whom Ricci had for so long claimed to despise.[45] In truth, there were many points of parallel between Buddhism and Christianity, aside from their shared commitment to celibacy. Both religions had a foreign origin, and a formal priesthood who took monastic vows, wore robes and engaged in ceremonial chants. Both observed a liturgical calendar, and made use of a variety of spiritual accessories including incense, images and relics. While differing in the particulars, Buddhists and Christians were united in believing in an afterlife. Both were committed to the virtues of charity, compassion and the suppression of the passions.[46] When the Jesuits arrived in China, it seems that Buddhist 'men of penitence' were attracted to Christianity because it appeared to chime with their ascetic lifestyle. But the Jesuits wanted their converts to be placed at the centre of secular affairs; they did not wish them to retreat from the world.

Their religious backgrounds aside, the majority of neophytes enjoyed little of the education and status of Xu and

Li. Ricci's letter of 1607 sent to Acquaviva provides an exceptional amount of data on the conversion of 'ordinary' people. It was the first letter that Ricci had been able to send to Rome in two years, since no boats had left China for India during that period. And it included news not just of the Beijing mission but also of the other Jesuit residences of Nanchang and Nanjing (based on reports filed by Ricci's colleagues Gasparo Ferreira and Diego de Pantoja), plus an account of a rural mission to Beijing's hinterland. Thus we learn that in Nanchang, during 1606, 33 Chinese were baptised, with a further 182 baptisms in 1607; in Nanjing, there were 96 baptisms, and in Beijing, 36 (excluding the foundlings who were periodically left at the Jesuit residence, and cared for by Ricci and his colleagues); in the rural area around Beijing, Ferreira and Pantoja had baptised 142. We also gain a more concrete sense of the social identity of at least some of the converts. For example, from Nanjing, we hear of 'more than twenty boatmen', who – after learning of Christianity from one of their passengers – often stayed all night at the Jesuit residence in order to study Christian doctrine.[47] Or the pious carpenter who showed steadfastness in his faith, despite being persecuted for it by his fellow artisans.[48]

So craftsmen and manual labourers were prominent among the Jesuits' followers. But there is another, more unexpected group: a remarkable number of *female* converts, of which our Nanchang mother is just one conspicuous example. Having been so glaringly absent from Ricci's narrative (let alone his pronouncements on mission policy) until the closing years of his life, women are suddenly ubiquitous. A neophyte woman named Elena shuns the devil, and rebuffs his repeated torments. Maria, wife of prominent Nanchang Christian Pietro, insists on seeking Christian instruction and baptism, despite the disapproval of her neighbours. A mother has her sickly children christened. A female convert drives out demons from a neighbour's house. Another – baptised without the permission of her husband – endures cruelty and beatings, but remains faithful to Christianity and a dutiful wife.[49] Here, we see the fledgling faith nurtured not at the banquets of literati, but in the female domain of the home. Ricci told Acquaviva that he himself took responsibility for teaching Christian doctrine to women, provided that they were married and of appropriate age.[50] And yet, for all they exemplify that classic Stoic virtue of constancy that was fundamental to the survival of the religious minority, these women are scarcely remembered in subsequent retellings of the Jesuit history, let alone trumpeted as the 'pillars of Chinese Christianity'.

If the majority of converts failed to conform to Ricci's blueprint as laid out in his letter to Pasio, the circumstances in which they adopted Christianity also diverged from the Jesuits' favoured model. The bulk of Ricci's 1607 letter to Acquaviva is taken up with a series of marvellous tales, in which Christian converts experienced miracles, and Gentiles were provoked to convert after witnessing miraculous events. Perilously sick children, including victims of a smallpox epidemic, were healed by the waters of baptism. A blind man had his sight miraculously restored to him after the removal of idols from his home and his subsequent baptism. Victims of possession were liberated from their demons when their idols were replaced by Christian images. A sick man was brought back from the brink of death when his wife sprinkled him with holy water, turfed out the idols, and promised that both she and he would convert. A Christian man falsely accused of homicide was found innocent. Similarly providential were the stories of divine punishment. We hear of a blasphemer who was blinded and an idolator stricken with illness. Or of divine mercy, as when God answered the appeal of Chinese Christians and cured a sinful man of tuberculosis. Each of the tales clearly carried a strong didactic message, which was written on the bodies of the protagonists. While the bodies of Christians were seen to enjoy the protection of God, those of idolators were racked and tormented. Baptism was shown to heal as well as to save. Put simply, conversion was not only the prerequisite of salvation; it was also the route to a healthier, happier life.

Ricci spoke of these events as 'marvels' and 'miracles' (*meraviglie* and *miracoli* in Italian), and he informed his superiors back in Rome of the value of these tales to the reputation of the Jesuits in China; on more than one occasion, he mentioned that news of a miracle had been 'publicised throughout the city with no small increase in credit to the law of God'.[51] All of this was to the Jesuits evidence of the providential course of the mission: 'God goes about helping this work, as he is accustomed to help the things that are dear to Him, on occasion granting miracles.'[52] In particular, miraculous episodes involving a cross or crucifix seemed to indicate 'the very special help afforded to the new Christianity by Our Lord'. A formulaic example followed on from this statement: 'A Christian man and his son fell ill with a third-degree fever; the man sent to ask Father Ricci for an image of the Holy Cross, and having received it with great devotion, both father and son were immediately cured.'[53] But Christ's image could play a more subtle role in expediting miracles. When the Saviour appeared to unconverted Chinese – for example, the pagan boy remembered as 'Michele of the thunderbolt', who was saved from death after being struck by lightning – Ricci made a point of reporting that they recognised the Lord, for they had previously seen works of religious art depicting him.[54] Images of Christ are pivotal in the accounts of conversion provided by Ricci: thus, our pregnant woman's husband prayed in front of a picture of the Saviour; the wrongfully accused man derived consolation from his image of the Saviour; the babies with smallpox were baptised at a makeshift altar, on which was placed an image of the Saviour, and after liberating a woman from possession and converting her, the Christians placed 'uno Giesù' (probably depicted as a baby) in her home.[55] It is clear that pictures and three-dimensional representations – presumably distributed by the Jesuits as cheap prints or ivory statuettes – were central to the devotional lives of the Chinese neophytes. With evident satisfaction, Ricci observed, 'There is no one who does not have in their house the image of the Saviour, and many keep by it a lamp lit day and night.'[56]

Just as powerful was the image of the Virgin Mary. The fervent carpenter, persecuted by his colleagues, said that he would rather they tore him to pieces than force him to burn his Madonna. Back in Zhaoqing in 1586, Ricci had recounted the narrative of the wife of the *lingxi dao*, who – after a history of fertility problems – gave birth first to a baby girl in 1584, and then 'with great happiness' to a male heir two years later. The providential pregnancies were accounted for by the Jesuits as the result both of their prayers, and of the intervention of the Madonna, the priests having given the woman an image of Mary that she venerated enthusiastically. Local women were equally convinced that a miracle had been wrought:

And thus it was that a rumour spread through the city that Our Lord had given her a son. And many sterile women came to the house of a Christian man to whom we had given an image of the Madonna, in order to adore her and to ask her for a son.[57]

And so we are led to picture Ricci and his friends focusing their campaign on a female audience, addressing the particular needs and anxieties of women, and drawing on the power of images and miracles in order to persuade them of the truth of the Christian message. Once again, we have drifted far from the Jesuits' stated aim of targeting the literati by means of 'reason, books, and science'.

*

These miraculous tales, rooted in Chinese soil, were typical of Catholic belief in early modern Europe – in the distant western lands that Matteo Ricci and his Jesuit colleagues had left behind. There, when a man feared for the safety of his wife, when the wise women and medics had failed, he could turn to Christ, the Virgin and other saints. (Or rather, as historians of 'medical pluralism' have taught us, he would probably pull out all the stops at once, combining the medical and the spiritual, often in a variety of forms.)[58] He looked to God and his intermediaries for a result, and when he got it he gave thanks. This was a religion of credits and debits, of favours exchanged.[59] And the expectations of the Catholic faithful that their requests might have automatic efficacy, or that they could do a deal with God, pervaded the religious culture that so profoundly offended Protestant reformers.

Spurred on by Protestant disapproval, early modern Catholics vaunted their miracles in countless representations, both verbal and visual. *Ex votos*, pieces of artwork commissioned in gratitude for miracles wrought, could take many forms: sailors whose boats had been spared during a storm might donate a model ship to hang in their church's nave, while wax models of body parts were used to commemorate the divine forestalling of corporeal afflictions. A particularly rich collection of *ex votos* is preserved in the museum of the Basilica at Tolentino, in the Italian Marches, Ricci's homeland. Although this includes some three-dimensional artefacts, the majority of the representations are paintings on wooden board: small, cheap and engagingly simple. Many depict women, kneeling by their cribs, clutching their rosaries or crucifixes and praying to their local saint, St Nicholas, to heal their ailing infants. But there are fathers as well as mothers, their faces racked with anxiety, keeping watch by the sickbed, waiting desperately for saintly intervention. More dramatic scenes are also conveyed: a young man caught up in a wool-winder; a woman falling out of a first-floor window; a bride possessed by the devil; a girl witnessing her father being attacked by armed brigands; fires, shipwrecks and accidents in the workplace involving boiling water or dropped tools.

Such images reminded Catholics of the steps they must take in order to set their disordered world aright. Theirs was a religion that provided numerous rituals and props that could be employed in times of crisis. It was a type of devotion with which Ricci would have been utterly familiar. His home town of Macerata stood roughly midway between Tolentino and the far more famous pilgrimage destination of Loreto, resting place of the Virgin's house, which had flown under the direction of Christ and a team of angels from Nazareth to central Italy in the thirteenth century, in order to save it from destruction by Muslim invaders. The Holy House still stands there today, at the centre of a vast and beautiful fifteenth- and sixteenth-century complex. From the Piazza della Madonna, designed by the architect Bramante, one enters the basilica, in the centre of which stands the House itself. Modest and brick-built inside, the Virgin's apartments are enclosed by an exquisite sculpted husk of marble. This miraculous building continues to draw the faithful in search of miracles. Chartered trains bring the sick on three-day missions of hope. The site teems with wheelchairs.

The Jesuits were already big in Loreto by the mid-sixteenth century. This was, indeed, one of the factors that prompted them to set up a college in nearby Macerata in 1561.[60] Here, in the same year, the young Matteo Ricci would commence his schooling; later Alessandro Valignano would spend a year as Rector of the college, before he was appointed Visitor to the Far East in 1573. Ricci was not the only Macerata boy to end up in East Asia. Among his compatriots, Oliviero Toscanelli accompanied Valignano in 1573, and was appointed Master of the elementary school in Macao in 1592; Giulio Piani, who served as Valignano's secretary, played a key role in the baptism of 12,000 people in Japan in 1577, while Giulio Mancinelli became Rector of the College of Macao in 1589.[61] Years later, Ricci would remember his holy homeland with pride. Writing in 1599 to Girolamo Costa (another Maceratese who was by now Procurator General of the order), Ricci told him, 'Sometimes I boast to these barbarians that I come from the land where Christ Our Lord transported the house that his mother had in this world, many miles away. And they are stunned when I tell them these and other marvels that God has made happen in these western lands.'[62]

Miracles belonged to the Europe that Ricci and his colleagues had left behind, but they also belonged to China. The similarities between European and Chinese concepts of the miraculous struck Michele Ruggieri and his Portuguese colleague António de Almeida forcefully during their travels in southern China in 1586. Visiting a temple near Nanjing, Ruggieri observed, 'Inside this church there hung many tablets on which miracles were recorded; there were also eyes and feet modelled in wax, silver and gold, as one sees in the famous houses of the Madonna in our Europe.'[63] He might well have been thinking specifically of Loreto.

Of course, one might wonder if Ruggieri was misreading the evidence before him and, in the spirit of European travellers throughout the world, desperately familiarising the exotic.[64] (After all, according to Jesuit commentators, Nanxiong and Nanchang were readily comparable to Florence, Suzhou and Shaoxing scarcely distinguishable from Venice.)[65] But, on this occasion, the Jesuit's comments are backed by Chinese evidence for the presence in late Ming temples of 'votive tablets' – inscribed plaques given by grateful believers – as well as a variety of figures or objects usually made of plaster or paper, left as testimony of prayers made and prayers answered. In her magisterial study of the temples of Beijing, Susan Naquin lists among the votive objects to be found in them baby shoes, silk painted with eyes, figures of babies or dogs (before a god that cured dog illnesses). According to Naquin, 'The active presence of a God was indicated not merely by prayers answered but also by miraculous events.' Some temples and their images had survived disastrous fires or floods. One temple had pillars in the Buddha hall that repainted themselves! The bitter water in the well of a courtyard of another temple had suddenly become wonderfully drinkable. There were temples with healing objects, for example, basins in which you could bathe your eyes and be cured of eye disease.[66]

We can add to Naquin's evidence from city temples that from Chinese pilgrimage sites, such as the Buddhist monastery at Nanhua, visited by Ricci in 1589. Such shrines were the locales for numerous apparitions and miracles, chronicled and publicised in gazetteers.[67] The eighteenth-century chronicler of Wudang shan, the mountainous site of a Daoist complex erected in the early fifteenth century, recorded that two years after the publication of his 'mountain monograph' – a guide to the pilgrimage site – 'I was blessed with the birth of a boy'; he further affirmed that 'every generation has transmitted tales of divine miracles'.[68] In the Daoist mind, miracles were associated with alchemy. When Ricci and Almeida arrived in Shaozhou in 1589, they were deluged by visitors 'on account of the fame of the miracles that the people had heard that we performed in Zhaoqing' and of 'the ability' that Ricci was thought to have in 'making silver'.[69]

So there were miraculous strands in both Buddhist and Daoist beliefs, and given the essentially syncretic nature of Chinese religion it is plausible that people were willing to accommodate marvels wrought by the Christian God within their repertoire of miraculous solutions. Chinese beliefs in divination and in demons, in alchemy and in supernatural healing, and their votive practices at shrines and temples meant that European-style miracles were easily assimilated. They transcended language barriers and they built bridges between cultures. They appealed not so much to the successful in life – to the literati whom Ricci courted – as to the vulnerable. And yet this powerful aspect of the Jesuits' religion, so pivotal to those Chinese who converted, is conspicuously absent from *The Lord of Heaven*.

*

In Ricci's Catechism, Chinese religion was misrepresented in myriad ways, the most significant distortions being the superimposition of a personal god on the impersonal 'supreme Heaven', venerated by Confucians, and the insistence on a pure and original body of doctrine in the context of a belief system that was – for all the Jesuits disliked it –

fundamentally fluid and syncretic. The Christianity depicted in Ricci's Catechism was equally warped, and while the
censors in Macao were prepared to give it their blessing, it
is unlikely that it would ever have passed the scrutiny of
the Inquisition in Rome. For while we have focused on the
religious truths propounded by Ricci in *The Lord of Heaven*,
we have thus far ignored the extraordinary omissions. These
relate principally to the account – dashed off in a meagre
paragraph of the final chapter – of Christ's life and death:

One thousand six hundred and three years ago, in the year *geng-
shen*, in the second year after Emperor Ai of the Han dynasty
adopted the reign title Yuanshou, on the third day following the
winter solstice, He selected a chaste woman who had never experienced sexual intercourse to be His mother, became incarnate
within her and was born. His name was Jesus, the meaning of
which is 'the one who saves the world'. He established His own
teachings and taught for thirty-three years in the West. He then
reascended to Heaven. These were concrete actions of the Lord
of Heaven.[70]

Amazingly, Ricci glosses over the nature of the death of
Christ. Perhaps put off by the reaction of the eunuch Ma
Tang to finding a crucifix in his luggage, or fearful of reviv-
ing memories of the crucifixion of twenty-six Christians,
including three Jesuits, in Nagasaki in 1597, Ricci decided
quite simply to write Christ's execution on the cross out
of the story. And with the Crucifixion gone, he also elimi-
nates the Last Supper. But what on earth were neophytes
to make of the Eucharist, if they were not allowed to know
how Christ had died?

We are reminded of Valignano's request to Rome to send
pictures 'of happy things, not of martyrs, wars, nor of the
mysteries of the Passion, since these do not serve the Chinese'. But the Jesuits' less than ingenuous approach to the

portrayal of Christian doctrine and its relationship to Chinese beliefs would come back to haunt the mission after Ricci's death. Reactions to *The Lord of Heaven* in the decades after it was published have been skilfully reconstructed by the sinologist Jacques Gernet. Using sources such as the *Poxie ji* or *Collection for the Destruction of Vicious Doctrines*, published in its complete eight-volume version in 1639, he reveals the extent of the disgust experienced by Chinese intellectuals on discovering the 'deceptions' that Ricci had wrought on them. The copious examples garnered by Gernet focus on exactly the three 'misrepresentations' identified above. Firstly, the sleight of hand whereby Ricci attempts to conflate the Christian 'Lord of Heaven' with the Confucian reverence for 'Heaven' itself. Here Zhang Chao, who was a friend and collaborator of various prominent Jesuits in the latter seventeenth century, nonetheless voiced significant reservations regarding their doctrines:

These people are extremely intelligent. Their studies concern astronomy, the calendar, medicine and mathematics; their customs are compounded of loyalty, good faith, constancy and integrity; their skill is wonderful. They truly have the means to win minds . . . The only trouble is that it is a pity that they speak of a Master of Heaven, an incorrect and distasteful term which leads them into nonsense which our men of letters have the greatest difficulty in accepting. If only they could leave [that idea] alone and not talk about it, they would be very close to our own Confucianism . . . Our Confucianism has never held that Heaven had a mother or a bodily form, and it has never spoken of events that are supposed to have occurred before and after his birth. Is it not true that herein lies the difference between our Confucianism and their doctrine?[71]

Secondly, we encounter a cynicism regarding Ricci's strategy of exalting Confucianism at the expense of Buddhism and Daoism. For example, Wang Qiyuan, writing in 1623, observed:

The Barbarians began by attacking Buddhism. Next, they attacked Daoism, next the later Confucianism [*houru*, i.e. neo-Confucianism]. If they have not yet attacked Confucius, that is because they wish to remain on good terms with the literate elite and the mandarins, in order to spread their doctrine. But they are simply chafing at the bit in secret, and have not yet declared themselves.[72]

Thirdly, there comes the realisation of the truth of Christ's ignominious death. This was the result, in part, of the different evangelical approach adopted by Ricci's successors. But Ricci's insistence on keeping silent about the Crucifixion was always bound to be a short-term strategy. In 1616, a lawsuit was brought against the Christians of Nanjing as a result of an anti-Christian movement led by the literatus Shen Que, who petitioned the Emperor with a raft of charges against the missionaries, including the fact that they were encouraging people to worship a criminal.[73] The priests were arrested and a proclamation was issued condemning Christian belief. Particular opprobrium was reserved for a work, entitled *Short Version of the Doctrine of the Master of Heaven*, that claimed that 'Yesu . . . died nailed by evil administrators to a structure in the form of a character that denotes ten.' With what 'audacity' did the Jesuits 'abuse the ears of the Emperor with such lying statements so contrary to propriety!' 'How could an executed barbarian convict be called the Master of Heaven?' A later commentator, Yang Guangxian, noticed the shift in Jesuit tactics:

In his books, Ricci took very good care not to speak of the lawful execution of Yesu. Thus all the literate elite have been deceived and duped. That is what makes Ricci a great criminal.

By contrast, Ricci's successor Adam Schall, based in Beijing from 1630 until his death in 1666, and – according to
Yang – 'less intelligent', had gone and spilled the beans.[74]
The case against Ricci and his colleagues is clear: by proceeding with characteristic 'caution and delicacy' in the first
instance, the Jesuits won influential friends. But, in the end,
their determination to obscure the fundamental teachings
of the Christian Church generated only confusion and war-
ranted accusations of deceit.

It is not the brief of this book to defend Ricci against
such attacks. On the contrary, in revealing the profound
disjuncture between the theory and practice of conversion,
a deep inconsistency in the history of the mission has been
brought to light. But evidence of conversion and of the
experiences of real Christians, in the capital and far beyond,
casts doubt on the assumption that the Jesuits were intending to hide the truth about Christ. If this had been the
case, how come the missionaries were distributing 'images
of the Saviour' wherever they went? On the ground, where
European priests interacted with the day-to-day realities of
human existence, it was possible to propound a far more
immediate and authentic version of the Lord of Heaven,
that transcended cultural boundaries and steered clear of
high-voltage claims for the compatibility of Chinese and
Christian ideas.

The final decade of Ricci's life witnessed two hugely
significant developments for the future of Christianity in China. The first was the publication and re-issue of
The True Meaning of the Lord of Heaven. The second was
an acceleration in the number of conversions, from around
100 in 1596 to 2500 by 1610.[75] It is a surprising fact that
these two occurrences bore so little relation to one another.
The tales of the miraculous that proliferated wherever the

Jesuits visited suggest a radically different account of why the conversions took place. Contrary to Ricci's insistence, ultimately conversion was not an intellectual matter, but an emotional response to human neediness. The Chinese neophytes craved a God who offered them support and consolation when they faced sickness, danger and pain; for them, this was the *true* meaning of the Lord of Heaven.

Conclusion: The Smell of Christianity

Among a series of edifying vignettes, written in an anonymous Jesuit hand shortly after the death of Ricci, we learn of a little old man from Shanghai who had converted to Christianity. As the priest records, the convert was marked by his simple piety, by his attachment to his Rosary, and by an unusual gift from God:

> He often recounted . . . how, whenever he prayed and wherever he happened to be, he could smell the odour of the church, and that when he went to hear Mass, it seemed that Our Lord wanted to console him with the smell of incense, so that he would not cease to offer Him the incense of his prayers.[1]

It is a telling story, suggesting at once the powerful sensory impact of the arrival of Christianity in China and the Jesuits' unease with that power. The tension reveals itself in the final twist of the account, the reference to 'the incense of his prayers'. The old man's curious olfactory experience is not simply to be celebrated as a marvel wrought by the grace of God; it has to be interpreted and controlled. The reader is reminded that incense is only an enhancement of, not a substitute for, Christian prayer. Any association between the rites of the Catholic Church and the incense-thick idol-worship of Buddhism is thereby discreetly denied. But how true was such an account to the convert's experience? For the old man, the impact on his senses was surely far removed from considerations of doctrine. Moreover, it was the commonalities (not the distinctions) between Buddhist and Catholic ways of doing religion (including their shared use of incense) that facilitated his embrace of the new faith.[2] The smell of Christianity was readily assimilable by a Chinese nose.

The Jesuit missionaries to China were at their most successful when they assailed the senses and worked on the emotions of the people they encountered. For all that the European priests insisted on the power of reason, books and science to convert the Chinese, we have repeatedly seen that non-verbal communication, by means of images, objects, healings and rituals, was the more effective way of bringing people to the font. This should not surprise us. Given the overwhelming demands of learning the Chinese language, it is understandable that the Jesuits would score highest when employing imagery and spectacle, and when tending directly to the material and physical needs of the people. Furthermore, the Jesuits were themselves rooted in a religious culture that was intensely sensory, emotive and theatrical. The sensuous appeal of Catholic religiosity was discussed most explicitly in relation to sight, and the use of visual images. Christians had been defending the use of images for many centuries. Most famously, at the start of the seventh century in an attack on the iconoclast Bishop Serenus of Marseilles, Gregory the Great extolled the value of pictures as 'the books of the unlettered'. Aquinas later elaborated the theme in a three-pronged argument. Church images were justified

first, for the instruction of the unlettered, who might learn from them as if from books; second, so that the mystery of the Incarnation and the exercises of the saints might remain more firmly in our memory by being daily represented to our eyes; and third to excite the emotions which are more effectively aroused by things seen than by things heard.[3]

The question of images was to come to the fore once again

during the Reformation conflicts of the sixteenth century, when the teachings of St Gregory and St Thomas would be reformulated in the decrees of the Council of Trent, emphasising the didactic function. However, to the young men who were gathering under the auspices of the newly formed Society of Jesus, it was Aquinas's last point that would prove especially relevant: the value of images lay in their ability to arouse the emotions.

Matteo Ricci and his colleagues were so doggedly cerebral in their approach to evangelisation that it is easy to forget that they belonged to an order whose trademark was emotive devotion. In the public domain, Jesuit preachers prided themselves on their ability to reduce audiences to tears.[4] Privately, meanwhile, members of the order and their lay followers were encouraged to subject themselves to a process of introspection that required them to call on the senses in order to excite their emotions. This they might achieve through 'imagination' – not just visual imagination but the mental invocation of *all* the senses with the aim of activating the emotions.[5] As an aid to this process, St Ignatius of Loyola, the founder of the order, developed a system of structured meditation, the *Spiritual Exercises*. His invitation to contemplate the horrors of Hell suggests just how that system was supposed to work. First, 'the exercitant' or practitioner of the *Exercises* is called on 'to look with the eyes of the imagination at the great fires and at the souls appearing to be in burning bodies'. Second, he or she is urged to 'hear with one's ears the wailings, howls, cries, blasphemies against Christ Our Lord and against all the saints'. The third challenge is 'to smell with the sense of smell the smoke, the burning sulphur, the cesspit and the rotting matter'. The fourth is 'to taste with the sense of taste bitter things, such as tears, sadness and the pangs of con-

science'. Finally, he or she must 'feel with the sense of touch
. . . how those in hell are licked around and burned with
the fires'. So, in invoking the smell of a Christian church
whenever he prayed, the old man of Shanghai was engaging
in a devotional exercise that was far from being unfamiliar
to the Jesuits.[6]

Only a tiny handful of converts is recorded as having
been guided through the *Spiritual Exercises* by Ricci; this
includes Qu Rukui, who was encouraged to pursue Ignatius's meditative programme as an antidote to his morbid
preoccupation with death.[7] It is notable that Ricci never
attempted to translate Ignatius's famous work into Chinese.[8] However, a far larger number of Chinese Christians
were to find their introduction to Ignatian piety in another
book – an illustrated aid to meditating on the life of Christ
by the Flemish Jesuit Jerome Nadal. The *Annotations and
Meditations on the Gospels* were the brainchild of Ignatius
himself, who shortly before his death in 1556 made Nadal
responsible for producing an illustrated aid to meditating on
the Gospels. Neither Ignatius nor Nadal (who died in 1580)
lived to see the end result; after a series of delays, due in part
to the conflicts that convulsed the Low Countries in the
latter half of the sixteenth century, the *Annotations* finally
made it into print in 1593–4. They consisted of two parts.
The first part was text: 595 pages of explanation about the
Gospels. The second part, separately entitled *Images of the
Gospel Story*, consisted of pictures: 153 exquisite plates, commissioned from the very best draughtsmen and engravers
in Europe, including the Wierix brothers. Each illustration
was marked with capital letters keyed to a legend at the foot
of the page, which directed the viewer's attention to the episodes on which they were to meditate.[9] As one art historian
has commented, the explanatory captions 'not only enlarge

the description of the various elements in the scene and call into play a range of purely theological associations'; they are also 'sensual and emotive'.[10]

Nadal's work was one of very few contemporary religious publications to make it to China, and Ricci was convinced of its evangelical value. In May 1605, he wrote from Beijing to his old friend Ludovico Maselli of how 'necessary' this book was to the mission. He explained how he had been in possession of a copy, but that it had been passed on to Manoel Diaz, the Superior of the southern mission, for use in the residences of Shaozhou, Nanchang and Nanjing. In return, Diaz had sent to Beijing a copy of Plantin's eight-volume polyglot Bible, 'another most necessary work'. Ricci asked Maselli to petition both Acquaviva and João Alvares, the Superior in charge of the Portuguese province, to send out at least one if not two more copies.[11] The matter was clearly on Ricci's mind, and a few days later, Ricci himself wrote directly to Alvares:

The book of the *Images* of Father Nadal has been kept by Father Manoel Diaz for use in his houses; I am writing to Father Lodovico Maselli to ask him to procure another for this house, since this book is even more useful for the present than the [Plantin] Bible. Because with the *Images* we clarify; in fact, we put before the eyes that which at times it is not possible to profess in words.[12]

It was a rare case of Ricci actually articulating what we have often seen to be the case. In the context of the China mission, images could speak louder than words.

Although Ricci lamented the fact that he had had to part with his copy of the *Images*, he was still in possession of some loose-leaf engravings, by the Wierix brothers and other artists whose work had featured prominently in the Nadal. When he was asked in 1605 by the wealthy merchant of ink-cakes Cheng Dayue to submit European illustrations to be reproduced in an album of wood engravings to be presented to the Emperor, Ricci leapt at the chance. *Master Cheng's Garden of Ink-Cakes* or the *Chengshi moyuan* was published the following year to considerable critical acclaim and, in contributing to the volume, Ricci had succeeded in finding a far wider audience for his Christian images than that afforded by one or two copies of the Nadal.[13] Moreover, this new venture provided opportunities for some tidy acts of accommodation, allowing Ricci to refashion both texts and images in order to concur with Chinese expectations and values. In Master Cheng's edition, Nadal's complicated glosses were streamlined, names and terms were Sinified, features of the Chinese land- and skyscape were incorporated, and the images were given a makeover to remove shading and to focus on the sharper lines prized by Chinese calligraphy. Best of all, Ricci got to choose the images that he would use. Predictably, he did not opt for any pictures relating to the suffering and Crucifixion of Christ, though these would be popularised by later Jesuits in China, notably in the 1630s and 1640s by Giulio Aleni.[14] Instead, Christ was depicted in proper manly roles, saving a friend from drowning ('The Apostle in the Waves') and engaged in conversation with his disciples ('The Way to Emmaus'). There was a Madonna and Child, since the image of Baby Jesus in his mother's arms had by now attained an iconographic respectability in China, and the cult of the Virgin was being actively encouraged through the creation of Marian confraternities.[15] Finally, Ricci included an image of 'Sodom's destruction'; in many ways, the discipline and authority of the Old Testament God was easier to present to a Chinese audience than the humility and vulnerability of Christ.

A deal of scholarly energy has been expended in analysing the ways in which Ricci manipulated the images that he used in the *Chengshi moyuan*. The pictures are pivotal to Jonathan Spence's innovative study, *The Memory Palace of Matteo Ricci*. And in a skilful piece of detective work, Spence has demonstrated that the first image, 'The Apostle in the Waves', fails to match the Bible story that it is supposed to illustrate. While the text, he points out, is an adaptation of Matthew 14, in which Christ invites his disciple Peter to join him in walking on water, the image published in the *Chengshi moyuan* shows Jesus with his two feet firmly on the ground, as he holds out a hand to Peter to pull him up to the shore. By cross-referring to Nadal, Spence is able to prove that the image used by Ricci here is actually an illustration of another Bible story, John 21, when Christ appears to his disciples after the Resurrection while they are fishing in the Sea of Galilee. The explanation given by Spence for the replacement of one image with another is simple. Ricci no longer had the Nadal volume at his disposal, so had to make do with the images that he had with him. These included a series of twenty-one Wierix engravings, starting with Christ's entry into Jerusalem and ending with the Ascension, from which the picture of 'The Apostle in the Waves' was taken. Of course, the text also had to be changed, with the reference to Christ's walking on water cunningly omitted. In Spence's translation, the text that appears in Master Cheng's volume reads as follows:

One day Boduoluo [the Chinese rendering of Pietro or Peter] was on a boat when he saw the distant outline of the Lord of Heaven standing on the seashore, so he said to him, 'If you are the Lord, bid me walk on the water and not sink.' The Lord so instructed him. But as he began to walk he saw the wild wind lashing up the waves, his heart filled with doubt, and he began to sink. The Lord reached out his hand to him, saying, 'Your faith is small, why did you doubt?'[16]

According to Spence, Ricci was forced to make a virtue of necessity. More recently, Carmen Guarino has suggested that the substitution was ideologically motivated. In her view, Ricci's eschewal of the miraculous narrative of Matthew's account was deliberate. In Chinese culture, she argues, miracles were for the masses; 'a Chinese man of letters would have scantly considered a salvation doctrine referring to prodigies'.[17] So the story of 'The Apostle in the Waves' had to be rewritten in a miracle-free version.

Guarino's interpretation echoes Ricci's elitist approach to mission and his determination to impose polarities on Chinese culture. Her clear division of popular and elite was exactly the sort of model that Ricci employed. He frequently established oppositions between Confucian and Buddhist, educated and common, scholar and monk, literatus and eunuch. And it is doubtless for this reason that miracles were sidelined in his accounts of mission strategy, although they were copiously recorded elsewhere in the *Letters* and his *History* of the mission. This was the difference, however, between theory and practice. The evidence presented in this book has shown not only that miracles were the principal factor leading Chinese people to Christianity, but also that the Jesuits' reputation for effecting supernatural interventions was by no means restricted to the common folk. Wherever Ricci and his colleagues travelled in China, they were sought out by literati in search of remedies for infertility or cures for sick relatives; others pleaded with the Jesuits to help them in their quest for the elixir of life and employed their services as exorcists.[18] We should not be surprised at these manifestations of elite vulnerability. Anxieties about death, disease and failure are human constants, and it is a function of religion to offer solace and succour to people in their hour of need. Not for nothing did Christ stretch out his hand to Peter. But this was not merely the support of one friend for another ('He who does not help a friend in need will have no one to help him when he finds himself in need'), and it was no ordinary friendship.[19] Even Ricci would not have wished to deny the supernatural dimensions of the New Testament story. Hence the caption to the image provided in the *Chengshi moyuan*: 'If you believe, you will walk on the sea, but if you doubt, you will sink.'[20]

One last marvel. When Ricci complained about the fact that he had parted company with the only copy of Nadal's *Images* to be had in China, he conceded that he had exchanged it for another 'very necessary' tome, the Plantin Bible. He later told João Alvares how the Bible had acquired an unexpected significance in the Beijing mission. It was a prestige item: eight folio volumes, gilded and lavishly bound, displaying the finest technology of Christopher Plantin's pioneering print workshop. Its unique selling point was to present parallel texts of the Bible in Hebrew, Latin, Greek, Syriac and Aramaic, a project that demanded the development of some extremely sophisticated new fonts and formatting techniques, and which resulted in a publication that was as beautiful as it was scholarly. The cost and effort of transporting these volumes from Europe to Macao must have been immense, and one can only imagine the despair of the Jesuits when, in the summer of 1604, freak flooding wrecked the boat that was carrying the Bible (along with a cargo of other necessities, including Communion wine) shortly before it reached Beijing. Amazingly, all was not lost. The Bible was well packed, and the box that contained it floated free of the wreck. Some Chinese sailors pulled it into their boat, and opened it up expectantly, presuming its contents to be valuable. But when they saw only incomprehensible books, they were disappointed, and offered to sell them back to the Jesuit lay brother from Macao who had been accompanying the cargo. Better still, being entirely ignorant of the value of the Bible, the sailors asked for a pittance in return. Only a little water had seeped into the box, and the Bible was scarcely damaged. As Ricci told Alvares, 'It seems that God wanted to console us and was listening to the prayers of Your Reverence; for I would have felt the loss of this Bible more than all the rest of the cargo.'[21]

The prodigious rescue of the Jesuits' Bible was not to be hidden under a bushel. On the contrary, the most public celebrations were organised to coincide with the August Feast of the Assumption. The Beijing church was apparently packed with the faithful and, after Mass, Ricci had the Bible carried in on boards. Censing the precious books, Ricci and his flock got down on their knees to pay homage. All gave double thanks to God, for having sent the Bible from afar, and for having recovered it from the waves and from the hands of Gentiles.[22] After this, reported Ricci, the Chinese often came to the Jesuit house to see the books, 'both in order to admire the printing and majesty of the volumes and to form an opinion of the beautiful doctrine that lay within it, even though they did not understand it'.[23] This was exactly the same sentiment as that expressed by Valignano seven years earlier, when he wrote his instructions on the gifts suitable for the Chinese Emperor. Concerning the acquisition of a New Testament, he advised that it was important to locate an exceptional manuscript with beautiful illumination and miniatures, but that if a suitable example could not be identified, a prayer book would do just as well. After all, the Chinese would not be able to understand what was written.[24] As logocentric as the Jesuits seemed, they were fully aware that the power of books lay not only in their words. A Bible could win over souls by its visual impact as well as by its teachings, and – in the case of Plantin's eight-volume wonder – the Chinese were 'stupefied' by such a beautiful book.[25] What is more, that impact could be ritually enhanced by the mystique of ceremony and by the scent of incense.

In the final years of Ricci's life, as the Jesuits attempted to turn their makeshift oratories into the first Christian churches in China, neophytes were transported into a strange new world of smells, sights and sounds.[26] There was the extraordinary buzz of Latin liturgy being mouthed by converts who – once again – did not understand the words, but realised their significance. And the sound of neophytes weeping as they recounted their sins.[27] There were the curious religious images that seemed to the Chinese 'to be sculpted, for they could not believe that they were drawn'.[28] The church had its own distinctive smell: a mixture perhaps of Chinese incense, European-style candles and the unfamiliar scent of Portuguese Communion wine. These were, in turn, the props to a completely new set of rituals. Not just the sacraments of communion, confession and baptism, but a whole calendar of feasts and ceremonies, as well as the veneration of certain books and images that defined one's identity as a Christian. And perhaps most significant in the life of a neophyte (and enthusiastically recorded in Ricci's narrative) there were the cleansing rituals of iconoclasm – the breakings and the burnings of the *wrong* books and images – that marked the departure from one faith and the admittance to another.[29]

In the conflict-ridden territories of Reformation Europe, the rituals of Catholicism were fundamental to the identity of the faithful. Under attack from Protestant reformers, who set up an opposition between the 'mere ritual' practised by

the Papists and the 'true religion' that was their own goal,
Catholics responded with outpourings of Eucharistic piety,
a growth in ceremonial confraternities and a proliferation
of local cults and processions.[30] But if we can describe the
Catholics of the early seventeenth century as belonging to
a ritual culture, the same can undoubtedly be said of the
Chinese of the late Ming. Theirs was a theatre state, complete with a Ministry of Rites, which oversaw and enforced
an elaborate paraphernalia of festivals, ceremonies and eti-
quettes.[31] As the anthropologist James Watson has commented, 'If anything is central to the creation and maintenance of a unified Chinese culture, it is the standardisation
of ritual.'[32] This shared heritage of ritual practices – and in
particular the practices surrounding key moments in the life
cycle – was the cultural foundation on which the Chinese
state was built. In this vast and ethnically diverse empire,
argues Watson, there was little attempt to regulate what
people believed. There was, in contrast with Christendom,
'no centralised hierarchy of specialists charged with responsibility of dispensing religious truth'. The emphasis was on
the enforcement of orthopraxy (correct practice) rather than
orthodoxy (correct belief), enabling state officials to incor-
porate people from different backgrounds and with varying
beliefs into an overarching social system.[33]

While the Jesuits stepped so carefully around the touchy
issues of Christian doctrine, they were at first slow to realise
that rituals could cause more problems than beliefs. They
energetically promoted their own practices, and reported
with pride when their converts adopted the rituals of a
good Christian death and burial, and eschewed 'Gentile
rites'.[34] But when in 1608 Ricci commented approvingly of
the funeral rites of the neophyte 'Fabio', that – according to
the dying man's express command – 'only those rites that

were not contrary to the Christian religion' were enacted, he could scarcely have anticipated the extent and consequences of the controversy that was to explode after his death.[35] Ricci's gloss on Fabio's funerary rites nodded in the direction of accommodation. The Jesuit was prepared to tolerate Confucian ancestral rites, including the practice of placing food on graves, because they did not collide directly with Christian belief. It was possible to interpret such gestures as secular rather than religious, and to elicit a didactic message from them: honouring one's parents was a doctrine shared by Chinese and Europeans.[36] But by the middle of the seventeenth century, the Jesuits were under attack, especially from their rivals in the mendicant orders who had embarked on their own programme of mission in China. The Jesuits' approach to indigenous rituals, especially those surrounding the dead, came under increasing scrutiny from Rome, and resulted in a series of decrees (in 1704, 1707, and 1715) banning Chinese rites, followed by a furious backlash from the Kangxi Emperor.[37] Missionaries were placed in an impossible position: either they could sign a patent agreeing to the authority of the Emperor in all matters relating to religion (and risk excommunication by the Pope) or they could remain loyal to Rome, and abandon the mission. With the ascent in 1723 of the new Emperor, Yongzheng, even that Hobson's choice – the last possibility of the mission – was rent from them. In the Sacred Edict of January 1724, Christianity was listed among the 'perverse sects and sinister doctrines', an indictment that led to the seizure of Jesuit buildings and the exile of priests. The Jesuit mission was to all intents and purposes over.[38]

The death of Matteo Ricci, when it came, was an elaborately choreographed affair, which exhibited both the distinctiveness of Christian practice and a talent for accommodation of the kind that failed so spectacularly during the Rites Controversy. Ricci predicted his own death when those around him assumed that he was merely suffering from a passing migraine. Lent 1610 had been an exceptionally demanding time for him. Beijing was swarming with candidates for the doctoral exam, and the influx of literati to the city made for many more visitors to the Jesuit residence than was usual. These learned visitors inevitably called during mealtime, interrupting what was in any case a meagre repast. (The Chinese found the European concept of fasting on fish and eggs laughably luxurious, so Ricci was limiting himself to rice and vegetables.) At the same time, Ricci was preoccupied by the illness of his close friend and collaborator Li Zhizao. And as if he didn't have enough on his mind, Ricci had since Christmas been overseeing the construction of a purpose-built church in Beijing. One day in May, Ricci took to his bed, informing his colleagues that 'This illness, caused by excessive over-work, will be fatal.'[39]

There was to be no rest for Ricci, even at the end of his extraordinarily busy life. His house in Beijing was crammed with stricken neophytes, wailing at the prospect of their spiritual father's imminent demise, and praying to God to extend Ricci's life at the expense of their own. Doctors came and went, leaving confusing and contradictory remedies. But from out of the chaos of the sickroom, Ricci reasserted ritual control. With enormous effort, the dying man pulled himself out of bed in preparation for receiving the Viaticum (the final Communion). On his knees, he prostrated himself and made the *Confiteor* or General Confession.

Then, during a most gentle conversation with the Lord, he wept profusely, spilling forth the sweetest tears that moved everyone who was present, both the neophytes and the servants of the house, and provoked them to similar tears of great devotion.[40]

In a state of delirium that lasted a day and a night, Ricci spoke of the new Christians, of the conversion of the Chinese, and of the Emperor. But the following day he regained his lucidity. He requested Extreme Unction, and he blessed the four other priests who were by his bedside. Having said a few words of encouragement for the future of the mission, he requested that a letter be sent, apologising to Pierre Coton, a controversial Jesuit preacher and writer at the court of Henri IV of France, for not having written to congratulate him on his work.[41] This final act of epistolary duty dispatched, Ricci was ready to go. Towards evening on 11 May 1610, 'propped up in bed, without any movement or contortion of the body, he surrendered his soul to God and, closing his eyes as if preparing to rest, he slept sweetly in the Lord'.[42]

It was a classic good death in the Christian tradition, or at least that is what the Jesuits who chronicled Ricci's last hours have led us to believe. But how would the next phase of the death rites be handled? In the immediate aftermath, conflict over the appropriate way to mourn for Ricci became apparent. The neophytes began to pour out their hearts in anguish at the parting of their beloved Father. The remaining Jesuit priests meanwhile imposed a 'brake' on their 'immoderate grieving'.[43] More welcome was the offer of the literatus Li Zhizao to purchase a high-quality casket in which Ricci's remains could be kept. Li's assurances that the corpse would not deteriorate while they awaited the construction of the coffin, for 'in the case of a man such as he, the normal laws of nature would not apply', turned out to be well founded. Although the body remained exposed for two whole days in the extreme heat, 'the face and lips retained their vivid colour, and he resembled a man more alive than dead'.[44] Ricci's case would never be brought to the canonisation courts of Rome, but his incorruptible flesh set him within the saintly league of the Catholic Church.[45]

Closed within the casket, the body was then taken into the church, where the funeral took place, with a celebration of the Mass and the Office of the Dead. Then Chinese custom took over, as the body was brought back to the home to be displayed on an altar where visiting friends could pay their respects. It was common for Chinese families to keep their dead relatives at home for a prolonged period, while they purchased and prepared a suitable burial site. For this reason, their coffins were of a very superior quality, lavishly coated with varnish. The point was to shut in the odours which, in Ricci's holy case, were not likely to be emitted: 'in such a way . . . bodies could be conserved for many years without emitting an evil smell'.[46] But perhaps it was better to be safe than sorry, for it took well over a year for Ricci's body to be returned to the earth. Months passed in furious bureaucracy, the Jesuits calling on every contact and playing every diplomatic card, until finally they were granted – by favour of the Wanli Emperor, no less – the temple and grounds belonging to a disgraced eunuch as the site of a Jesuit cemetery. For a foreigner to be accorded a burial site by the emperor was an extraordinary coup, which testified to the success not just of their immediate campaign but of nearly thirty years of careful networking and diplomacy.[47]

Before Ricci could be buried in this foreign soil, certain purifications would be necessary. The temple priest needed to be evicted, the site cleared of its copious idols.[48] To quash the eunuch's claims on his land, a lengthy lawsuit had to be fought and won. But the Jesuits' success was sealed by the arrival at the residence of an inscription sent by the Governor of Beijing to adorn Ricci's tomb, reading 'TO HE WHO

CAME TO CHINA, ATTRACTED BY OUR JUSTICE SYS-
TEM, AND TO THE AUTHOR OF SO MANY BOOKS'.[49] The
cemetery was at last ready, and Ricci's body was solemnly
transported, 'not with the usual pomp of the Chinese', but
accompanied by a procession of neophytes bearing candles
and following a Cross.[50] That well-varnished coffin was
deposited for the time being in the former temple, now the
newly appointed chapel of the would-be graveyard. Fortunately, it was already surrounded by cypress trees, emblems
of mourning in China as in Europe. The Jesuits were still
busy preparing a suitable burial plot within the grounds.
'God wished that he who had during his entire life attacked
idols should now, upon his death, be buried with them; the
cement for the construction of the tomb was deliberately
recycled from the broken shards of a gross idol.'[51] The other
idols that were torn from the altar were thrown on the fire
(if made of wood) or reduced to dust (if clay). They were
replaced by a painting of the Saviour surrounded by angels
and apostles.[52] The burial took place on the Feast of All
Saints, 1 November 1611.[53]

The interment of Ricci was the occasion for the most
subtle interplay of accommodation and aloofness. For every
element in it that demonstrated the superiority of Christianity to native 'idolatry' and superstition, there was another
that capitalised on chance overlaps, convenient coinciden-
ces could be exploited to win the Jesuits the favour of
their Chinese hosts. If the very materials out which Ricci's
tomb was made demonstrated the destruction of intolerable
blasphemies, the cypresses that grew around it suggested
that death could assume a familiar shape in the most distant lands. Ricci's gravestone, which survives today in a new
location (Beijing's Jesuit graveyard), is likewise an impressive amalgam of East and West, with its parallel Latin

and Chinese text incised in grey stone surmounted with a design of clouds and serpentine coils. Here again, the smell of Christianity was to the fore – Christian beliefs about the saint's incorruptible flesh rubbing up against the Chinese expectation that burial would be a long-delayed affair.[54]

The management of the rites surrounding Ricci's death was a success story, a matter for celebration in both Europe and China. As Nicholas Trigault, the Jesuit responsible for publicising Ricci's achievements in Europe after his death, commented:

Who will not marvel that these poor foreigners have obtained from the Emperor a house and an honorific tomb: a privilege that in this realm has never before been conceded to any foreigner, and moreover has only exceptionally been granted to the highest Chinese magistrates, the most worthy men of the country.[55]

For the rulers of China, Ricci was to become the acceptable face of the West. In the throes of the Rites Controversy, the Kangxi Emperor issued a series of edicts, lauding 'Ricci's ways'. Responding with fury and frustration to the 1715 Bull of Clement XI banning Chinese rites, Kangxi warned the missionaries, 'Again, I say, if you do not follow the rules of Ricci, the teaching preached for two hundred years in China will have to be discontinued; all the Westerners will have to leave.'[56] But if Ricci and his immediate colleagues are to be congratulated for their control of ritual, we should not fall into the trap of intellectualising a process that was to a large extent beyond reason.[57] We cannot reduce the tears of the Chinese Christians who stood by Ricci's grave on All Saints Day 1611 to Jesuit strategy.

Acknowledgments

I embarked on this book for childish reasons: I was ignorant, and I was curious. This is not how the academic historian normally proceeds. More often, she writes about what
she knows best, and new projects arise at the intersection of
several fields with which she is intimate. I am truly grateful
therefore to those institutions that have given me the freedom and the means to pursue my curiosity, and especially
to the Master and Fellows of Jesus College, for providing
me with such a supportive community in which to work.
'Community' is not a word that one can apply quite so readily to the Cambridge History Faculty, but I have learned
that there are wells of kindness to be tapped here too. I am
particularly indebted to those colleagues and administrative
staff who have supported me during the last few, busy years;
among these, Liz Partridge deserves special mention for her
perpetual helpfulness and forbearance.

I am glad of the opportunity to express my gratitude
to those many historians whose knowledge underpins my
book. The best thing about this project for me has been the
obligation to immerse myself in the social and cultural history of late Ming China. This is a thrilling field, populated
by extremely gifted scholars. Thanks to them, I have been
able to avoid reading the Jesuit mission through unremit-
tingly western eyes and have gained a much richer sense of
the world in which Ricci moved. I have also profited greatly
from personal contacts with scholars of China. In Beijing,
Professor Han Qi and his family gave hospitality, and much

helpful guidance on opportunities for Jesuit-related sight-seeing. Dr Sun Chengsheng, meanwhile, spent a whole day escorting me around those sights, and sharing with me his own deep knowledge of the Jesuit encounter with China. Back in Cambridge, Christopher Cullen, Catherine Jami and John Moffet welcomed me to the Needham Institute, Adam Chau treated me to a series of stimulating conversations, and Oliver Weingarten provided invaluable advice on the romanization of Chinese words. Thanks too to Chloë Starr and Judith Green, who supplied helpful references, and to Craig Clunas for his advice on images. I was very lucky indeed to run into Henrietta Harrison of the University of Harvard, who helped me to understand something of religion in China and whose own microhistorical study of a Catholic village in Shanxi from its establishment in the late seventeenth century to the twentieth century continues to inspire me. It is a particular pleasure to record my thanks to Joe McDermott, whose friendship is one of the many long-term assets I acquired during a Research Fellowship at St John's College, Cambridge. Looking back over the period of writing this book, I have the impression that Joe was running a 24-hour helpline to cater for my many queries and incomprehensions. I hope that's an illusion. But what is clear is that without Joe's reading lists, emails, phone calls, and consultations (these last memorable occasions being held amid many reference books in the Aoi Pavilion of the University Library), *this* book would not have been written. Needless to say, I take full responsibility for the errors that undoubtedly remain in it.

I have also been the beneficiary of much guidance from scholars in my own field of European history. Robert Goulding, Scott Mandelbrote and Francesca Trivellato all helped me to solve the riddle of the prisms; Julia Poole offered me expert advice on the present list. My friends and colleagues Tara Alberts, Peter Burke, Manuel Buttigieg, Melissa Calaresu, Nick Davidson, Filippo de Vivo, Simon Ditchfield, Michael Edwards, Rebecca Flemming, John-Paul Ghobrial, Robert Gordon, Deborah Howard, Larry Klein, Margaret Meserve, Simon Macdonald, William O'Reilly, Barbara Placido, Ulinka Rublack, and Jane Stevens-Crawshawe provided wise counsel and encouragement just when they were needed. In addition, Peter Garnsey, Peter Mandler, Brian Pullan and Lyndal Roper dropped what they were doing to read and comment incisively on drafts of the book at short notice. John Cornwell helped me to define the book at the outset, and has been reading versions of it ever since. I am grateful for the patience and courtesy of my editors at Faber, Walter Donohue and Kate Ward, and to my agent Clare Alexander for her wisdom and encouragement. In the run-up to completion, Alex Bamji, Mike O'Brien and Jason Scott-Warren gave my manuscript the sort of going-over that you can only expect from your best friends. As Ricci would have said: 'The end of friendship is none other than this: if the friend is superior to me, I imitate and learn from him; if I am superior, I improve him.' I know on which side of that equation I sit.

Over the last four years, I have had the opportunity to teach a 'Special Subject' on Matteo Ricci and the Jesuit Mission to China. This has been a delightful experience, and my students – undergraduate and graduate – have proved another significant force for my improvement. Constructive criticism and intellectual sustenance have also been drawn from seminars and conferences in Cambridge, London, Los Angeles, and Venice. I am not nearly so well-travelled as was Ricci, but my investigations have nevertheless taken me on some wonderful journeys, to Macerata, Macau, Canton, Zhaoqing, and Beijing. Thanks to Kit Fan for practical advice on getting to China, to Yves Camus for helping me find my way around the Macau Ricci Institute, and to the University of Cambridge and Jesus College for paying my fares. During two research trips to Rome, I was especially grateful for the help and efficiency of the Director and staff of the Archivum Romanum Societatis Iesu. In le Marche, Linda Lyne allowed us to invade her beautiful home and – together with Raphael, Clare, Thomas and Sophie – showed us a marvellous time.

As every academic parent knows: no childcare, no publications. So heartfelt thanks are due to Jennie Tegetmeier in York, and Elizabeth Wiggam and her staff at the Mrs Cameron (aka Caius) nursery in Cambridge, who have looked after our children with affection as well as expertise, and who have contributed greatly to our well-being too. Just as indispensable to our lives and to our work have been those unpaid heroes, Doreen Laven, and Celia and Anthony Scott Warren, who have held the fort on numerous occasions, including during two trips to China. I have exploited and relied upon our friends and relatives in more ways than I care to remember. But I can't forget that Stephen Siklos spent a week in the summer of 2009 sitting in the car-park of the Perse School while our (and his) boys participated in virtuous sporting activities. When I protested that it wasn't exactly fair that he should bear this burden single-handed, he told me that I needed the time in order to have 'aperçus'; how right he was. Most of all, for doing rather more than his fair share, thank you Jason.

Notes

INTRODUCTION: MAPPING THE WORLD

1 Sheet N-31-133 General Staff CAMBRIDGE 1: 10,000 (1989) *Secret*. Translated by Charles Aylmer for Soviet Military Maps Study Day, Cambridge University Library, 8 October 2005.

2 John Davies, 'Uncle Joe knew where you lived: The story of Soviet mapping of Britain (part 1)', *Sheetlines* 72 (April 2005), 26–31.

3 *Sheetlines* 73 (August 2005), 59–60.

4 John W. O'Malley, *The First Jesuits* (Cambridge, MA, 1993), 5–6.

5 O'Malley, *The First Jesuits*, 234, 54.

6 O'Malley, *The First Jesuits*, 67.

7 O'Malley, *The First Jesuits*, 73.

8 M. Antoni J. Üçerler, 'The Jesuit enterprise in sixteenth- and seventeenth-century Japan', in Thomas Worcester (ed.), *The Cambridge Companion to the Jesuits* (Cambridge, 2008), 153–68 (156).

9 Henry James Coleridge (ed.), *The Life and Letters of St Francis Xavier*, 2 vols (first published London, 1874; reprinted New Delhi, 1997), 568.

10 Marco Polo, *The travels of Marco Polo: the complete Yule-Cordier edition* (New York, 1993), 374–5, 390–91.

11 Anthony Grafton, *New Worlds, Ancient Texts: The Power of Tradition and the Shock of Discovery* (Cambridge MA, 1992), 70–73.

12 *Travels of Sir John Mandeville*, trans. C. W. R. D. Moseley (London, 1983), 140.

13 Eugene Rice and Anthony Grafton, *The Foundations of Early Modern Europe, 1460–1559*, 2nd edn (New York, 1994), 36.

14 C. R. Boxer, *The Portuguese Seaborne Empire* (London, 1969), 43.

15 Boxer, *The Portuguese Seaborne Empire*, 46–7.

16 Donald Lach, *Asia in the Making of Europe*, 3 vols (Chicago, 1965–93), 1, 731.

17 Clive Willis, *China and Macau* (Aldershot, 2002), 1–5.

18 Willis, *China and Macau*, 1.

19 Willis, *China and Macau*, 3.

20 Willis, *China and Macau*, 4.

21 Willis, *China and Macau*, 1–2.

22 Lach, *Asia in the Making of Europe*, 1, 735.

23 Rice and Grafton, *The Foundations of Early Modern Europe*, 38.

24 C. R. Boxer (ed.), *South China in the Sixteenth Century* (London, 1953), 261.

25 Lach, *Asia in the Making of Europe*, 1, 324.

26 Among those colleagues in the Society of Jesus who offered constructive advice and criticism to Maffei, and who attempted to direct his attention to reliable sources, was Matteo Ricci, *Lettere* (1580–1609), ed. Francesco D'Arelli (Macerata, 2001; hereafter *Lettere*), 21–5, 33–41.

27 O'Malley, *The First Jesuits*, 6.

28 O'Malley, *The First Jesuits*, 1.

29 Lach, *Asia in the Making of Europe*, 1, 315.

30 Lach, *Asia in the Making of Europe*, 1, 318–19.

31 Compare, for example, Ricci's comments on Nanjing (distinguished by its nobility, civility and healthfulness) and Shaozhou (marred by bad air, and annual epidemics), *Fonti ricciane*, 3 vols (Rome, 1942–9; hereafter *FR*), 1, 350 and 284.

32 For the pioneering role of Alessandro Valignano in allowing his evaluation of new territories to shape his mission policies, see M. Antoni J. Üçerler, 'Alessandro Valignano, Man, Missionary, and Writer', *Renaissance Studies* 17 (2003), 337–66 (352).

33 Üçerler, 'Alessandro Valignano', 353.

34 Üçerler, 'Alessandro Valignano', 354–5.

35 Üçerler, 'Alessandro Valignano', 357.

36 Üçerler, 'Alessandro Valignano', 364.

37 *FR* I, 91; Archivum Romanum Societatis Iesu, Jap. Sin. 101, Michele Ruggieri, 'Relaciones' (hereafter, 'Relaciones'), 16v.

38 *FR* II, 25.

39 *Lettere*, 172.

40 On the fundamental characteristics of the Jesuit mission, see Nicolas Standaert, 'Jesuits in China', in Worcester (ed.), *The Cambridge Companion to the Jesuits*, 169–185 (172–3).

41 O'Malley, *The First Jesuits*, 81–2.

42 The portrait was taken to Rome in 1614 by Nicholas Trigault, the Jesuit who also discovered, and published for the first time (in Latin) the manuscript of Ricci's full account of his mission to China. The painting is now conserved in the sacristy of the Gesù.

43 *Lettere*, 116. See 269 and 323 for similar claims made in later letters.

44 http://www.riccimac.org/eng/introduction/index.htm (last accessed 10 January 2010).

45 Jacques Gernet, *China and the Christian Impact: A Conflict of Cultures*, trans. Janet Lloyd (Cambridge, 1985), 45–6.

46 *Lettere*, 264.

47 For Ricci's complaint in 1585 that he had no books, apart from two astronomical works (by Clavius and Piccolomini), and for the arrival of an edition of Ortelius in 1608, see *Lettere*, 116 and 481.

48 Pasquale d'Elia, *Il mappamondo cinese del P. Matteo Ricci* (Città del Vaticano, 1938), 22, speculates that Ricci's map might have been one of one of the works of Ferdinando Vaz Dourado, published in Goa in 1568 or 1571.

49 *Lettere*, 160.

50 D'Elia, *Il mappamondo cinese*, 23–35. This first edition bore the title: 'Complete geographical map of the mountains and seas'. Wang Pan's complete title was *lingxi anchasi fushi* (see Henry Bernard, *Le père Matthieu Ricci et la societé chinoise de son temps* (1552–1610) (Tientsin, 1937), 106 and 121).

51 *Lettere*, 140.

52 This corresponds roughly to the copy now kept at the Vatican Library, each panel of which measures 1.79 by 0.69 metres; D'Elia, *Il mappamondo cinese*, 109.

Notes

53 D'Elia, *Il mappamondo cinese*, 37–84.

54 *Lettere*, 92, 103.

55 *Lettere*, 338.

56 D'Elia, *Il mappamondo cinese*, 185; Jonathan Spence, *The Memory Palace of Matteo Ricci* (London, 1984), 97.

57 Gernet, *China and the Christian Impact*, 46.

58 *Lettere*, 57–87.

59 *Lettere*, 57.

60 *Lettere*, 62.

61 J. N. Hillgarth, *The Spanish Kingdoms, 1250–1516*, 2 vols (Oxford, 1976–8); II, 472–4.

62 *FR* II, 549; A. Adversi et al. (eds), *Storia di Macerata*, 5 vols (Macerata, 1971–7); see especially II, 357–96, for biographical notes on Ricci; IV on the University; V on religion.

63 *Lettere*, 166. Among the three books that Ricci took with him to the Jesuit novice house of Sant'Andrea di Quirinale in Rome was a well-known pharmacopoeia by Pantaleone da Confienza; Adversi et al. (eds), *Storia di Macerata*, II, 359 and *Lettere*, 534.

64 Filippo de Vivo, *Information and Communication in Venice: Rethinking Early Modern Politics* (Oxford, 2007), 107; de Vivo, 'Pharmacies as centres of communication in early modern Venice', *Renaissance Studies* 21 (2007), 505–21; Evelyn Welch, *Shopping in the Renaissance: Consumer Cultures in Italy, 1400–1600* (Yale, 2005), 151–8; David Gentilcore, 'For the Protection of Those Who Have Both Shop and Home in this City: Relations between Italian Charlatans and Apothecaries', *Pharmacy in History*, 45 (2003), 3, 108–21 (111).

65 Among the work produced by Jesuits, the three-volume edition of *Fonti ricciane* (*FR*), foundational to all subsequent scholarship, must be singled out. Other important studies written or edited by Jesuits include George H. Dunne, *Generation of Giants: The Story of the Jesuits in China in the Last Decades of the Ming Dynasty* (Notre Dame, 1962); Nicolas Standaert (ed.), *Handbook of Christianity in China*, 2 vols (Leiden, 2000–2010), I; Charles Ronan and Bonnie Oh (eds), *East meets West: The Jesuits in China, 1582–1773* (Chicago, 1988). Publications by members of other religious orders include the seminal study by Johannes Bettray (a member of the missionary order founded in the nineteenth century, the Societas Verbi Divini), *Die Akkomodationsmethode des P. Matteo Ricci S.J. in China* (Rome, 1955) and Gianni Criveller (a member of the Pontifical Institute for Foreign Missions), *Preaching Christ in Late Ming China: The Jesuits' Presentation of Christ from Matteo Ricci to Giulio Aleni* (Taipei, 1997). Accounts of Ricci's mission written by lay authors include Vincent Cronin, *Wise Man from the West* (London, 1955), Jonathan Spence, *The Memory Palace of Matteo Ricci*, and Michela Fontana, *Matteo Ricci: Un Gesuita alla corte del Ming* (Milan, 2005). Sinologists who have turned their attention to the Jesuit mission include Jacques Gernet, *China and the Christian Impact*; Erik Zurcher, 'Jesuit Accommodation and the Chinese Cultural Imperative', in David E. Mungello (ed.), *The Chinese Rites Controversy: Its History and Meaning* (Sankt Augustin, 1994), 31–64, and Haun Saussy, *Great Walls of Discourse and Other Adventures in Cultural China* (Cambridge MA, 2001), chapter 2, 'In the

workshop of equivalences: Translation, institutions, and media in the Jesuit re-formation of China', 15–34.

66 Pasquale d'Elia, *Galileo in China: Relations through the Roman College between Galileo and the Jesuit Scientist-Missionaries (1610–1640)* (Cambridge MA, 1960); David E. Mungello, *Curious Land: Jesuit Accommodation and the Origins of Sinology* (Stuttgart, 1985); Howard Goodman and Anthony Grafton, 'Ricci, the Chinese, and the toolkits of textualists', *Asia Minor* (1990), 95–148; Catherine Jami and Hubert Delahaye (eds), *L'Europe en Chine: Interactions scientifiques, religieuses et culturelles aux XVIIe et XVIII siècles* (Paris, 1993); Federico Masini (ed.), *Western Humanistic Culture Presented to China by Jesuit Missionaries* (Rome, 1996); Peter M. Engelfriet, *Euclid in China: The Genesis of the First Chinese Translation of Euclid's Elements Books i–vi (Jihe yuanben; Beijing, 1607) and its Reception up to 1723* (Leiden, 1998); David Porter, *Ideographia: The Chinese Cipher in Early Modern Europe* (Stanford, 2001).

I THE TOWER OF HIGH FORTUNE

1 On the strange features of the house, see *Lettere*, 100 and 108. On the shared use of building materials, see *FR* I, 190.

2 *FR* I, 184–5.

3 *Lettere*, 115. Ricci mistakenly counts eighteen floors.

4 *FR* I, 180–83.

5 *FR* I, 258.

6 *FR* I, 185.

7 *Lettere*, 160–61.

8 *Lettere*, 112–13.

9 *Monumenta historica Soc. Iesu*, vol. 103, *Documenta Indica* XI (1577–80), ed. by Joseph Wicki (Rome, 1970), 161.

10 *Documenta Indica* XI (1577–80), 333–79, 631–41.

11 *Documenta Indica* XI (1577–80), 640; *Lettere*, 20.

12 *Lettere*, 14, 17–18.

13 In 1586, Macao was granted city status and was henceforth officially known as 'Cidade do Nome de Deos na China'; C. R. Boxer, *Fidalgos in the Far East, 1550–1770* (Hong Kong, 1968), 4.

14 Boxer, *Fidalgos in the Far East*, 3–4.

15 Boxer, *Fidalgos in the Far East*, 6.

16 *FR* I, 155–6.

17 For an account of the role of Captain-Major, see Boxer, *Fidalgos in the Far East*, 4, and Francesco Carletti, *My Voyage Around the World* (London, 1965), 139. According to d'Elia, the Captain at this time was either João de Almeida or his successor, Aires Gonzales de Miranda, *FR* I, 162; cf. Boxer, *Fidalgos in the Far East*, 40–41.

18 *FR* I, 161; Tacchi-Venturi, *Opere storiche del p. Matteo Ricci, S.I.*, 2 vols (Macerata, 1911–13; hereafter Tacchi-Venturi), II, 414.

19 *FR* I, 160–62.

20 *FR* I, 162.

21 *FR* I, 164; Tacchi-Venturi II, 415.

22 *FR* I, 165–6

23 Tacchi-Venturi II, 415.

24 *FR* I, 167.

25 *FR* I, 168–9.

26 *FR* I, 172–3; Tacchi-Venturi II, 414.

27 *FR* I, 173.

28 *FR* I, 177.

29 M. Howard Rienstra (ed.), *Jesuit Letters from China, 1583–4* (Minneapolis, 1986; hereafter *Letters from China*), 20; on the population of Rome in 1580, see Peter Partner, *Rome: A Portrait of a Society, 1500–1559* (Berkeley CA, 1976), 83.

30 Tacchi-Venturi II, 430.

31 *Letters from China*, 27–8. For the original and full version, see Tacchi-Venturi II, 430.

32 *Letters from China*, 28.

33 *Lettere*, 100.

34 *Lettere*, 92, 100, 108.

35 *Lettere*, 100.

36 *Letters from China*, 28.

37 *Lettere*, 108.

38 *Letters from China*, 22–3; Ricci describes the gift in *FR* I, 199–200.

39 *Lettere*, 100.

40 *Lettere*, 116; cf. *Lettere*, 51, and Tacchi-Venturi II, 416. On clothing, see Peter Stallybrass and Anne Rosalind Jones, *Renaissance Clothing and the Materials of Memory* (Cambridge, 2000).

41 Claude Pavur (ed.), *Ratio Studiorum: The official plan for Jesuit education* (Saint Louis, 2005), 32–3.

42 *Lettere*, 45.

43 Tacchi-Venturi II, 411–12. On the challenge of learning the Chinese language, cf. Tacchi-Venturi II, 401.

44 *Letters from China*, 21.

45 *Lettere*, 93.

46 *Lettere*, 103.

47 *Lettere*, 93.

48 Gaetano Ricciardolo, 'Matteo Ricci e la lingua italiana' (*Mondo cinese*) 1992, 73–90 (especially 83 and 88–9).

49 *Lettere*, III.

50 *FR* I, 192, 195.

51 *FR* I, 193–4.

52 Criveller, *Preaching Christ in Late Ming China*, 91–3.

53 Criveller, *Preaching Christ in Late Ming China*, 105–7. *Li* is a traditional Chinese unit of measurement, today standardized at 500 metres.

54 Tacchi-Venturi, II, 421; *Letters from China*, 22.

55 *Lettere*, 97–8; cf. 107 and 115.

56 *Lettere*, 122.

57 Tacchi-Venturi II, 429; *Letters from China*, 26–7; *FR* I, 219.

58 *FR* I, 185–6.

59 *Lettere*, 98.

60 *Lettere*, 115.

61 *Lettere*, 107.

62 *Lettere*, 121–2.

63 *Lettere*, 159.

64 Tacchi-Venturi II, 418.

65 *Lettere*, 98, 100.

66 *FR* I, 202–3.

67 Ruggieri, 'Relaciones', 91r.

68 *FR* I, 204. For another allegation of child abduction, in Canton, see Tacchi-Venturi II, 413. Cf. Ruggieri, 'Relaciones', 32v, 38r.

69 *Lettere*, 101; *FR* I, 234.

70 *FR* I, 239.

71 *FR* I, 239–43.

72 *FR* I, 244.

73 *FR* I, 245.

74 *FR* I, 245–7. D'Elia suggests that 'black' slaves of Malaysian origin were a common luxury in Cantonese society at this time; *FR* I, 246 n. 4. Alternatively, the reference may be to one of the African slaves that the Portuguese brought with them to Asia.

75 *FR* I, 252–3.

76 *FR* I, 253.

77 *FR* I, 265.

78 *FR* I, 264; for the earlier history of the Jesuits' relations with Tansiaohu, see *FR* I, 187, no. 6.

79 *FR* I, 265.

80 *FR* I, 269.

81 *FR* I, 270.

82 *FR* I, 272; *Lettere*, 161.

83 *Lettere*, 160–61.

84 *Lettere*, 67, 121.

85 Tacchi-Venturi II, 404.

86 Tacchi-Venturi II, 420; *Letters from China*, 21.

87 Alonso Sánchez, 'Memorial to the Council: The proposed entry into China', in Emma Blair and James Robertson (eds), *The Philippine Islands, 1493-1898*, 55 vols (Cleveland, 1903-1909), VI, 197–233 (200, 210).

88 *FR* I, 202.

89 *Lettere*, 84, 107.

90 *Lettere*, 270.

2 PRESENTS FOR THE EMPEROR

1 Ruggieri, 'Relaciones,' 115r.

2 Archivum Romanum Societatis Iesu (ARSI), Fondo Gesuitico, 722/2.

3 On the colour symbolism of the Ming, see Valery Garrett, *Chinese Clothing: An Illustrated Guide* (Hong Kong, 1994), 9.

4 On the prominence of 'men in the marketplace', see Welch, *Shopping in the Renaissance*, especially 212–25.

5 *FR* I, 229, 250.

6 Cronin, *Wise Man from the West*, 86. On the overshadowing of Michele Ruggieri by Matteo Ricci, see Eugenio Lo Sardo, *Atlante della Cina di Michele*

Ruggieri (Rome, 1993), 12 and 19; and for Ruggieri as Ricci's precursor (with echoes of John the Baptist's relationship with Christ), *FR* I, xcviii.

7   Lo Sardo, *Atlante della Cina di Michele Ruggieri*, 30.

8   *FR* I, 250, n. 2.

9   Valignano commented on Ruggieri's ability to write in the Chinese language in his letter to Acquaviva of 10 November 1588; J. L. Alvarez-Taladriz, 'El proyecto de embajada del papa a la China y el padre Alejandro Valignano, S. J. (1588)', *Tenri Daigaku Gakuho*, 89 (1973), 60–94 (81).

10 Ruggieri, 'Relaciones', 84r.

11 *Lettere*, 119.

12 For Ruggieri's account of this trip, see 'Relaciones', 39r–45r.

13 Tacchi-Venturi II, 435, 18 October 1585.

14 *Lettere*, 102, 106.

15 Robert B. Marks, *Tigers, Rice, Silk and Silt: Environment and Economy in Late Imperial South China* (Cambridge, 1998), 21–2.

16 Ruggieri, 'Relaciones', 39v.

17 Ruggieri, 'Relaciones', 40r–41r. For an equally enthusiastic nineteenth-century account, see Revd William Charles Milne, *Life in China* (London, 1857), 357–62.

18 Ruggieri, 'Relaciones', 41v–42r.

19 Ruggieri, 'Relaciones', 42v. See 42r for an account of how a pontoon was opened for Ruggieri's party, allowing them to pass through without paying the normal customs duties.

20 Ruggieri, 'Relaciones', 43r.

21 J. H. Gray, *China: A History of the Laws, Manners, and Customs of the People*, 2 vols (London, 1878), II, 233.

22 Ruggieri, 'Relaciones', 44v.

23 Ruggieri, 'Relaciones', 45v; *FR* I, 229.

24 Ruggieri, 'Relaciones', 45r.

25 Cf. *Lettere*, 122: baptism took place on Easter Day, 6 April 1586.

26 *FR* I, 229.

27 *FR* I, 230.

28 Ruggieri, 'Relaciones', 49r–51v.

29 Ruggieri, 'Relaciones', 49r.

30 Ruggieri, 'Relaciones', 50r.

31 Ruggieri, 'Relaciones', 50r.

32 Ruggieri, 'Relaciones', 50r–v.

33 Ruggieri, 'Relaciones', 50v–51r.

34 Ruggieri, 'Relaciones', 51r–v.

35 Ruggieri, 'Relaciones', 51v–52v.

36 Ruggieri, 'Relaciones', 52v.

37 Pamela Smith and Paula Findlen (eds), *Merchants and Marvels: Commerce, Science, and Art in Early Modern Europe* (New York, 2002), 1–2.

38 See Craig Clunas's characterisation of China as a 'visual culture', *Empire of Great Brightness: Visual and Material Cultures of Ming China, 1368–1644* (London, 2007), 11.

39 Boxer (ed.), *South China in the Sixteenth Century*, 124–7.

40 Boxer (ed.), *South China in the Sixteenth Century*, 283–4; cf. Garrett, *Chinese Clothing*, on Chinese clothes and social status, 12.

41 Peter Burke, 'The sources: Outsiders and insiders,' *The Historical Anthropology of Early Modern Italy* (Cambridge, 1987), 15–24.

42 Willis (ed.), *China and Macau*, 1.

43 Boxer (ed.), *South China in the Sixteenth Century*, 14.

44 Boxer (ed.), *South China in the Sixteenth Century*, 287.

45 Norbert Elias, *The Civilizing Process*, trans. Edmund Jephcott (Oxford, 2000).

46 Carletti, *My Voyage Around the World*, 141.

47 Carletti, *My Voyage Around the World*, 150.

48 Lach, *Asia in the Making of Europe*, 1, 315.

49 Josef Franz Schütte, *Valignano's Mission Principles for Japan*, trans. John J. Coyne, 2 vols (St Louis, 1980–1985), 1, part 11, 184–5.

50 Carletti, *My Voyage Around the World*, 148.

51 *FR* 1, 32.

52 *FR* 1, 29.

53 *Lettere*, 282, 348; *FR* 1, 40–42.

54 *Lettere*, 517.

55 The list of gifts also included possible coded references to Christian doctrine: coral was often used in Catholic devotional art, depicted in the hands of the Christ child as if to prefigure the blood of the Crucifixion; the prisms or 'glass triangles' commissioned by Valignano (and discussed in greater detail in chapter 4) might have functioned as silent symbols of the Trinity.

56 For a trenchant account of the incommensurability of Chinese and European ideas, see Gernet, *China and the Christian Impact*; for a critique of Gernet, see Haun Saussy, 'In the Workshop of Equivalences', 15–34 (30–31).

57 On the Japanese envoys and their gifts, see Lach, *Asia in the Making of Europe*, 1, 688–706; J. F. Moran, *The Japanese and the Jesuits: Alessandro Valignano in Sixteenth-century Japan* (London, 1993), 6–19, and Luis Frois, *La première ambassade du Japon en Europe, 1582–1592*, ed. by J. A. Abranches Pinto et al. (Tokyo, 1942).

58 Oliver Impey, *The art of the Japanese folding screen* (Oxford, 1997), 9–14. 'Namban-byobu' or screens depicting foreigners became popular after the arrival of the Portuguese in Japan. They often feature a European boat, a Western man wearing baggy trousers, and Jesuit priests; Boxer, *Fidalgos in the Far East*, 20–26.

59 Craig Clunas, *Superfluous Things: Material Culture and Social Status in Early Modern China* (Cambridge, 1991), 58–60.

60 Clunas, *Superfluous Things*, 51.

61 Ruggieri, 'Relaciones', 54v–55r.

62 Ruggieri, 'Relaciones', 54r–v.

63 Ruggieri, 'Relaciones', 58r.

64 Ruggieri, 'Relaciones', 62r.

65 His hosts included Cardinal Albrecht of Austria, then Viceroy of Portugal; Teotónio de Braganza, Archbishop of Evora and a scion of one of the most important families in Portugal; and through the Archbishop, Duchess Catarina of Braganza, a claimant to the Portuguese throne.

66 Ruggieri, 'Relaciones', 66v.

67 Ruggieri's connections with the Orsini, long-time patrons of his family, were

to prove crucial in securing the Jesuit hospitality and contacts in Italy; see Francesco A. Gisondi, *Michele Ruggeri. Missionario e primo sinologo europeo (Spinazzola, 1543–Salerno, 1607)* (Milan, 1999), 21.

3 ON FRIENDSHIP

1   *Lettere*, 311, 219.
2   *Lettere*, 297–321.
3   *Lettere*, 197–267: Ricci to Duarte de Sande, Nanchang, 29 August 1595.
4   The Prince of Jian'an, named here by Ricci as 'Qian Zhai', is better known as 'Zhu Duojie'; Matteo Ricci, *Dell'amicizia*, ed. Filippo Mignini (Macerata, 2005; hereafter, *Dell'amicizia*), 48. All quotations are taken from Mignini's Italian edition and are translated by the author. For a recent English edition, see Matteo Ricci, *On Friendship: One Hundred Maxims for a Chinese Prince*, trans. Timothy Billings (New York, 2009).
5   The Peak of the Plum Trees or Mount Meiling is at the border between the southern province of Guangdong and the adjacent province of Jiangxi, the capital of which is Nanchang, where Ricci was at the time of the composition of *On Friendship*. The 'changes of stars and snows' indicate the years spent in Guangdong.
6   *Dell'amicizia*, 63.
7   The expression used by Ricci, translated here as 'taking my hands' indicates not a simple handshake but the pressing of the hands and part of the forearms between the hands of the host.
8   By placing the request for the work in the mouth of the Prince, Ricci reinforced its dignity and importance. The model of friendship to which Qian Zhai alludes here is something very similar to that understood in the ancient West; it expressed more a respect for conventions of ritual and justice than a sentiment or relationship experienced between individuals.
9   Michel Jeanneret, *A Feast of Words: Banquets and Table Talk in the Renaissance* (Cambridge, 1991), 27–32.
10 Boxer (ed.), *South China in the Sixteenth Century*, 134.
11 Boxer (ed.), *South China in the Sixteenth Century*, 134.
12 Boxer (ed.), *South China in the Sixteenth Century*, 141.
13 Clunas, *Empire of Great Brightness*, 145–6.
14 *Lettere*, 172.
15 *Lettere*, 171–2.
16 *Lettere*, 199–200.
17 *Lettere*, 236.
18 *Lettere*, 237. Ricci used the term *chayuan* to refer to members of the Institute of Censorship; *Lettere*, 564.
19 *Lettere*, 246–7.
20 *Lettere*, 294.
21 On the importance of this theme to Renaissance discussions of friendship, see Guy Fitch Lytle, 'Friendship and Patronage in Renaissance Europe', in F. W. Kent and P. Simons (eds), *Patronage, Art and Society in Renaissance Italy* (Oxford, 1987), 56–7.
22 *Lettere*, 240–41.

23 David Konstan, *Friendship in the Classical World* (Cambridge, 1997), 5, guards against a conception of Greek and Roman friendship as limited to obligatory reciprocity. On the particularities of friendship between strangers, see Gabriel Herman, *Ritualised Friendship and the Greek City* (Cambridge, 1987), 10–13. On the great variety of forms friendship could take in the early modern period, see Natalie Zemon Davis, *The Gift in Sixteenth-Century France* (Oxford, 2000), 30–32.

24 For a helpful explication of classical conceptions of friendship in terms of a pyramid, see Reginald Hyatte, *The Arts of Friendship: The Idealization of Friendship in Medieval and Early Renaissance Literature* (Leiden, 1994), 4–6.

25 Sofia Mattei, in her notes to *Dell'Amicizia*, proposes Plutarch, *De liberis educandis*, 6, 4, as the source for this adage, and suggests that Ricci deliberately changed Plutarch's choice of metaphor – 'if you live next door to a cripple, you will start to limp' – to one of greater relevance to his Chinese readers, *Dell'amicizia*, 173. For a discussion of the place of friendship in relation to the other four relationships, see Norman Kutcher, 'The Fifth Relationship: Dangerous Friendships in the Confucian Context', *American Historical Review* 105 (2000), 1615–29.

26 Kutcher, 'The Fifth Relationship', 1618.

27 Kutcher, 'The Fifth Relationship', 1622.

28 Chinese homosexuality will be discussed at greater length in chapter 5. For a discussion of how male homosexuals observed the hierarchy of gender in Renaissance Florence, see Michael Rocke, *Forbidden Friendships: Homosexuality and Male Culture in Renaissance Florence* (New York, 1996), 13–14.

29 Joseph McDermott, 'Friendship and its Friends in the Late Ming', *Family Process and Political Process in Modern Chinese History* (Taipei, 1992), 82.

30 McDermott, 'Friendship and its Friends', 81–2.

31 McDermott, 'Friendship and its Friends', 83–5.

32 For Huang Daozhou's ideas, see McDermott, 'Friendship and its Friends', 85–7.

33 McDermott, 'Friendship and its Friends', 73–4.

34 *Lettere*, 165.

35 *Lettere*, 167–8.

36 *Lettere*, 181.

37 *Lettere*, 389–93.

38 *Lettere*, 329, 505.

39 *Lettere*, 329.

40 *Lettere*, 329.

41 *Lettere*, 401.

42 For biographical details of Ludovico Maselli, see Tacchi-Venturi II, 11, n. 3.

43 *Lettere*, 19.

44 *Lettere*, 108–9.

45 *Lettere*, 294; for details of Girolamo Costa, Ricci's compatriot and almost exact contemporary, who could be relied on to forward his brother in China Macerata news, even if he could not be relied on to be reliable, see Tacchi-Venturi II, 119, n. 1. For more tears, cf. *Lettere*, 273, addressed to an anonymous recipient.

46 *Lettere*, 187.

47 *Lettere*, 49.

48 *Lettere*, 269.

Notes

49 *Lettere*, 158.

50 See Konstan, *Friendship in the Classical World*, on the role of self-disclosure in early modern and modern conceptions of friendship, 15–18.

51 *Dell'amicizia*, 55.

52 *Dell'amicizia*, 59.

53 *Lettere*, 507.

4 HEAVENLY KNOWLEDGE

1 For an account of Qu Rukui's baptism, see *FR* II, 342–5.

2 *FR* II, 345.

3 *Lettere*, 418.

4 For details of Qu Rukui's father, see *FR* I, 295–6.

5 For Ricci's complaint about the quality of converts, see *Lettere*, 122.

6 Ugo Baldini, 'Christopher Clavius and the scientific scene in Rome', in G. V. Coyne et al. (eds), *Gregorian Reform of the Calendar* (Città del Vaticano, 1983), 137–69 (144–5).

7 *FR* II, 55.

8 Copies of Clavius's *Practical Arithmetic*, first published in 1583, and his *Commentary on the Sphere of Giovanni Sacrobosco*, first published in 1570, both appear in later inventories of the Jesuits' Beijing library in editions published in 1585, suggesting (though not verifying) that Ricci might have had them in his possession by 1589–90. (In 1605, Ricci was still complaining that he did not have a single astronomical book in China; see *Lettere*, 408, and below in text.) Clavius's 1591 edition of Euclid's *Elements*, first published in 1574, is also inventoried, but would obviously have arrived too late to have been of direct benefit to Qu Rukui during his year of mathematical study. On the other hand, in 1585, Ricci wrote to his colleague, Giulio Fuligatti, that the only books he had were 'the works of Clavius and Piccolomini'; *Lettere*, 116. Given the pairing of these authors, the latter of whom was famous for his own work of positional astronomy, the first printed star atlas, entitled *De la sfera del mondo* (Venezia, 1540), it is likely that the work of Clavius alluded to here was *his* work on the celestial sphere, the commentary on Sacrobosco.

9 Schall and Verbiest were, in 1645 and 1669 respectively, appointed Directors of the Beijing Observatory.

10 On reform of the Chinese calendar, see D'Elia, *Galileo in China*, 5. On the reforms instigated by Pope Gregory XIII, see G. V. Coyne et al. (eds), *Gregorian Reform of the Calendar*. On the controversies generated by the Gregorian reform, see R. Poole, *Time's Alteration: Calendar Reform in Early Modern England* (London, 1998), especially 37–44.

11 Robert S. Westerman, 'The astronomer's role in the sixteenth century: a preliminary study', *History of Science* 18 (1980), 131.

12 *Lettere*, 407–8.

13 *Lettere*, 166, n. 3. See *FR* II, n. 4, for a more balanced account.

14 The three levels of Chinese degree were sometimes likened to the European 'Bachelor', 'Master' and 'Doctor', although the European equivalents scarcely convey the vocational and competitive nature of the Chinese qualifications. On the frequency of exams and the numbers of men participating, see Benjamin

Elman, *A Cultural History of Civil Examinations in Late Imperial China* (Berkeley CA, 2000), xxvii.

15 *FR* I, 46.

16 Kai-Wing Chow, *Publishing, Culture, and Power in Early Modern China* (Stanford, 2004), 94, quoting Ai Nanying.

17 *FR* I, 47.

18 *FR* I, 47–8.

19 Boxer (ed.), *South China in the Sixteenth Century*, 13.

20 *FR* I, 36.

21 Pavur (ed.), *Ratio Studiorum*, 44.

22 Pavur (ed.), *Ratio Studiorum*, 119–20.

23 Pavur (ed.), *Ratio Studiorum*, 121.

24 *FR* I, 37.

25 Confucius, *Analects*, 1:3 and 17:17. I am grateful to Joe McDermott for shedding much light on the absence of oratory as a Chinese ideal.

26 O'Malley, *The First Jesuits*, 217.

27 O'Malley, *The First Jesuits*, 222–3.

28 On the relationship between rhetoric and dialectic, see Peter Mack, *Renaissance Argument: Valla and Agricola in the Traditions of Rhetoric and Dialectic* (Leiden, 1993), 1–21, especially 6–7.

29 *FR* I, 39.

30 *FR* I, 40–41.

31 *FR* I, 358–9.

32 *Lettere*, 282.

33 *Lettere*, 316. The full passages in which Ricci discusses the factors attracting the Chinese to the Jesuits in Nanchang are *Lettere*, 281–2, 292–3, 315–17.

34 Home to more than 180 publishers, Nanjing was (after Jianyang in Fujian province) the second largest publishing centre in China in the late sixteenth century; Chow, *Publishing, Culture, and Power in Early Modern China*, 82.

35 *FR* II, 283.

36 *FR* I, 31; Chow, *Publishing, Culture, and Power in Early Modern China*, 38–56.

37 On paper production, see Chow, *Publishing, Culture, and Power in Early Modern China*, 28–33.

38 On travelling salesmen and the social space of the bookshop, see Clunas, *Empire of Great Brightness*, 108. The Cheng'en temple at Sanshan Street, Nanjing, was a renowned centre of book trading; Chow, *Publishing, Culture, and Power in Early Modern China*, 83.

39 Saussy, 'Workshop of Equivalences', gives a full discussion of this contrast.

40 *Lettere*, 140.

41 *Lettere*, 392.

42 *Lettere*, 496.

43 *Lettere*, 337–8.

44 *Lettere*, 364, Ricci complained to his friend Girolamo Costa that to publish something himself he would have to go through a cumbersome rigmarole in order to obtain the correct licences from the order.

45 *Lettere*, 490–91

46 *Lettere*, 491.

47 *Lettere*, 490.

Notes

48 *Lettere*, 470.

49 *Lettere*, 505.

50 *Lettere*, 501.

51 *Lettere*, 496.

52 *Lettere*, 336.

53 *Lettere*, 347.

54 Michael Lackner, 'Jesuit *Memoria*, Chinese *Xinfa*: Some preliminary remarks on the organisation of memory', in Masini (ed.), *Western Humanistic Culture*, 201–19 (205).

55 Lackner, 'Jesuit *Memoria*', 204.

56 *Lettere*, 378, 385–6.

57 Gernet, *China and the Christian Impact*, 49.

58 Gernet, *China and the Christian Impact*, 50.

59 Lackner, 'Jesuit *Memoria*', 212.

60 *Lettere*, 293.

61 *Lettere*, 158; *FR* II, 121.

62 *Lettere*, 52.

63 *Lettere*, 252.

64 *Lettere*, 293–4.

65 *Lettere*, 116.

66 *Lettere*, 108, 211, 435.

67 *FR* I, 255; *FR* II, 37. On the sale of Manhattan, see Nicholas Thomas, *Entangled Objects: Exchange, Material Culture, and Colonialism in the Pacific* (Cambridge MA, 1991), 83.

68 *Lettere*, 211.

69 Seneca had described various experiments reflecting sunlight by means of 'certain rods of glasse very narrow, wherein there are divers angles, and knots or points'; see Thomas Lodge's 1614 translation of *The Naturall Questions*, 768. On Newton's experiments with prisms, see Simon Schaffer, 'Glass works: Newton's prisms and the uses of experiment', in David Gooding et al. (eds), *The Uses of Experiment: studies in the natural sciences* (Cambridge, 1989), 67–104.

70 Antonio Neri, *The Art of Glass, wherein are shown the wayes to make and colour glass, pastes, enamels, lakes, & other curiosities* (London, 1662), A1r.

71 On the history of Chinese attitudes to glass, see H. E. Winlock, 'The History of Glass: An Exhibition', *The Metropolitan Museum of Art Bulletin* (1936), 192–7 (194) and Emily Byrne Curtis, *Glass Exchange between Europe and China, 1550–1800: Diplomatic, Mercantile and Technological Interactions* (Farnham, 2009), 1–5.

72 Carletti, *My Voyage Around the World*, 153.

73 John Hall, *A Most Excellent and Learned Woorke of Chirurgerie* (London, 1565).

74 Girolamo Cardano had given his own account of the story in his *De subtilitate*, published in Nuremberg in 1550.

75 David Gentilcore, *From Bishop to Witch: The System of the Sacred in Early Modern Terra d'Otranto* (Manchester, 1992), 100–101; David Gentilcore, *Healers and Healing in Early Modern Italy* (Manchester, 1998), 187–98.

76 Sébastien Michaelis, *The Admirable Historie of the possession and conuersion of a penitent woman* (London, 1613).

77 *Lettere*, 292.

78 *FR* I, 104–7.

79 P. Smith, *The Business of Alchemy: Science and Culture in the Holy Roman Empire* (Princeton NJ, 1994), especially 179–81; C. Webster, 'Alchemical and Paracelsian Medicine', in C. Webster (ed.), *Health, Medicine and Mortality in the Sixteenth Century* (Cambridge, 1979), 301–34.

80 Joseph Needham, *The Shorter Science and Civilisation in China*, abridged by Colin Ronan (Cambridge, 1978), 219–20. *Qi* may be translated as 'energy flows'. Needham tells us that 'between AD 389 and 404 the Northern Wei emperor established at the capital both a professorship of Daoism and a Daoist laboratory for the making of medicinal preparations. Indeed the Western Mountains were allocated to supply firewood for the alchemical furnaces, and those guilty of capital offences were made to test the elixirs in person.' In Europe, at the very centre of the so-called 'scientific revolution', Newton was devoting much of his career to carrying out experiments in Trinity; Jan Golinski, 'The Secret Life of an Alchemist', in J. Fauvel et al. (eds), *Let Newton Be!* (Oxford, 1988), 147–67.

81 *FR* II, 490–91. See also Francesco Carletti's reference to the Chinese inclination to 'spend time searching for things that they can swallow which will make them immortal', *My Voyage Around the World*, 146.

82 *FR* II, 37. The same topos worked its way into Francesco Carletti's account of the Chinese delight in 'triangular-shaped glasses'. He claimed that 'these were sold at up to five hundred ducats each, and such was the wonder with which they struck those people the first time that they saw them that they began to praise them aloud, saying that what one saw by means of them was the matter from which the heavens are made', *My Voyage Around the World*, 153.

83 This story was reprinted in Neri's *Art of Glass*, 229–31.

5 JESUITS AND EUNUCHS

1 G. Carter Stent, 'Chinese eunuchs', *Journal of the North-China Branch of the Royal Asiatic Society*, new series, 11 (1877), 143–83 (170–71).

2 Stent, 'Chinese eunuchs', 143.

3 In his determination to avoid sensationalism, Shih-Shan Henry Tsai's impressive study, *The Eunuchs in the Ming Dynasty* (New York, 1996) skirts over the physical and psychological impact of castration. Susan Naquin, *Peking Temples and City Life, 1400–1900* (Berkeley CA, 2000), restricts her discussion of eunuchs to their role in the upkeep and patronage of temples.

4 Tsai, *The Eunuchs in the Ming Dynasty*, 11.

5 *FR* I, 100.

6 *FR* II, 17, n. 6; Hoshi Ayao, 'Transportation in the Ming Dynasty', *Acta Asiatica* 38 (1980), 1–30 (2).

7 *FR* II, 20.

8 *FR* II, 21.

9 *FR* II, 29–30.

10 Stephen Turnball, *Samurai Invasion: Japan's Korean War, 1592–1598* (London, 2004).

11 *FR* II, 81; Tsai, *The Eunuchs in the Ming Dynasty*, 170–79.

12 For figures testifying to the increase of eunuchs under the Wanli Emperor, see Tsai, *The Eunuchs in the Ming Dynasty*, 25.

13 *FR* II, 81–2.

14 Tsai, *The Eunuchs in the Ming Dynasty*, 12.

15 Tsai, *The Eunuchs in the Ming Dynasty*, 26; Saussy, *Great Walls of Discourse*, 23–4.

16 *FR* II, 109–10.

17 *FR* II, 110.

18 *FR* II, 112.

19 *FR* II, 116.

20 *FR* II, 120, 131.

21 Naquin, *Peking Temples and City Life*, 126.

22 Tsai, *The Eunuchs in the Ming Dynasty*, 43–4; Taisuke Mitamura, *Chinese eunuchs: the structure of intimate politics*, trans. Charles A. Pomeroy (Rutland Vermont, 1992) 110–20.

23 Tsai, *The Eunuchs in the Ming Dynasty*, 44.

24 Tsai, *The Eunuchs in the Ming Dynasty*, 33.

25 Tsai, *The Eunuchs in the Ming Dynasty*, 45.

26 One picul equalled 100 catties, and approximates to 60 kilos.

27 Tsai, *The Eunuchs in the Ming Dynasty*, 45–6.

28 Tsai, *The Eunuchs in the Ming Dynasty*, 50.

29 Tsai, *The Eunuchs in the Ming Dynasty*, 48.

30 Tsai, *The Eunuchs in the Ming Dynasty*, 46.

31 Tsai, *The Eunuchs in the Ming Dynasty*, 46–7.

32 Tsai, *The Eunuchs in the Ming Dynasty*, 47.

33 Tsai, *The Eunuchs in the Ming Dynasty*, 45.

34 Naquin, *Peking Temples and City Life*, 181; Tsai, *The Eunuchs in the Ming Dynasty*, 55.

35 *FR* II, 162–5.

36 Tsai, *The Eunuchs in the Ming Dynasty*, 19, 58.

37 *FR* I, 98.

38 *Lettere*, 315, on beards, and 83, on the rituals of male toilette and 'femminucce'. *FR* I, 88, for a discussion of the physiognomy of Chinese men, and – in particular – their paltry facial hair.

39 *FR* I, 69–70.

40 Gaspar da Cruz in Boxer, *South China in the Sixteenth Century*, 223–6. On the non-bellicose nature of the Chinese, see also the comments of Tomé Pires and Duarte Barbosa, in Willis, *China and Macau*, 3 and 5, and Carletti, *My Voyage around the World*, 166.

41 Timothy Brook, *The Confusions of Pleasure: Commerce and Culture in Ming China* (Berkeley CA, 1998), 232.

42 Brook, *The Confusions of Pleasure*, 231; Giovanni Vitiello, 'Exemplary Sodomites: Chivalry and Love in Late Ming Culture', *Nan Nü: Men, Women and Gender in Early and Imperial China*, II, no. II (Leiden, 2000), 253–4.

43 Kutcher, 'The Fifth Relationship', 1615–29 (1615).

44 On the *sancong* or 'three obediences', which required women to submit to the authority of their fathers, husbands and sons, see Dorothy Ko, *Teachers of the Inner Chambers: Women and Culture in Seventeenth-Century China* (Stanford, 1994), 6.

45 *FR* I, 88–9. On the history of footbinding, see Dorothy Ko, *Cinderella's Sisters: A Revisionist History of Footbinding* (Berkeley CA, 2005); on the part played by Protestant missionaries in the campaign against the practice, see especially 14–17.

46 *Lettere*, 71.

47 Boxer, *South China in the Sixteenth Century*, 149.

48 *FR* I, 83.

49 For accounts of patriarchy in early modern European context, see especially Steven Ozment, *When Fathers Ruled: Family Life in Reformation Europe* (Cambridge MA, 1983); Lyndal Roper, *Holy Household: Women and Morals in Reformation Augsburg* (Oxford, 1989); Ulrike Strasser, *State of Virginity: Gender, Religion and Politics in an Early Modern Catholic State* (University of Michigan Press, 2004).

50 Matteo Ricci, *The True Meaning of the Lord of Heaven*, eds D. Lancashire and P. Hu Kuo-chen (St Louis, 1985; hereafter *Lord of Heaven*), 439.

51 *Lord of Heaven*, 437. On Jesuit masculinity, see Ulrike Strasser, '"The First Form and Grace": Ignatius of Loyola and the Reformation of Masculinity', in Susan C. Karant-Nunn and Scott H. Hendrix (eds), *Masculinity in the Reformation Era* (Kirksville, Missouri, 2008), 45–70.

52 *Lord of Heaven*, 409–11.

53 *Lord of Heaven*, 415.

54 *Lord of Heaven*, 419.

55 *Lord of Heaven*, 421–3.

56 *Lord of Heaven*, 427.

57 *Lord of Heaven*, 429.

58 *Lord of Heaven*, 431.

59 *Lord of Heaven*, 431–3.

60 *Lord of Heaven*, 437.

61 Confucius, *Analects*, 4:19.

62 Gernet, *China and the Christian Impact*.

63 On the nature of celibacy in Buddhism, which – in contrast to the conventions of Christian monasticism – was not necessarily a life-long commitment, see Etienne LaMotte, 'The Buddha, His Teachings and His Sangha', in Heinz Bechert and Richard Gombrich (eds), *The World of Buddhism: Buddhist Monks and Nuns in Society and Culture*, (New York, 1991) 41–58 (especially 55–6).

64 *FR* I, 282.

65 *FR* I, 283.

66 *FR* I, 125–6. 'Bonze' (or *bonzo* in Italian) was the term the Jesuits used to refer to Japanese or Chinese Buddhist monks.

67 *FR* I, 336–7.

68 Elman, *A Cultural History of Civil Examinations in Late Imperial China*; see especially chapter 6, entitled 'Emotional Anxiety, Dreams of Success, and the Examination Life', 295–370.

69 Elman, *A Cultural History of Civil Examinations in Late Imperial China*, 298.

70 Kenneth K. S. Ch'en, *The Chinese Transformation of Buddhism* (Princeton, 1973), 15–17 and 45.

71 On the physical characteristics of eunuchs, see Stent, 'Chinese eunuchs', 178–9; on charges of unfiliality, see Stent, 181.

72 Dympna Callaghan, 'The Castrator's Song: Female Impersonation on the Early Modern Stage', *Journal of Medieval and Early Modern Studies* 26:2 (1996), 321–53 (325–34).

73 Tsai, *The Eunuchs in the Ming Dynasty*, 11. On castrati singers in Europe, see R. Sherr, 'Guglielmo Gonzaga and the Castrati', *Renaissance Quarterly* 33 (1980), 33–56.

6 THE TRUE MEANING OF THE LORD OF HEAVEN

1 *Lettere*, 437.

2 *Lettere*, 509–20.

3 *Lettere*, 516–17.

4 *Lettere*, 517.

5 *Lettere*, 517.

6 For scholarly debate on the impact of print, see E. Eisenstein, *The Printing Press as an Agent of Change* (Cambridge, 1979); A. Johns, *The Nature of the Book: Print and Knowledge in the Making* (Chicago, 1998), and Sabrina Baron et al. (eds), *Agent of Change: Print Culture Studies after Elizabeth L. Eisenstein* (Amherst MA, 2007).

7 *Lettere*, 517–18.

8 *Lettere*, 518–19.

9 *Lettere*, 519.

10 *Lettere*, 519.

11 *Lettere*, 520.

12 David Porter argues compellingly for 'Ricci's rhetorical insistence on distilling the original essence of the early Confucian belief system from the syncretic potpourri of religious practices that he encountered in the pluralistic climate of the late Ming dynasty', in *Ideographia*, 81.

13 *Lord of Heaven*, 15.

14 *Lord of Heaven*, 75.

15 *Lord of Heaven*, 77–8.

16 *Lord of Heaven*, 81–3, 89.

17 On the history of the Catechism, and the Jesuits' place within it, see O'Malley, *The First Jesuits*, 87–90 and 116–26.

18 O'Malley, *The First Jesuits*, 125.

19 *Lord of Heaven*, 307.

20 The Donglin Academy flourished in the years 1608–25. On Ricci's alliance with those who would come to stand at the heart of its protests, see Saussy, *Great Walls of Discourse*, 24–9.

21 *Lord of Heaven*, 101.

22 *Lord of Heaven*, 99.

23 Saussy, *Great Walls of Discourse*, 22–6.

24 *Lord of Heaven*, 99.

25 *Lord of Heaven*, 131.

26 *Lord of Heaven*, 225.

27 *FR* II, 232. On Xu's background and life, see Willard Peterson, 'Why did they become Christians? Yang T'ing-yün, Li Chih-tsao, and Hsü Kuang-ch'i', in Ronan and Oh (eds), *East meets West*, 143–5, and Catherine Jami et al. (eds),

Statecraft and Intellectual Renewal in Late Ming China: The Cross-Cultural Synthesis of Xu Guangqi (1562–1633) (Leiden, 2001), 1–15.

28 *Lettere*, 459, 469, 491; *FR* II, 168–78.

29 *Lettere*, 469; *FR* II, 178–9.

30 *FR* II, 178, n. 3.

31 For this account, we are dependent on Giulio Aleni (Ricci's successor in Beijing); see Peterson, 'Why did they become Christians?', 139.

32 Peterson, 'Why did they become Christians?' See also Nicolas Standaert, 'The Four Principal Converts', in Standaert, *Handbook of Christianity in China*, I, 404–20.

33 *Lettere*, 122.

34 Porter, *Ideographia*, 89.

35 *Lettere*, 100.

36 *Lord of Heaven*, 243.

37 *Lord of Heaven*, 251.

38 *Lord of Heaven*, 255.

39 *Lord of Heaven*, 259–61. For a brilliant discussion of 'baptism by meat' as a strategy of Christian missionaries in China from the seventeenth to the twentieth centuries, see Eric Reinders, *Borrowed Gods and Foreign Bodies: Chinese Missionaries Imagine Chinese Religion* (Berkeley CA, 2004); chapter 10 entitled 'Blessed are the meat-eaters', 146–69. Although Buddhists, who held that not eating meat was a religiously meritorious form of fasting, did not necessarily commit permanently to vegetarianism, the association of Buddhism and a non-meat diet was so strong in the European imagination that many Christian missionaries, from Ricci onwards, felt the need to attack vegetarianism.

40 *Lord of Heaven*, 265–7.

41 *Lord of Heaven*, 91.

42 I am grateful to Henrietta Harrison for pointing out to me that vegetarianism (along with the Ten Commandments and the Lord's Prayer) would become one of the defining features of Chinese Catholicism in the seventeenth and eighteenth centuries.

43 *Lettere*, 172–3.

44 *Lettere*, 98.

45 *Lettere*, 189–90, 390, 438, 439, 447.

46 Porter, *Ideographia*, 86.

47 *Lettere*, 443.

48 *Lettere*, 445.

49 *Lettere*, 437–41.

50 *Lettere*, 448.

51 *Lettere*, 439, 441; c.f. *Lettere*, 139: on the Jesuits' arrival in Shaozhou in 1589, Ricci commented on the fact that their reputation for working miracles preceded them. When Ricci's colleague Michele Ruggieri travelled to Shaoxing in January 1586, he also remarked that the Jesuits' reputation for curing the sick brought them 'great credit', Ruggieri, 'Relaciones', 46v–7r.

52 *Lettere*, 397.

53 *FR* II, 512.

54 *Lettere*, 390; see also, on the same page, the case of the judge who was moved to release an innocent Christian man following an apparition of Jesus.

55 *Lettere*, 123, 436, 437, 438, 439, 445. On the use and availability of Christian imagery in China during Ricci's mission, see Gauvin Alexander Bailey, *Art on the Jesuit Missions in Asia and Latin America, 1542–1773* (Toronto, 2001), 82–111, and 'The Image of Jesus in Chinese Art During the Time of the Jesuit Missions (16th–18th Centuries)', in R. Malek (ed.), *The Chinese Face of Christ*, 4 vols to date (Sankt Augustin, 2002–), II, 395–415.

56 *Lettere*, 441.

57 *Lettere*, 123.

58 David Gentilcore, *Healers and Healing*.

59 In this respect, the expectations of the Catholic chimed with those of the Chinese; see Cynthia Brokaw, *The Ledgers of Merit and Demerit: Social Change and Moral Order in Late Imperial China* (Princeton NJ, 1991).

60 Adversi et al. (eds), *Storia di Macerata*, v, 183–6.

61 Adversi et al. (eds), *Storia di Macerata*, v, 189.

62 *Lettere*, 361. On the importance of miracles to Jesuit work in Europe, see Trevor Johnson, 'Blood, Tears and Xavier-Water: Jesuit Missionaries and Popular Religion in the Eighteenth-Century Upper Palatinate', in Bob Scribner and Trevor Johnson (eds), *Popular Religion in Germany and Central Europe, 1400–1800* (London, 1996), 183–202 (185), and Gentilcore, *From Bishop to Witch*.

63 Ruggieri, 'Relaciones,' 44v.

64 Anthony Pagden has referred to this impulse as 'the principle of attachment'; *European Encounters with the New World: From Renaissance to Romanticism* (New Haven, 1993), chapter 1.

65 *Lettere*, 71 and 346, for comparisons between Nanxiong and Nanchang and Florence; *FR* II, 36, on the similarity between Suzhou and Venice; and for that between Shaoxing and Venice, see Ruggieri, 'Relaciones', 45v.

66 Naquin, *Peking Temples and City Life*, 40–45.

67 Susan Naquin and Chün-fang Yü (eds), *Pilgrims and Sacred Sites in China* (Berkeley, 1992).

68 John Lagerwey, 'The Pilgrimage to Wu-tang Shan', in Naquin and Yü, *Pilgrims and Sacred Sites*, 308. On the endurance of miraculous culture in China, see Adam Chau, *Miraculous Response: Doing Popular Religion in Contemporary China* (Stanford, 2006), who argues that 'at the core of Chinese popular religion is the concept of magical efficacy (*ling*), which is conceived of as a particular deity's miraculous response (*lingying*) to the worshipper's request for divine assistance (granting a son, granting magical medicine, bringing rain, resolving a dilemma through divination, granting prosperity, etc.)' (2).

69 *Lettere*, 139.

70 *Lord of Heaven*, 449.

71 Gernet, *China and the Christian Impact*, 39–40. Zhang Chao's remarks appear in the preface to a short work produced in collaboration with the Jesuit priests Buglio, Magalhães and Verbiest, entitled the *Xifang yaoji* or *Essential Ideas about the Countries of the West*, completed in Beijing in 1669.

72 Gernet, *China and the Christian Impact*, 52.

73 On the Nanjing persecution, see David Mungello, *The Great Encounter of China and the West, 1500–1800* (2nd edn, Oxford, 2005), 55–7.

74 Gernet, *China and the Christian Impact*, 57.

75 For a digest of the available figures for the number of Chinese Christians during Ricci's life, see *FR* III, 108–9.

CONCLUSION: THE SMELL OF CHRISTIANITY

1 *FR* II, 515.

2 In speaking of 'doing religion' and in shifting the emphasis from beliefs to practices, I am here borrowing Adam Chau's approach; see his *Miraculous Response*.

3 Cited in David Freedberg, *The Power of Images: Studies in the History and Theory of Response* (Chicago and London, 1989), 162; this is Aquinas's argument, as paraphrased by Peter Lombard in the *Sentences*.

4 Johnson, 'Blood, Tears, and Xavier-Water', 192.

5 The emotionality of Jesuit devotion is a theme recently addressed by Olwen Hufton in her Birkbeck Lectures at the University of Cambridge, given in 2009.

6 Ignatius of Loyola, *Personal Writings* (London, 1996), 298–9. On the importance of the imagination to Ignatian piety, see Freedberg, *The Power of Images*. For a later Jesuit account of Heaven, also structured around the five senses although this time detailing the delightful fulfilment of each sense, see Pietro Camporesi, *Incorruptible Flesh* (Cambridge, 1988), 27.

7 See *FR* I, 315, for an account of the first Chinese Christian, a merchant from Nanxiong and a friend of Qu Rukui, to undertake part of the *Spiritual Exercises* in 1591; *FR* II, 490, for Qu Rukui's own pursuit of the *Exercises*.

8 While there was no Chinese edition of the *Exercises*, according to D'Elia (*FR* II, 490), a Latin edition was published in Amakusa, Japan in 1596.

9 Jeffrey Chipps Smith, *Sensuous Worship: Jesuits and the Art of the Early Catholic Reformation in Germany* (Princeton and Oxford, 2002), 41–6.

10 David Freedberg, 'A Source for Rubens's Modello of the Assumption and Coronation of the Virgin: a Case Study in the Response to Images', *Burlington Magazine* (July 1978), 432–41 (434).

11 *Lettere*, 380.

12 *Lettere*, 406.

13 Carmen Guarino, 'Images of Jesus in Matteo Ricci's Pictures for *Chengshi Moyuan*,' in Malek (ed.), *The Chinese Face of Christ*, II, 417–36 (421).

14 Gianni Criveller, 'Christ Introduced to Late Ming China by Giulio Aleni (1582–1649)', in Malek (ed.), *The Chinese Face of Christ*, II, 437–60; Sun Yuming, 'Cultural Translatability and the Presentation of Christ as Portrayed in Visual Images from Ricci to Aleni', in Malek (ed.), *The Chinese Face of Christ*, II, 461–98.

15 *FR* II, 492.

16 Spence, *The Memory Palace of Matteo Ricci*, 59–64; translation appears on p. 60.

17 Guarino, 'Images of Jesus', 422–3.

18 Historians of Europe in this period are no longer content to speak of 'popular' and 'elite' religion, as if they were separate and opposed entities. They recognise that princes as well as peasants participated in unofficial, superstitious beliefs and practices, and that mentalities cannot easily be categorised along class lines. A survey of the interactions between the Jesuits and their would-be converts in China suggests that the beliefs

and practices of the local people also resisted such classification. On the
European historiography, see, for example, William Christian, *Local Religion
in Sixteenth-Century Spain* (Princeton, 1981), 8, and Craig Harline, 'Official
Religion – Popular Religion in Recent Historiography of the Catholic
Reformation', *Archiv für Reformationsgeschichte* 81 (1990), 239–62.

19 *Dell'amicizia*, 53.

20 Spence, *The Memory Palace of Matteo Ricci*, 60.

21 *Lettere*, 405–6, and *FR* II, 280–82. The quote is from *Lettere*, 405.

22 *Lettere*, 406.

23 *FR* II, 282.

24 See discussion in chapter 2, 96.

25 *Lettere*, 405.

26 On plans for the first purpose-designed Christian church in Beijing, as
conceived by Ricci shortly before his death, see *FR* II, 535.

27 *Lettere*, 376. For further references to the tears of neophytes, see *Lettere*, 98,
173, 174.

28 *Lettere*, 392.

29 *Lettere*, 98, 115, 189, 387.

30 Edward Muir, *Ritual in Early Modern Europe* (Cambridge, 1997), 7, on the
opposition between 'mere ritual' and 'true religion'.

31 Joseph McDermott (ed.), *State and Court Ritual in China* (Cambridge, 1999)
and Clunas, *Empire of Great Brightness*, 50–55.

32 James L. Watson, 'The Structures of Chinese Funerary Rites: Elementary
Forms, Ritual Sequence, and the Primacy of Performance', in James L.
Watson and Evelyn S. Rawski (eds), *Death Ritual in Late Imperial and
Modern China* (Berkeley CA, 1988), 3.

33 Watson, 'The Structures of Chinese Funerary Rites', 10.

34 *Lettere*, 444, 457–8, 467–8, 497–8; *FR* II, 764.

35 *Lettere*, 498. For an account of Ming funeral rituals, as prescribed in the classic
text *Family Rituals (Jiali)*, see Nicolas Standaert, *The Interweaving of Rituals
in the Cultural Exchange between China and Europe* (Seattle, 2008), 11–14.

36 Mungello, *Curious Land*, 64.

37 David Mungello, 'An Introduction to the Chinese Rites Controversy', in
Mungello (ed.), *The Chinese Rites Controversy*, 3–14 (4).

38 Liam Brockey, *Journey to the East* (Cambridge MA, 2007), 199–200.

39 *FR* II, 534–7.

40 *FR* II, 539.

41 *FR* II, 541.

42 *FR* II, 542.

43 *FR* II, 542.

44 *FR* II, 544.

45 Camporesi, *Incorruptible Flesh*, 8, 190.

46 *FR* II, 545.

47 *FR* II, 568.

48 *FR* II, 600.

49 *FR* II, 616.

50 *FR* II, 620.

51 *FR* II, 621.

52 *FR* II, 625.

53 *FR* II, 626.

54 On the Chinese use of air-tight coffins, and the expectation that the corpse will remain within the community for a lengthy period after death, see Watson, 'The Structures of Chinese Funerary Rites', 14–15.

55 *FR* II, 630.

56 John Dragon Young, 'Chinese Views of Rites and the Rites Controversy, 18th–20th Centuries,' in Mungello (ed.), *The Chinese Rites Controversy*, 83–108 (94).

57 As the German philosopher Ernst Cassirer observed, to share in a ritual performance means to live 'a life of emotion, not of thoughts', *The Myth of the State* (New Haven, 1946), as quoted in Muir, *Ritual in Early Modern Europe*, 2.

Index

Acquaviva, Claudio: petition to, 231; Provincial's letter to, 73; Ricci's letters to, 18, 24, 45, 47, 51, 53, 104, 146, 195, 213, 214; Ruggieri's letters to, 51, 64, 76, 85

alchemy: Chinese conception, 158; Daoist practitioners, 159, 221; experiments, 158–9; Qu Rukui's work 128, 131; Ricci's views, 158, 180; rumours of Jesuit knowledge, 57, 128, 140, 157–8, 166; triangular glass, 159–60

Aleni, Giulio, 232

Alexander, King, 114, 116

Alvares, João, 130, 231, 235–6

Ambrose, 104

Analects (Confucius), 103, 188, 190

ancestor worship, 183, 202, 239

Anhui province, 143

Annotations and Meditations on the Gospel (Nadal), 230

apothecaries, 10, 28–9

Aquinas, Thomas, 30, 201, 228, 229

Aristotle: influence, 30, 111, 124; in Jesuit education, 135, 138–9; Ricci's use of, 104, 106, 202; translations of, 116

Armada, Spanish, 100

The Art of Glass (Neri), 153–4

astronomy, 129, 139, 206–7

Augustine, 104

banquets, 107–10

Barradas, João, 122

Bei Jiang, 77

Beijing: arrival of polyglot Bible, 231, 235–6; church, 236, 240; converts, 207–8, 213; embassy plans, 72, 75, 84, 103; examinations, 132, 133, 240;

Hanlin Academy. 206; Imperial City, 173–7; Jesuit mission in, 119, 195, 213, 225, 235; Jesuit view of, 65; permission to enter, 76, 130, 151, 172; prostitution, 180; publishing, 125, 147, 151, 199; Ricci's arrival, 165; Ricci's contacts, 170; Ricci's death, 208, 240–1; Ricci's description of, 17–18; Ricci's gravestone, 242–3; site, 6; temples, 220; transport links, 164

Benci, Girolamo, 67, 122

Boccaccio, Giovanni, 191

Book of Odes, 114, 169

book production, Chinese, 142–3

Borromeo, Carlo, 101

Brazil, 5

Buddhism: celibacy, 190–2, 212; comparison with Christianity, 212, 227; conversion from, 209, 212; dietary principles, 210–11; dress, 19–20, 45, 191, 200; eunuchs, 177, 178; opposition to, 178, 207; Ricci's view of, 55, 150, 191–2, 196, 198–200, 205, 209–12, 223–4, 234; shrines, 220–1; status in China, 146; temple of Ama, 36

Cabral, Francisco, 42, 53

calendar, 130–1

Calicut, 8, 9

Calvin, John, 203

canals, 164

Canisius, Peter, 5, 203–4

Canton: authorities, 40, 54, 59; communications, 33; converts, 38; eating and drinking, 107, 123; markets, 79, 86, 90; Portuguese relations, 11, 37–8, 64; publishing,

271

Index